Managing Growth and Expansion into Global Markets

LOGISTICS, TRANSPORTATION, AND DISTRIBUTION

THE GLOBAL WARRIOR SERIES
Series Editor: Thomas A. Cook

Managing Growth and Expansion into Global Markets:
Logistics, Transportation, and Distribution
Thomas A. Cook (2016)

Driving Risk and Spend Out of the Global Supply Chain
Thomas A. Cook (2015)

Mastering the Business of Global Trade: Negotiating Competitive
Advantage Contractual Best Practices, Incoterms®
and Leveraging Supply Chain Options,
Thomas A. Cook (2014)

The Global Warrior Series

Managing Growth and Expansion into Global Markets

LOGISTICS, TRANSPORTATION, AND DISTRIBUTION

Thomas A. Cook

CRC Press
Taylor & Francis Group
Boca Raton London New York

CRC Press is an imprint of the
Taylor & Francis Group, an **informa** business

A PRODUCTIVITY PRESS BOOK

First published 2016 by Productivity Press

Published 2019 by CRC Press
Taylor & Francis Group
6000 Broken Sound Parkway NW, Suite 300
Boca Raton, FL 33487-2742

© 2016 by Taylor & Francis Group, LLC
CRC Press is an imprint of Taylor & Francis Group, an Informa business

No claim to original U.S. Government works

ISBN 13: 978-1-4822-5917-9 (hbk)

Library of Congress Cataloging-in-Publication Data

Cook, Thomas A., 1953-
  Managing growth and expansion into global markets : logistics, transportation, and distribution / Thomas A. Cook. -- 1 Edition.
     pages cm
  Includes bibliographical references and index.
  ISBN 978-1-4822-5917-9
  1. Consolidation and merger of corporations. 2. Business logistics--Management. 3. International trade. 4. Globalization--Economic aspects. I. Title.

  HG4028.M4C66 2016
  658.1'62--dc23

2015009576

Visit the Taylor & Francis Web site at
http://www.taylorandfrancis.com

and the CRC Press Web site at
http://www.crcpress.com

To many who have passed by … Loyalty, Obligation, Respect, and Responsibility in personal and business relationships define your character and who you are … now lost … may you find your way.

Contents

APPENDICES

Prologue

U.S. supply chain companies are expanding at an expeditious rate into foreign markets. At the same time, overseas transportation and logistics companies are expanding into the United States.

Aligned with this, many companies throughout the world are entering into the global economy, with supply chains that expand into foreign markets servicing all four corners of the international marketplace. Transportation and logistics companies are following their clients' expansion into these foreign markets. They must be able to service all their clients' global supply chain needs. This means they must grow expediently and comprehensively with expansive capabilities and customer service value-added facilitations.

When we think about where global companies were in 1980 in global trade and where they are today, we are dealing with triple-digit growth and expansion. Are these growth challenges managed organically or through mergers and acquisitions?

Companies are facing the challenges of growing organically. Many professional growth consultants are taking the position in 2015 that organic growth for transportation and logistics companies in keeping up with the demands of their client base is nearly impossible. But some companies are exceeding: how and why?

How does a company assess growth strategies? How does it best enter in foreign markets and avoid all the pitfalls? How do some companies transition new business units successfully, whereas others have very poor experiences? How does a company assess its best options in growth and expansion?

This book, *Managing Growth and Expansion into Global Markets*, will review all these questions and outline specific answers, strategies, and a best-practice outline for corporate executives to follow. There is also an array of legal and regulatory implications that need to be reviewed, understood, and brought into the decision-making process. The book will become a handbook for mergers and acquisitions in the supply chain and global arena for corporate executives and a tutorial on the subject matter for students and business-school attendees.

The show doesn't go on because it's ready; it goes on because it's 11:30.

Lorne Michaels

Sweat equity is the most valuable equity there is. Know your business and industry better than anyone else in the world. Love what you do or don't do it.

Mark Cuban

Acknowledgments

Special acknowledgment and thanks extended to Kelly Raia (KellyRaia @dragonfly-international.net) and Richard Furman (rfurman@cmk.com), who helped write some of the content in this book, Kelly with trade compliance and Richard with legal aspects of global trade. Kelly also participated in helping me to edit the material and was inspirational in her continued support for the book. Kelly and Richard's participation and comprehensive viewpoints are valuable and appreciated (Meridian Finance Group, http://www.meridianfinance.com).

Author

APEX GLOBAL SUPPLY CHAIN MANAGEMENT

Thomas A. Cook has been involved in domestic and global business for over 35 years in an array of diverse supply-chain management and international business trades. He graduated from Maritime College at Fort Schuyler, New York, from which he earned a bachelor's degree in transportation science and a graduate degree in transportation and business management.

His career began in the US Naval Reserve and the US and Dutch Merchant Marines, where he served as an officer in various commercial and military capacities on passenger, tug, oil, chemical, break bulk, and container vessels all over the globe. Tom has also been involved in the international insurance, manufacturing, exporting, importing, and marketing, in the trade finance arenas, and in senior management and ownership positions, with an emphasis on air and ocean freight, supply chain, distribution, logistics, compliance, and security, along with domestic and global sales, purchasing/sourcing, and business development concerns.

He has authored over 225 articles and published 15 books on international trade, with 3 of the latest as follows: *Post 911 "Compliance in Today's Global Supply Chain," Mastering Import and Export Management, Purchasing Management,* and *Driving Risk and Spend out of the Supply Chain.* He has lectured all over the world on varied subjects involved with global trade. He is considered by many leading professionals to be top in the field of global logistics and international operations.

Tom has skill sets in global supply chain, operations, purchasing and vendor management, leadership, general management, sales, business development, negotiation, and problem resolution management.

Tom has numerous interests in third-party logistics, global trade, and international business. He has acted as an advisor or trainer or was on the board of many companies and organizations, such as but not limited to, Axis WorldLink, American River International, FSI Global Logistics, The Trade Resource Group of Customs in Washington, DC, The Small Business Exporters Association, North American Exporters Association, *World Trade Magazine*, American Management Association, ISM, CCSMP, APPA, IOMA, AFA, TIA, and The World Academy, New York District Export Council.

Tom was awarded the prestigious International Partnership Award, sponsored by the US government, The State University of New York, and the World Trade Council, delivered by former US President Clinton. Tom currently serves as a senior consultant and managing director of Blue Tiger International.

Tom is a frequent participant course leader and lecturer with such organizations as the AMA, ISM, CCSMP, NAPM, APPA, and numerous others involved in supply chain management.

Tom has entered into an eight-book contract with Taylor & Francis to publish a series of books called The *Global Warrior*, referencing all the skill sets required to compete in a global world. Supply chain, logistics, communication, general management, negotiation, customer service, and dealing with government regulations are all critical components of the series.

Tom frequently speaks to and consults with companies that do business in Asia, more specifically China. He has spent considerable time studying the Chinese market, manufacturing prowess, and the supply chain needs of importers and exporters. He often assists companies in *Best Practices* that export and import to and from China.

Tom also serves as the COO of the Apex North American Holding Company and has responsibility for all operations, sales, business development, and branch offices.

1

Understanding the Business Model for Growth and Expansion on a Global Basis

Company executives in every field and enterprise recognize the importance of going global. As companies go global, this extends their supply chains into new parts of the world, new economies, and turbulent markets.

This chapter looks at the basis of how the decisions are made to go global, the impact these decisions have on the global supply chain, and, more importantly, the companies that provide services to the global supply chain.

THE CASE FOR GOING GLOBAL

Every company must give consideration to going global. For those that have already entered international market(s), they are looking to expand, raise their margins, and grow their presence in more and more countries.

Every company will validate its rationale for global expansion, but there are many common areas for all companies to consider:

- Domestic vs. international
- Margins
- Meeting aggressive growth targets
- Protection from competition
- Diversification
- Security
- Access to local market benefits and value add
- Creating a "panache"
- Going public
- Selling strategy

Domestic vs. International

Doing business domestically is very different from expanding into the global arena. The key difference is the array of risks and exposures a company faces as soon as it crosses international borders. These risks, which are outlined below, are perilous, extreme, and rampant. For the unprepared, the stakes are high.

The most successful companies that have engaged in global trade after a long learning curve are now prepared proactively. These successful companies would outline key risk factors in the following areas:

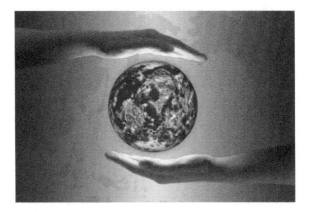

- Political
- Economic

- Demographic
- Physical
- Cultural and language
- Legal
- Compliance

Political

Political risk is one of the major deterrents to companies expanding into global markets, particularly outside "westernized countries." History shows us numerous examples of political disasters that wreaked havoc to the interests of businesses and companies globally. In the last 50 years, these political occurrences include the following:

- Destabilization of Southeast Asia throughout the 1960s and 1970s, impacting countries such as Cambodia, Vietnam, Laos, Myanmar, and Thailand
- The Iranian Revolution in the early 1980s
- Nationalization issues in Latin America, which still continued in 2014 in countries such as Venezuela, Cuba, and Peru, to name a few
- Iraq's invasion of Kuwait in 1992
- The events of 9/11 in the United States
- The wars in Afghanistan and Iraq and the overall destabilization in Africa and the Middle East
- Piracy in the east coast of Africa
- Nuclear threats from Iran and North Korea
- Continued terrorist initiatives worldwide

All of the above are just a small sampling of the political risks and exposures companies face in entering global markets. Even on doing business in westernized countries, the events listed above have a huge impact.

Political risk is a risk insurable by several government and private insurance companies. Some even consider war; strikes, riots, and civil commotions (SRCCs); and terrorism as political exposures.

Insurance companies group these exposures into four primary areas: confiscation, nationalization, expropriation, and deprivation (C, N, E, and D). While all four are closely linked, there are some differences between them.

Confiscation

Confiscation occurs when a government confiscates assets from another government or private entity. We saw this in the Iranian Revolution, where the new government seized all the local assets of foreign governments and private interests. When Iran acted so hastily and aggressively, it woke up many companies who had or were going to expand globally to look to insurance as a mitigating option. Politically risky markets expand significantly in capacity and scope of cover, following the Iranian Revolution and similar events that followed.

Nationalization

Nationalization occurs when a host government declares the "nationalization" of private assets. This occurred in 1984 in Peru, when the government took over the assets of private companies in the petroleum industries and made these a national asset.

Sometimes nationalization is done swiftly and in one shot. Sometimes it is "creeping" and accomplished over a period of time.

Typically, the host country justifies its nationalization initiative to be in the best interest of that country and its people.

Expropriation

Expropriation can be defined as the act of taking of privately owned property by a government to be used for the benefit of the public. Typically, the government under eminent domain has the right to expropriate but with just compensation. In the context of expropriation being a political risk, either there is no compensation or the compensation is not adequate. In the 1970s the Chilean government was notorious for expropriating foreign private interests for the benefit of their general public.

Deprivation

Deprivation, unlike nationalization, confiscation, and expropriation, is not the taking of an asset but the deprivation of access by a host government to a private interest's assets. For example, a U.S. mining company acquires land in a particular country and builds its mining capability. After the company has been in the country for several years, the host country, because of political reasons, denies that company access to its assets or the right to run its business. The company still owns the land

and the equipment but is unable to run its business as it is prohibited or deprived of access.

Other Political Risks

There are other forms of political risks not included in the primary four outlined above. Some of these are devaluation, war and SRCCs, terrorism, currency inconvertibility, sanctions, contract frustration, loss of licenses, unfair calling of financial guarantees, and piracy.

Devaluation   Many countries take steps in devaluating their currency, in the hopes of stabilizing an imbalance in trade and mitigating inflation concerns, along with a host of other economic reasons. This means that if importers in such a country were buying goods and services from another country, they would have to come up with more local currency to pay for those goods or services, as the impact of the devaluation had caused the exchange rate to be in disfavor of the buyer. A foreign company could be impacted in its ability to get paid on sales in that country or through the appropriation of funds back to that country from local resources.

Venezuela, Great Britain, South Korea, and Japan are recent examples of countries that have devalued their currency in the hope of minimizing inflation and rising costs, along with the opportunity of slowing down imports and increasing export sales.

War and SRCCs   War and strikes, riots, and civil commotions stand as they are and obviously are a daily threat in various parts of the world. Threats exist all over the world, but in areas such as East Africa, the Middle East, and North Korea, exposures to global trade and foreign expansion are present daily.

Terrorism   The events of 9/11 in New York City might represent the most recent and significant act of terrorism that led to numerous political risk exposures all over the globe, including war, sanctions, more acts of terrorism, and significant multi-government initiatives, rules, and regulations impacting how countries in the world conduct themselves in trade, in travel, and with one another.

By the dictates of security professional, terrorism poses the greatest threat to global expansion; any company's expansion initiatives must include evaluating the threats of terrorism and the protection of its personnel, interests, and assets 24/7.

Sanctions   The United States, along with most of its allies, attempt to utilize sanctions as an effective political tool of managing risks globally. By definition, a sanction is the utilization of economic, political, and restrictive actions in dealing with a government's behavior of not responding to regulations, laws, or world agreements.

In 2014 the most recent sanction of the Group of Eight (G8) countries against Russia was for its involvement in the destabilization of Ukraine. Most of the sanctions are leveraged against the leadership in Russia, prohibiting them from financial and travel access. Additionally, recent examples of sanctions are those currently in place by the USA against Cuba and those dealing with nuclear proliferation against Iran and North Korea.

Sanctions are a method whose results are dubious when viewing the historical effects. There have been sanctions against Iran for over 10 years regarding their development of a nuclear bomb; these sanctions have been highly criticized as a total failure.

Sanctions have several negative impacts on global supply chains:

- Cause a duplicate action upon those being sanctioned, which creates an economic war where everyone loses
- Tend to punish the general public of the country and not the sources who are making the decisions, making the sanctions ineffective and trade and expansion becomes stalled

- Forestall trade, investment, and stability by design; who really wins?
- Increase acts of terrorism by those who become desolate and desperate

Currency Inconvertibility The United States has a federal reserve but has no central bank. Most countries in the world have central banks, which control the flow of money in and out of a country.

A U.S. company sells machinery to a buyer in Poland. When it comes time to pay for the goods, the buyer in Poland instructs its local bank to remit its payment. The local bank then contacts the Polish Central Bank (Narodowy Bank Polski), which, depending on its disposition of funds, will remit payment to the seller's bank in the United States. The Polish Central Bank remits on that transaction based upon its ability to do so. If funds are restricted, payment may take up to four months to happen. In some countries payment can take several years to occur.

Typical payment terms of net 30 have potentially no meaning in countries around the world that have imbalances of trade and cannot honor obligations timely. The buyer pays, but the central bank cannot transfer funds to the beneficiary bank.

Such a situation is called currency inconvertibility; over 60 countries have problems with this issue every day. Your banking team would be in the best position to advise which countries overseas have inconvertibility issues. This does not mean that you should not sell to these countries. What this means is that after you recognize that there is a risk, you approach the sale cautiously and then take steps in evaluation options to mitigate that risk, which is covered in various chapters of this book.

Algeria, Chad, Venezuela, and Russia are but three examples of countries with currency inconvertibility issues.

Contract Frustration/Repudiation When one is selling to a foreign government or a public-sector buyer, contract-frustration risk or contract-repudiation exposure is the nonpayment or arbitrary nonhonoring of your contract, either before or after shipment of your goods or performance of services. This exposure can be mitigated through political risk insurance available to protect against nonhonoring of sovereign government payment guarantees, whether the buyer is in the public or private sector.

Other kinds of policies can be written to insure against the political risks of nonpayment on your sales to private-sector buyers, such as, for example, to cover sales to your company's own subsidiary located in a market with high political risks or to any buyer for whose receivables you will not or cannot purchase comprehensive export credit insurance but, in any event, who might be unable to pay due to expropriation, currency inconvertibility or transfer risks, political violence, or other government actions or political events that would be out of their control.

In Chapter 3 are several brokerage/insurance company options with recommended support from this author.

Loss of Licenses   In most countries import licenses are required for goods entering from foreign sources. These licenses are typically controlled by the host governments and their import and related agencies. There have been numerous cases where in the middle of an import transaction, these licenses get pulled or are cancelled by various host government authorities, arbitrarily or due to unforeseen political reasons. These risks are more real than we would like to admit and are another reason in certain developing countries that we proceed with caution, identify the risks, and look for the various options we have to obtain insurance or mitigation techniques.

Unfair Calling of Financial Guarantees   Many times, sales to foreign markets will entail use of certain various forms of financial instruments to make payments. A widely utilized form of financial guarantee that is utilized on behalf of buyers to government entities and may produce terms is the letter of credit (L/C), which is provided by an exporter to guarantee certain performance requirements. The unfair calling on of that guarantee or L/C is another form of political risk present in global transactions. The guarantee is drawn upon with little recourse that the guarantor has against a foreign government entity. This exposure qualifies as a political risk. It can be successfully managed and mitigated once identified and quantified and steps outlined in Chapter 4 are followed.

Piracy   One only needs to see the 2013 film *Captain Phillips*, depicting the 2010 real-life event where the ocean freighter *Maersk Alabama* was boarded and taken over by Somali pirates just off the east coast of Africa. The film received great accolades and awards for showing what continues to be a serious issue in various trade lanes in ocean freight commerce.

Areas such as the east coast of Africa, the straits of Malacca, parts of northern Latin America, and the Caribbean all pose various levels of risk and exposure to pirates for both ocean freight and passenger/luxury vessels. Some experts say that pirates travel from the Philippines to Peru to Somalia and back around.

Piracy is a difficult risk to combat or avoid, but it can be mitigated through various supply-chain insurance and loss-control techniques, which are outlined in Chapter 4.

Economic

Economic issues are present in every country and where global trace occurs. They cannot be avoided but they can be mitigated.

It is critical for companies that sell internationally or source globally to

- Track economic impacts on the goods they sell or purchase, market by market; and
- Recognize that economic circumstance will impact
  - Costs;
  - Ability to get paid or pay; and
  - What currency to utilize.

Demographic

Just dealing with the size of the world and the distances involved creates exposure and challenges to those who enter the global business arena. To move freight from one corner to another could mean transit distances of over 10,000 miles, through numerous and difficult terrains and five to six countries and with several modes of transit. With potential interruptions-in-transit along with delays, physical restrictions are all the world has to offer as obstacles to movement and trade.

Physical

The physical challenges of global supply chains can be quickly summarized in the description outlined in the previous "Demographic" discussion. Great distances and extreme conditions tied into poor infrastructures pose along the way great exposure to managing expansive supply chains to and from the world.

Moving freight from Toledo to Minneapolis has risks and uncertainty; but moving that same freight from Toledo to Kazakhstan means increasing the physical risks tenfold.

Cultural and Language

I love the various cultures of the world and appreciate my global interface of over 35 years. That love has certainly not been without certain challenges.

Managing relationships in some cultures is both an art and a science. Latin America, Asia, the Middle East, and the Near East are but a few of the areas that pose unique differences in culture, which we must learn to deal with successfully in managing global expansion.

Here in the United States we have cultural differences all over, like how we in the northeast speak compared to those in the Deep South or how we go about our approach to business in the Midwest compared to that of Californians.

Add distance and language and hundreds of years of cultural development and the differences can be huge. Those individuals and companies who expand globally master the cultural and language differences by embracing these not as a right-or-wrong matter but as mere differences—differences that we must both respect and be able to navigate successfully with and should not be changed but caressed with honesty, care, and appropriate behavior as we want from them.

Legal

The legal differences in the world are huge. A significant amount of due diligence and reasonable care must be weighed and factored into every decision as we grow internationally. The ramifications and consequences of not paying attention to local laws, regulations, and business practices can be disastrous.

There are hundreds of examples of companies like General Motors (GM), U.S. Steel, Clorox, and Nike who would freely admit certain blunders from a legal perspective as they moved forward in global expansion. Today they are global giants with significant expertise in the legal side of international business, which is the certain consequence of stumbling along the way.

Compliance

When freight crosses international borders, the local customs authorities require that the importers are in compliance with the import regulations of that country. While many of the regulations are similar from one country to another, there are also numerous differences.

Typically there are very stringent guidelines in dealing with issues, such as the following:

- Origin
- Valuation
- Documentation
- Transfer pricing
- Harmonized classification (harmonized tariff schedule of the United States or HTSUS)
- Record keeping
- Shipping details

In many countries, such as the United States, customs is responsible for security concerns as well. After the events of 9/11 in the USA, the U.S. Customs' name was changed to Customs Border and Protection (CBP) to better suit its new enhanced responsibilities as our frontline against global security threats.

Margins

Margins are a mixed bag internationally. From my interviews with many corporations engaged in global trade, you will hear different stories about margins. From margins are better domestically; to margins are thinner globally. Our experience has shown that at the end of the day, there is greater margin expansion and opportunity for larger indexes in international markets over the course of time, which falls in line with another reason to expand internationally.

There are challenges with margin management, with currencies and exchange rates as examples of areas that need to be carefully scrutinized to make sure anticipated margins are protected and earned.

The author has clearly learned the tough lesson that over time, managing margins is one of the most important and singularly relevant responsibilities of company executives who enter into global expansion mode. It can be the cause of both failure and sustainable success!

Meeting Aggressive Growth Targets

All the challenges that a company faces in growing internationally may present serious obstacles to keeping aggressive growth strategies on target. I am as aggressive as the next guy, but I always err on the side of conservatism when determining growth targets. But in planning global strategies, it is best recommended to be cautious and keep expectations contained. Make sure that expectations are

- Relevant;
- Predictable;
- Measurable;
- Sustainable; and
- Reasonably obtainable.

Protection from Competition

Competition can be fierce from sources spanning the globe. The number of competitors, the capabilities of competitors, and some of the unfair trade practices in the global arena all pose serious challenges to growing internationally when every turn presents stiff competition. Knowing who the competitors are, their strengths and weaknesses, and their strategies are all critical elements of managing the challenges of global competition.

Control over intellectual property (IP) related issues is also a challenge in operating globally, as many of the protections here in the USA are not existent in certain markets or are not very robust. Local legal support is a critical risk management strategy in dealing with IP concerns in the various markets you are entering; recognize that control over IP in some markets, at the end of the day, does not functionally exist.

Diversification

A key strategy in global expansion is to diversify your approach in a number of ways and business processes:

- Focus on various regions and individual countries in those regions.
- Focus on the diversity of products and services.
- Focus on an array of approaches and strategies; do not rely on just one.

Diversity in itself is a strategy that should be included in your overall growth and global business development initiatives.

Security

I attend several security conferences a year and pay attention to the threat of security in global trade. In some trade lanes, markets, and companies, security concerns are the number one threat and obstacle to expansion in the global arena. The past and current turbulence in Africa and the Middle East raises this security concern to heightened levels.

Security concerns threaten

- Personnel traveling and living overseas;
- Local employees working overseas;
- Physical assets, both here and foreign domiciled;
- Financial transactions;
- IP, trademark, patent, etc.;
- Economic and financial well-being;
- Communication infrastructure;
- Plans for expansion, growth, and merger and acquisition (M&A) activity;
- Consequential propaganda; and
- Deal reluctance.

All threats outlined above pose threats to global expansion, threats that can be managed with a proactive and comprehensive global security program.

GLOBAL SECURITY CHALLENGE

Example 1.1: Customs-Trade Partnership against Terrorism

Customs-Trade Partnership against Terrorism (C-TPAT) seeks to safeguard the world's vibrant trade industry from terrorists, maintaining the economic health of the United States and its neighbors. The partnership develops and adopts measures that add security but do not have a chilling effect on trade, a difficult balancing act.

A GROWING PARTNERSHIP

Begun in November 2001 with just seven major importers as members, as of June 2011, the partnership has grown. Today, more than 10,000 certified partners that span the gamut of the trade community have been accepted into the program. These include U.S. importers, U.S./Canada highway carriers, U.S./Mexico highway carriers, rail and sea carriers, licensed U.S. Customs brokers, U.S. marine port authority/terminal operators, U.S. freight consolidators, ocean transportation intermediaries and non-operating common carriers, Mexican and Canadian manufacturers, and Mexican long-haul carriers. These 10,000-plus companies account for over 50 percent (by value) of what is imported into the United States.

EXTENDING THE ZONE OF U.S. BORDER SECURITY

By extending the United States' zone of security to the point of origin, the customs-trade partnership allows for better risk assessment and targeting, freeing CBP to allocate inspectional resources to more questionable shipments.

The partnership establishes clear supply-chain security criteria for members to meet and, in return, provides incentives and benefits like expedited processing. A corollary is to extend the partnership's antiterrorism principles globally through cooperation and coordination with the international community. Back in 2005, the World Customs Organization created the Framework of Standards to Secure and Facilitate Global Trade, which complements and globalizes CBP's and the partnership's cargo security efforts.

HOW IT WORKS

When they join the antiterror partnership, companies sign an agreement to work with CBP to protect the supply chain, identify security gaps, and implement specific security measures and best practices. Additionally, partners provide CBP with a security profile outlining the specific security measures the company has in place. Applicants must address a broad range of security topics and present security profiles that list action plans to align security throughout their supply chain.

C-TPAT members are considered low risk and are therefore less likely to be examined. This designation is based on a company's past compliance history, security profile, and the validation of a sample international supply chain.

AN EMERGING FOCUS: MUTUAL RECOGNITION ARRANGEMENTS

CBP has numerous mutual recognition arrangements with other countries. The goal of these arrangements is to link the various international industry partnership programs so that together they create a unified and sustainable security posture that can assist in securing and facilitating global cargo trade.

The goal of aligning partnership programs is to create a system whereby all participants in an international trade transaction are approved by the customs function as observing specified standards in the secure handling of goods and relevant information. C-TPAT signed its first mutual recognition arrangement with New Zealand in June 2007 and since that time has signed similar arrangements with South Korea, Japan, Jordan, Canada, the European Union (EU), Taiwan, Israel, and Mexico.

Bringing security into the global expansion plans is very important to meeting all the requirements of maintaining secure and compliant supply chains.

Access to Local Market Benefits and Value Added

Going global means access to local markets. Adding value to your supply chain obtains differentiation in those local markets, which creates opportunity. Meeting this challenge and turning it into opportunity creates a path for expansion and growth with the best chance of success.

Creating a "Panache"

Working with companies such as Coca-Cola, Revlon, Nike, Apple, and numerous others meets the challenges of global expansion by creating a panache on a macrolevel crossing all cultures and geographic boundaries. On a microlevel these panache strategies have to be localized and created to successfully deal with cultural, language, and geophysical differences that exist between regions, countries, provinces, and cities.

Going Public

In international growth strategies extending growth, acquisitions, and penetration into foreign markets is a challenge that can prove very beneficial to increasing the initial public offering (IPO) value.

Having tenured international expansion creates stockholder value that stabilizes stock price and aids in the overall market viability of the equity in time.

Selling Strategy

Companies face the challenge of selling themselves. Having M&A activity sided with global expansion creates a sense of greater value and worth that can

- Attract investors;
- Have larger payouts; and
- Gain larger interest in diverse markets.

Too many companies believe people are interchangeable. Truly gifted people never are. They have unique talents. Such people cannot be forced into roles they are not suited for, nor should they be. Effective leaders allow great people to do the work they were born to do.

Warren G. Buffet

2

Unique Challenges of Supply-Chain, Transportation, and Logistics Companies in Merger and Acquisition and Growth Strategies

This chapter outlines the numerous challenges that companies engaged in global supply chains face in successfully growing their business models. It sets the structure and the balance of material and content covered throughout the balance of this book.

DEFINE THE GLOBAL SUPPLY CHAIN

The *global supply chain* is defined as the connectivity and relationships of the parties to an international transaction that typically interface with each other for the purpose of delivering a final product and/or service. The success of any global supply chain is totally dependent on how well that connectivity works between all the vested parties.

The following two outlines depict the typical domestic and international supply-chain processes and parties. These parties are complex and convoluted and have an array of connection points that work both directly and indirectly between all the vested and stakeholder parties.

Domestic Supply-Chain Parties

- Manufacturers
- Distributors
- State and federal agencies
- Warehouses
- Carriers (truck, rail, car, aircraft, boat)
- Buyers
- Consignees
- End users

International Supply-Chain Parties

- Manufacturers
- Distributors
- Domestic carriers
- Warehouses and consolidators
- Outbound government authorities (customs plus)
- Foreign carriers
- Inbound government authorities (customs plus)
- Domestic carriers
- Warehouses and deconsolidators
- State and federal agencies
- Buyers
- Consignees
- End users

LANDED COST MODELING

Landed cost modeling is an essential element of any global supply chain. It creates the financial case for sourcing overseas and helps to create competitive leverage on export activity. It is often missed by many corporate executives, who realize too late that what they thought was going to work out financially does not!

This chapter gives an overview of the necessity of landed cost modeling and the implications of this modeling on strategic and tactical decision making.

Why Do Landed Cost Modeling?

The reasons that a company engaged in global supply chains needs to do landed cost modeling are the following:

- Landed cost modeling creates the financial argument for overseas sourcing as a strategic option in choosing suppliers and vendors outside the country of destination.
- It determines the margins of opportunity.
- It provides information flow and intelligence that allow better decision making in the various options we have in how the global supply chain operates and ultimately performs.

Creates the Financial Argument for Overseas Sourcing as a Strategic Option in Choosing Suppliers and Vendors outside the Country of Destination

In over 35 years of consulting and working with companies engaged in global trade, I have come across numerous examples of where decisions were made to source products in overseas markets and the model a year down the line was not working out financially, making the overseas sourcing decision an unsuccessful option. The typical scenario might be scripted as follows:

Zenon Corporation, which is based outside Nashville, Tennessee, manufactures industrial valves and pumps. Their U.S.-completed manufacturing costs for their most popular sale come in at US$2,200.00 when the product is manufactured at their plant.

Their purchasing department is approached by a contract manufacturer located near Nimbo, China. After product specifications, examples are completed and quality control (QC) signs off. A free-on-board (FOB), or port-of-export, outbound cost comes in at US$2,000.00 per unit when bought in 1,000 MOQs. Zenon's intention is to order over 20,000 units annually. They determine freight costs of US$25.00/unit for bringing a unit to the port of Los Angeles, and their duties and tax estimates are at 1.5%, which places the landed cost in their estimate at $2,000 + $25 + $20 = US$2,045.00. They estimate that they will save US$155.00 per unit. When you multiply this cost by 20,000 units, the savings exceed US$3 million annually. The case for utilizing this source for manufacturing can easily be made.

However, after a year of sourcing from Nimbo, a financial audit determines that the savings are considerably less than anticipated, and when you tie in a host of additional issues that pop up, the sourcing option is at a breakeven or even a potential loss. Why?

The landed cost model utilized did not capture all the costs correctly and did not anticipate some of the extra expenses associated with returns and warranty issues. The first problem arose when the goods started to come into the United States and were being cleared through Customs Border and Protection (CBP) in Los Angeles, the port of entry.

The first few shipments cleared through the customs pretty easily. However, in a random CBP inspection, the goods were held up and after a two-week hold, it was determined that the incorrect harmonized tariff schedule (HTS) number was being utilized. This had been supplied by the supplier and proved to be incorrect. The correct HTS number was determined, but this moved the duty rate to 4.5%. This raised unit costs by $60.00.

When the third shipment arrived at the U.S. facility in Nashville, there was damage, leading to a claim against the supplier and the carrier. It turned out that no one had insured the shipment after the FOB point in Nimbo. This led to insurance being purchased, as it should have been from the beginning. This added another $10.00 per unit.

In the audit, it was also determined that no one had calculated the clearance costs in Los Angeles. This added another $5.00 per unit. The audit also showed another $10.00 per unit for inland transit from Los Angeles to Nashville.

Two additional expense items from the customer service group regarding product failures showed up in the audit as well. These failures caused replacement of several parts that were under warranty. The Chinese supplier provided the parts for free as part of the purchase price, but the shipping costs, insurance costs, duties, taxes, and ancillary costs added another $350,000.00 annually. The second additional expense item had to do with production and inventory management delays. These caused a considerable amount of air freight shipping. The supplier contributed a small portion to this expense, which annually amounted to an additional $500,000.00 of expense.

There also was almost $250,000.00 of expenses with purchasing, engineering, and QC personnel having to visit the China plant in dealing with manufacturing issues. The real landed costs were significantly higher:

$$\text{Actual landed cost: } \$2,000 + \$45.00 + \$60.00 + \$10.00 + \$5.00 + \$10.00 = \$2,130.00.$$

The costs were as much as $85.00 higher than those budgeted. For 20,000 units this reduced the anticipated savings by $1,700,000.00. When you add back in the problem with returns ($350,000), air freight ($500,000), and travel ($250,000), the savings totaled $1,100,000.00. The real landed costs annually reduced the anticipated profits of over $3 million (budgeted) to maybe $200,000–$300,000, a far cry from the original decision to move manufacturing from the home base to a foreign location. With the amount of internal disruption with the personnel and the plant, all the benefits of controlled and owned on-site manufacturing dissipated quickly.

Summary of Conclusions

- Landed cost modeling must be done on all options for sourcing, including domestic choices.
- Due diligence, along with comprehensive analysis, must be done to make sure that the business model for foreign sourcing has financial integrity.
- Landed costs must include all the expenses associated with the foreign sourcing option, including the cost of managing and dealing with likely problems.*
- Contingency planning must be part of the landed-cost-modeling process, where strengths, weaknesses, opportunities, and threats (SWOT) analysis is brought into the equation so that the budget is as close to reality as possible.

---

* Some accounting practices will allocate some of these costs outside of landed cost models and away from cost of goods purchased and place the expenses into different categories in the general ledger, which the author acknowledges as another option. But, having said that, these are still costs in doing business this way and should in some fashion be accounted for against budgeted savings.

Landed cost modeling should or could include the following:

- Cost of purchase: either ex works or FOB/free carrier (FCA) outbound gateway
- Freight costs: domestic and international (depending on choice of international commercial terms [Incoterms])
- Storage, consolidation, and deconsolidation costs
- Insurance costs
- Duties, taxes, value-added taxes (VATs), etc.
- Customs clearance costs
- Costs of import licenses or applications
- Costs of inspection services
- Return and warranty costs
- Air freight or special time-sensitive or expedited freight costs when required
- Travel and personnel costs for purchasing, senior management, engineering, QC, etc.

The bottom line is that companies need to be sure that foreign sourcing is a legitimate option financially. Landed cost modeling is one of the best tools to accomplish this.

Determines the Margins of Opportunity

The previous discussion of landed cost modeling clearly states the case for determining the costs of global sourcing options. This then creates the starting point for considering your margins on a product for sale to customers or your selling prices.

As we move past the recession of 2008/9, margins are clearly a major issue facing every company in business today. The reality is that margins have shrunk considerably since 2007, and, while stability has arisen in most businesses and industries, the clear majority of corporate executives believe thinner margins are a new reality going forward for everyone. Therefore, for a company determining what the opportunity for margin reward exists, there is a firm need to compute what their costs are to bring the product to a point of sale or point of value. The landed cost modeling process is this tool that ultimately can be utilized to set margins and profitability.

Improper utilization of landed cost modeling can lead to margin variation, unhappy customers, and loss of sales.

Provides Information Flow and Intelligence That Allows Better Decision Making in the Various Options We Have in How the Global Supply Chain Operates and Ultimately Performs

Foreign sourcing and overseas contract manufacturing is an option. It must be weighed and calculated. The process includes establishing an information flow into your organization that will allow better and more informed decision making. This will create the best opportunity for decision making that will lead to

- Greater profits
- Business development growth
- Higher margins
- Better customer service

The gained information flow allows you to make better choices in many of the following areas:

- Choice of suppliers and vendors
- Price points and margin structure
- Supply chain and distribution structure
- Choice of carriers, modes of transit, and service providers
- Marketing options
- Customer service variables

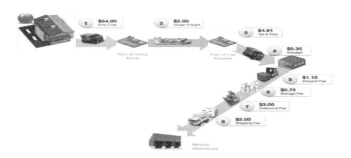

Although landed cost modeling is a necessary evil, it is also a way to be assured of foreign sourcing decisions and ultimately allows the best run and managed global supply chain. Landed cost modeling is mostly a science if you follow the metrics outlined in the preceding paragraphs.

But, having said that, there is a creative side to landed cost modeling where the "artsy" side can help with making the process run more smoothly and with more cost-effectiveness and allow better and more precise decisions.

Example 2.1

The company we reviewed previously, Zenon Corporation in Nashville, Tennessee, has to decide which suppliers in China will be the best long-term partner for their contract manufacturing. They approach this process by creating a very competitive request for proposal (RFP) from a list of six vendors that they believe offer serious potential for this agreement. They actually create a competitive bidding process, taking price out of the equation, working with the vendors and giving them a lot of room to be creative, and then providing an RFP in the following areas:

- Ability to create products that provide market differentiation
- Ability to provide products that allow sustainability
- Ability to provide products that meet "going green" standards
- Ability to meet products with significant competitive advantage
- Ability to meet manufacturing specifications that are energy efficient and provides best environmental practices

The RFP allows the vendors the ability to be creative without the immediate pressure of trying to be also at the lowest price.

When we handled foreign sourcing in this fashion in the past, we were always amazed with what happened when the pricing restrictions had been loosened. We truly get the creative juices flowing from our vendors and suppliers and we all become winners. Once we have made the choice by design, we then can go back. If we benchmark our pricing correctly, we will be in a position to now negotiate pricing, which allows a compromise between this creative process and the market conditions.

This creative process, outlined previously, also truly allows a partnership to exist between the vendor and the buyer and gives the best opportunity for long-term global supply chain success. This process becomes integrated with business growth strategies as a company expands its global footprint and can become an excellent method for forming sustainable and competitive relationships.

Price should always be a driving factor, but it must also be weighed against and compromised against services, timing, creativity, value add, and total costs measured.

Leaders must be close enough to relate to others, but far enough ahead to motivate them.

John C. Maxwell

3

Organic Growth versus Merger and Acquisition

Companies growing their global supply chains have many options in planning their growth strategically; these options fall into two primary camps: through merger and acquisition (M&A) and through organic growth. This chapter reviews the strategic pros and cons in both areas and creates a planned-out thought process on how to move ahead in both areas.

ORGANIC GROWTH

Most companies start outgrowing but directly capturing business themselves. In the early years, growth is based upon preexisting relationships leveraged into clients.

Organic growth can make its mark in a number of ways:

- Lower costs
- Relationship driven
- Unique services
- Controlled or protected capabilities
- Hiring key personnel
- Forming strategic partnerships
- Aligning with key relationships

Lower Costs

Organic growth as compared to aggressive M&A growth can usually be done at a much lower cost outlay to the parent company. Additionally, it usually is a more lethargic process for which costs can be easily controlled and limited. It also can be targeted and can allow time for tactical actions to take place and show results before more monies are expended. It generally allows a slower pace to be developed, which allows control over expenses, as results are achieved. Additionally, it allows greater flexibility because changes, modifications, and tweaking can take place more easily. Commitments become a little more tentative, affording a change in direction when needed, quickly and precisely.

Relationship Driven

Relationships and referrals are two great ways to develop business organically. Many companies will hire sales personnel who have "books of business" and critical relationships, which, when these personnel become part of the organizations, can help grow the business.

One of the most successful organic growth strategies is the finding and hiring of key sales personnel who have a following of clients and opportunities. Obviously, noncompete and trade-secret agreements must be identified and managed successfully. These can be expensive problems when not handled correctly.

Relationships with trade associations, networking groups, and government agents will also present opportunities for global growth organically.

Unique Services

Your company's ability to provide unique services that differentiate you from your competition can be a critical factor in organic growth. This typically provides a creative approach to product design, service capabilities, control over market venues, trade lanes, and other aspects that will make you more competitive. You will be more competitive in providing a product, service, or capability that others cannot access or do as well.

An example of providing unique services lies in how Google dominated the search-engine market or how Mercedes continues to lead in high-end automobile sales or how TaylorMade dominates the world of golf products. In transportation and logistics, Expeditors' domination, APL's growth engine, and C.H. Robinson's third-party logistics (3PL) and trucking services are examples.

Making initiatives and creating a structure that encourages innovation, creativity, and unique expansion verticals can be a full-time job and is typically a responsibility shared among a team of executives directly supported by senior management.

Some areas to be considered are as follows:

- Verticals not being pursued by other competitors
- Geographic areas not being pursued by competitors, such as those in the world of developing and third-world countries in Africa, Latin America, the Caribbean, and Southeast Asia, which all fit into this opportunity
- Offering better and/or more competitive payment options and extending credit liberally, but with protections (protections such as those that can be absorbed by credit, political risk, or receivable insurance)
- Utilizing foreign trade zones and bonded warehouses to gain competitive advantage

Controlled or Protected Capabilities

In mergers and acquisitions, secret and proprietary information exchanges hands. When you are the acquirer and gain trade secrets, patents, proprietary rights, and capabilities are typically a gain; but when you sell, although these can all be lucrative collateral and assets, they can also be part of your demise.

Some companies, therefore, prefer to grow internally and organically so that they can control the proprietary factors in their business model. This is a double-edged sword. As this will allow a controlled growth, the growth will most likely be at a slower pace than that by acquisition. An evaluation needs to take place in this regard for you to be able to think about what will work best for your company's growth strategies.

Here are some of the considerations to think about in evaluating your protectionist approach:

- How much longer will the patent be in place? How much time is left on your holding exclusivity to that trade lane? When will that capability or trade secret be mitigated by time, technology, or competitive sources?

- Are time, money, and resources being spent on protectionist policies and actions providing a cost-benefit balance to the overall business model? Or, in other words, are they providing value against spending, with more results, benefits, attributes, and revenues?
- Does what you are protecting have a life span? Is it truly protectable? Or, as an example with a slight modification, would it lose its proprietary properties?

Hiring Key Personnel

Many companies grow by obtaining key personnel in marketing, sales, and business development, those that "control business" and have a following of prospects and clients. Some companies develop their growth by relying on key personnel that they hire and giving these personnel the responsibility, the authority, the support, and the funding necessary to grow the business. Some strategies start at the top with a chief executive officer (CEO) who has growth experience and capability.

Forming Strategic Partnerships

Global expansion can often take a route of forming strategic relationships that create benefit for both companies. It can often be done to minimize both risk and cost of the endeavor. Two varied companies can bring different but compatible skill sets, assets, and capabilities to the partnership, creating a win-win collaboration that works for everyone's interests.

Aligning with Key Relationships

Strategic partnerships are structured and formalized. A less intrusive way may be to align with key relationships under temporary, loose, or convenient agreements that allow mutuality to work for everyone's interests. It generally creates opportunity at less cost and with fewer risks than those for strategic partnerships and can sometimes prove just as valuable in growing and developing global expansion and opportunity.

WHAT THE CORPORATE ICONS HAVE TO SAY

So, what do the big boys have to say about M&A?

We spoke with or attended conferences highlighting more than fifteen senior executives from the supply-chain world who had been engaged in M&A activity and global expansion all over the world. Here is an outline offering a summary of their common thoughts:

- Acquisition growth creates a faster path to gaining market share quickly.
- Organic growth is a slower process but is a strategy that should be done in sync with any acquisition strategy.
- Earnings before interest, taxes, depreciation, and amortization (EBITDA) is a tool and not an end-all in the evaluation process.
- Make sure that you understand the "why of any international business development activity" and not just do it because it is "the trend or market driven" activity.
- Exercise due diligence in every deal, paying attention to detail and turning over as many stones as possible.
- Make sure that all key executives in the acquisition have bought into the new deal and are on board for the transitional strategies utilized.
- Carefully scrutinize all non-compete and trade-secret agreements.
- Communicate articulately and carefully to all staff, clients, and vendors.
- Make sure that key clients, along with any critical vendors, are contacted proactively and that they are on board with the deal.

- Transitional strategies are a very important element of making the deal work.
- Allow sufficient time for the deal to be analyzed, and do not be hasty in the final decision-making process.
- Information at the granular level is very critical.
- As you approach deal closure, check, recheck, and check again. Diligence, scrutiny, and "stone turning" make the difference between success and failure of the deal.

AS REPORTED BY PRICEWATERHOUSECOOPERS IN AUGUST 2014

When beer brewers SABMiller plc and Molson Coors Brewing Co. announced plans to merge their U.S. operations in October 2007, the companies said that they expected to achieve $500 million in annual cost savings from, among other things, streamlining production and reducing shipping distances. Achieving the projected cost savings would be the key to the success of the merger as the united brewers contend with rising prices of aluminum, grains, and other commodities. In addition, the cost cuts would help strengthen the new company's hand in a potential price war with Anheuser-Busch, which held an almost 50 percent share of the U.S. market (versus the combined SABMiller–Molson Coor's roughly 29 percent).

Supply-chain considerations rarely are the driving factor behind mergers and acquisitions. But as the beer brewers' linkup suggests, the supply-chain function typically plays a crucial role in ensuring the success of any union of two or more companies. This article explores the best practices for ensuring that the supply chain can rise to the challenges and meet the promise presented by a merger or an acquisition.

PLAN EARLY, PLAN REALISTICALLY

A survey of 154 supply-chain and other business executives at large U.S. corporations that was conducted last year for Accenture revealed what most supply chain executives probably had already known in the majority of cases (77 percent in the survey): supply-chain executives became involved in a merger only at or after the announcement of the deal.

"That's too bad," says Jay Welsh, a partner in the supply-chain-management practice at Accenture, and this is because companies that bring their supply-chain leadership into the merger-planning process earlier are more likely to be successful in meeting their goals. "It's important to have supply-chain executives involved early in the planning process, getting them involved not only during the synergy estimation and analysis but also during the due diligence," Welsh says. "That's the number one success factor."

Bringing the supply chain into the planning process early helps on a couple of different fronts. First, doing a thorough, upfront analysis of the potential M&A synergies—that is, the cost savings that can be expected from combining two or more companies' operations—from a supply-chain perspective can help ensure that senior management sets goals that the supply-chain organization can actually meet, Welsh says. Conversely, supply-chain executives may be able to identify additional synergies that the C-level group has not considered. Either way, establishing goals that are achievable makes it more likely that the merger will be viewed as a success once the dust settles.

Second, involving supply-chain executives at an early stage can help the supply-chain function understand how they are expected to meet the goals for the merger, says Marc Tanowitz, a principal with Pace Harmon, an information technology and supply-chain consulting firm based in Vienna, Virginia. "Sometimes you'll hear a CEO say that the supply chain is going to drive X amount of savings, but the people in the supply-chain organization don't necessarily know what that means," says Tanowitz, who estimates he has been involved in some $200 billion worth of merger activity for various companies. Does the CEO mean that the supply organization is supposed to re-source major spending categories for per-unit cost savings or figure out how to reduce inventory to drive savings through lower working-capital expenditures? Bringing the supply chain into the analysis process can help the organization focus on the correct set of target metrics from the start of the merger process and begin planning that much earlier on how to accomplish those targets.

SUPPLY-CHAIN CHECKLIST FOR M&A SUCCESS

- Involve supply-chain executives as early as possible in the M&A planning to
  - Understand potential synergies,
  - Set realistic goals, and
  - Prepare the supply-chain organization for focusing on the appropriate goals.
- Do not rely on intuition; rely on the data.
  - Make sure that you understand how the data in each company's systems relate to each other.
  - Leverage supply-chain solutions that can tap into the data from each company's core back-end systems without causing service disruptions.
- Embrace the change and look for opportunities to make fundamental transformations in how you manage your supply chain.
  - Be sensitive to, and do not underestimate, the cultural issues involved in combining two organizations.

Concentrate your energies, your thoughts and your capital. The wise man puts all his eggs in one basket and watches the basket.

Andrew Carnegie

4

Strategic Planning

Strategic planning is both an art and a science. Those that succeed best in strategic planning know how to balance out both areas and develop an ideology that assures consistent success.

This chapter provides a very comprehensive overview of strategic planning and offers the reader a structured approach to this area that can provide an easy, simplified approach to thinking out strategic planning consistently and achieve desired results.

THE STRATEGIC PLANNING PROCESS

Strategic planning can be best addressed by viewing the following steps:

- Identifying stakeholders and leadership
- Setting deliverables
- Alignment of goals and expectations
- Managing a strengths, weakness, opportunities, and threats (SWOT) analysis
- Establishment of timelines and action plans
- Cost and return-on-investment (ROI) analyses
- Senior management buy-in
- Initial salvos
- Implementation
- Problem anticipation and proactive mitigation
- Tweaking period
- Closure

Many companies fail at growth internationally due to a lack of a strategic plan or a plan that is riddled with faults, holes, and mines. From my consulting practice of over 30 years and looking at various global organizations that have been successful or have failed, the key ingredients to having succeeded are

- Quality strategy,
- Leadership, and
- Execution.

The best opportunity to make these three qualities happen is to adhere to the following steps.

Identifying Stakeholders and Leadership

The first step in strategic development is to identify who the stakeholders are. My definition of *stakeholders* is those personnel who have a **direct vested interest** in the consequences of the strategy.

While all personnel in a company may be impacted by any strategy, the differences of those who would participate in the strategic development are that they

- Are significantly impacted by the strategic plan;
- Have an ability to make an impact on developing or executing the strategy;
- Have the skill sets, resources, and capabilities to offer value in the strategic planning process; and
- Are part of the senior management team(s) that help run the company and are involved in moving it forward.

Once the stakeholders are identified, there will be a need to determine who will take ownership and leadership of the strategy. While committees and team activity will be a comprehensive part of the strategic plan, it usually will require a leader to drive the initiative.

Successful strategic leaders possess the following traits:

- Has already established successful leadership
- Can lead a group to successful completion
- Is not afraid of challenge or confrontation
- Sees obstacles as challenges and not as preventive issues
- Can lead without creating too much angst
- Can motivate with both little and expansive incentives
- Can see the forest through the trees
- Can create camaraderie and team building
- Knows how to negotiate a favorable close

Setting Deliverables

One of the first steps following leadership appointment is to set up the deliverables, expectations, and/or goals. These will set in motion what the leadership is trying to achieve. In the international business world, this is typically set by a board of directors in alignment with the CEO and senior management team of their company.

Goals will usually address the following areas, relative to this book:

- Margins and profitability
- Growth targets, organically and through M&A
- Specific target areas
- Allowances and funding (budgeting) for global expansion
- Structure of the global "mantra"

Expanding globally requires a comprehensive strategy coming from the board of directors and in conjunction with the senior management.

Deliverables must contain the following traits:

- Have reasonable expectations
- Reach far and beyond
- Tap into creative talents
- Maximize use of resources and capabilities
- Be both short and long term
- Be comprehensive

Have Reasonable Expectations

Much thought must be given to the development of deliverables. One of the most important thoughts must be the reasonableness of the deliverable or goal.

Often I bear witness to goals that are too high and mighty and, in evaluation, are never really achievable. On the other hand, I have observed goals that did not go far enough or were much too conservative.

Most companies that enter the global arena do so because this creates the best opportunity for longevity and prosperity for the company. But the strategy must be well thought out, balancing out unrealistic expectations and realistic likelihoods. This requires intense

- Mining of information necessary to make informed decisions;

- Comprehensive metrics and analysis; and
- Time and resource allocation.

While strategies can change, the real goal is not to change the strategy. Tactics and action plans are made to change, but the strategy should be well thought out as to be "cast in stone."

Some flexibility will be allowed in strategic planning but not much. This makes strategic planning a very critical element that must be well thought out before finalizing and executing. I compare it to complex surgery: once the knife enters the body, there is not much room for change. Make sure that the surgical process you are committed to is the right one! Analysis, assessment, fact finding, and studying the information flow become critical before making that first incision. Business strategic planning is very similar. Setting expectations, rather than deliverables, requires exact planning.

Reach Far and Beyond

Leadership must set goals and deliverables that will make an impact. These are often, while good leaders are called "movers and shakers" and "captains of industry"; they set the pace. Their goals reach the extremes of possibility—extreme but realistic.

"Reaching for the moon" may be lofty but is achievable and a good mantra for setting goals and deliverables. "Cutting edge" and "futuristic" are also good identifiers of far-reaching goals. The bottom line is that "blinders" need to be removed, and leadership needs to look very far ahead and often take some positions that will be controversial to create a path for growth and business development that leads rather than follows the competition.

Innovation and creative process is a leadership tool that must be brought into the global-expansion business model. Look at some of the major companies of our time with innovation as their second name: Apple, Microsoft, Intel, Coca-Cola, Mercedes-Benz, Expeditors, and Kuehne + Nagel, to name a few.

Every one of the mentioned companies balances a conservative approach with innovation and leading-edge customer service and product ideas, which allows them huge international growth, prosperity, and shareholder value. All these companies reach into six continents and have double-digit growth internationally. All have different strategies in both organic and M&A activities and have been very successful in developing a global brand and international outreach; they are all leaders in their respective industries. They all are mature in fundamental growth strategies but are also all engaged in leading-edge activities that are innovative, creative, and very futuristic. They all have been successful in balancing out the approach to conservatism and protection of assets while leading the charge into some uncertain areas where risk may be prevalent but manageable.

Tap into Creative Talents

Most organizations have a wealth of talent. And where there are deficiencies, they must seek to hire talent.

Talent is the number one acquisition for growth and international business development opportunity. An exceptional talent has

- Global reach and access to local expertise;
- Skill sets in areas that allow growth in sales, marketing, business development, customer service, acquisition relationships, etc.; and
- Skill sets that protect assets: legal, risk management, accounting and financial controls, consulting, and operational audit and oversight.

Opportunity is always available to access external talent, and many companies choose that option over the choice to create internal talent. There are arguments set in both cases but most companies eventually lead to develop their own expertise as the company matures internationally. Utilizing external talent and expertise is typically a short-term strategy.

People and their talents and skill sets set the stage for global expansion and growth.

Maximize Use of Resources and Capabilities

What capabilities are needed for global growth?

- Marketing
- Sales
- Business development
- Operations
- Legal expertise
- Finance
- Trade compliance
- Audit
- Supply chain and logistics
- Research and development (R&D)
- M&A
- International operations

Marketing

Creating the case for global opportunity often rests on the talent pool of the marketing group. It is in their initial assessments that marketability is determined. This is to help determine a marketing strategy with the best opportunity for success.

Sales

At some point an international sales force with "boots on the ground" will need to be created. This will be structured with both sales personnel who travel overseas and those developed at a regional or local level. They become the leadership who turns opportunities into revenue.

Business Development

Some companies will choose to handle international growth and expansion within a defined business-development group that will tend to specialize their talents in the area of business development. They typically combine the skill sets of sales, marketing with strategic planning, and business implementation. Business-development talent will usually possess several skill sets and have years of experience in M&A and global expansion deals.

Operations

Operations personnel make the business happen. They can include several areas inclusive of manufacturing, warehousing, customer service, strategic planning, business development, etc. They are the talent pool that executes what marketing and sales has sold. It is said that they often have to make houses from clay when steel, wood, glass, and stone have been promised. Operations makes this happen, protects margins, and drives business implementation.

Legal Expertise

The complexities of any business as it grows require legal talent. Make a business international and the complexities grow tenfold. In Chapter 9, this topic is covered in detail.

International law is so detailed and complex that no one source can provide expertise in all areas. Most general counsels of global firms are

"Quarterbacks" managing a pool of international legal expertise that addresses all of the following areas of concern:

- International laws
- Country-specific laws
- Product-liability laws
- Contract laws
- Intellectual-property-right (IPR) issues
- Human-resource concerns
- Trade-compliance management

The general counsel of a large company in Nassau County, New York, emphasizes the importance of his responsibilities in leading and structuring a team of qualified legal and consulting professionals in all areas of global operations to assure his company creates the best path for international growth and profitability.

Finance

Accounting practice on the global scale requires a huge pool of talent. Legal and financial implications in foreign sales and operations require very intense fiduciary controls. Chief financial officers (CFOs) of international companies often see their role at orchestrating a team of professionals and their skill sets as benefiting the financial bottom line of the organization.

The methods and options available in global business widely vary. When accessing all the options, knowledge of the up and down sides of financial decisions has to be weighed every day both in strategic planning and in execution.

Public companies also have Sarbanes–Oxley Act of 2002 (SOX) legal ramifications to deal with. For this, they typically rely on close relationships with some of their major accounting firm's expertise and talent pools here in the United States and in all the countries they operate in.

The **big four accounting firms** are recognized especially for their ability to provide sound financial expertise for companies engaged in global expansion and with major international reach to cover companies located all over the world.

Trade Compliance

While trade compliance has always been an important aspect of global trade, the event of 9/11 in New York City has the greatest importance in this area for companies involved in international operations. Trade-compliance management requires operators of global supply chains to pay attention to details on how products, services, and foreign entities operate in the world of international business. This is covered in great detail in Chapter 10.

Areas that are very critical include, but not limited to, the following:

- Harmonized tariff schedule of the United States (HTSUS)
- Valuation
- Revenue recognition
- Utilization of international commercial terms (Incoterms) of sale
- Payment methods
- Currency utilization
- Record keeping
- Creation of standard operating procedures (SOPs)
- Training of all global personnel
- Dealing with and managing customs issues
- Import and export licenses/permits
- Dealing with the departments of treasury, commerce, and state
- Denied party scrutiny

The consequences of not paying attention to trade-compliance regulations and best practices can lead to unsuccessful global initiatives and unprofitable operations. Doing these right can lead to better-run global supply chains, improving financial results, and setting the stage for growth and sustainability.

Audit

Setting up systems, protocols, and business-process controls to assure responsible and accountable global operations is an evil but necessary component of international growth and expansion. Larger companies typically will have internal audit personnel and access external resources as well to assist in global audit responsibilities. Self-regulation is a great best practice and for public companies is a component of SOX.

Auditing is an evil but necessary component of global operations.

Supply Chain and Logistics

The very basic responsibility of a supply chain is moving goods and services from A to B. This needs to be done as follows:

- Timely
- Safely
- Cost-effectively
- Securely/trade compliantly

Supply chains operating 100 years ago or in 1970 or as we enter 2016 all need these four components. What do these mean in brief?

Timely All goods and services typically have a time frame for occurrence, delivery, or utilization. The supply-chain manager's principal responsibility is to maintain schedules and leverage all supply-chain functions for the company's benefit.

Safely Goods and services must arrive in a usable condition for processing or sale. This is a responsibility of the supply-chain team. Make sure that goods and services arrive safely in a usable and of-value condition.

Cargo-loss control is the science of packaging, labeling, marking, materials handling, and shipping in a way to reduce risk and leverage spend. Cargo-loss control is an important responsibility of supply-chain managers; the results of quality decision making make for better international operations.

International shipping is an integral part of the global-supply-chain manager's responsibilities. Cargo-loss control is an important skill set.

Cost-Effectively Supply-chain managers are always looking to reduce costs. The key is to reduce cost without increasing risks. In my third book in *The Global Warrior Series, Reducing Risk and Spend in the Global Supply Chain,* I discuss this subject in great detail.

Arranging the cheapest service or cost usually impacts on risk unfavorably. The trick is to find a balance between cost and risk that keeps costs competitive and risks low.

Securely/Trade Compliantly   Supply chains run well when there is a balance between cost, safety, and timeliness. Having said that, there needs to be an element of inclusion of making sure that goods and services move securely and compliantly. This has been reemphasized by the events of 9/11 and will be an ongoing concern for current and future global supply chains. It generally adds minimal costs to accomplish and must be factored into operational budgets to round out supply-chain operational responsibilities, best practices, and successful growth and M&A targeting.

Research and Development

Research and development in all industries (not just chemical, pharmaceutical, and food companies) needs to be a focused part of any plan to grow globally and expand into international markets. As we approach 2016, most companies coming out of the economic recession are back again to spending more money in R&D activity as it sets the stage for creation, development, and expansion to increase the most competitive products and services possible. R&D makes a company take the leading edge.

Merger and Acquisition

Many companies choose to distinguish themselves in growth and expansion in global markets by setting up and managing independent M&A activities. This allows the company personnel not to be distracted from M&A responsibilities and "wearing other hats." This also allows a distinct focus on M&A activities, which in the long run can prove to have the most favorable results.

Some companies may call this business development or acquisition, but whatever it is called the design is to allow a team of professionals targeting M&A opportunities as the primary focus. It is a good position for many companies that are expanding internationally and have aggressive plans and strategies.

International Operations

Many corporations involved in global business will run their business units as a separate and distinct international operation. They will have both U.S. corporate and international operations, covering all business out of the United States. Others might show distinction between North America (inclusive of Canada and Mexico) and all other countries where there are international operations. Their personnel have developed an expertise in foreign sales, operations, and business development as a separate discipline.

The international divisions in larger companies may regionalize the world in how it is managed, recognizing the need to specialize in all the differences in global business but under a singular leadership and talent pool. These international divisions are often run as entirely separate companies, reporting to different boards with different agendas from those of their domestic counterparts.

International operations can be developed as its own area of expertise in many corporate strategies.

Be Both Short and Long Term

Deliverables and goals need to address both short-term and long-term goals. American executives are often blamed for thinking too short term and not having the necessary patience for decisions with impacts that are out more than a few years. While that statement can be subject to a debate, it probably has some validity over the past number of years since 2007, when the recession began to surface. Executives here in the USA and abroad were forced to make numerous short-term decisions, which had huge impacts immediately and also down the road.

The reality is that decisions need to be made in considering both short- and long-term consequences. Additionally, it should be recognized that short-term decisions will have both immediate and longer-term implications.

Example 4.1

To reduce payroll costs, a company decides to cut back on the executive workforce, including some senior tenured managers, whose compensation has grown to be sizable. Their reduction would have a huge impact. The favorable consequence of that decision in the short run is a reduction in payroll, which is felt immediately.

The potential negative impacts are as follows:

- What will happen to the morale of those personnel left who feel exposed in their own situations?
- Who will pick up the slack and the slew of the cut-back executives' workload?
- Will these executives go to competitors and take the company's clients, IPR, and other assets with them?
- Will other employees follow them?
- Will there be lawsuits?

- When the economy improves, will we be able to replace them? Will the replacement have the same or better experience?

The benefits of firing are achieved, but at what consequences? The real question to ask is, Was there a better option to reducing costs without firing or laying off personnel that could have a potentially negative impact?

The analysis of options and their use may present a less risky approach that can resolve the short-term budgetary issue without negatively impacting future issues. The answer lies with a balanced approach that allows more reasonable decisions that provide short- and long-term solutions with the least amount of impact in both the short and long terms.

Be Comprehensive

Deliverables and goals are usually emphasized by bullet points in a brief presentation. That is okay as an overview. But for the long term, goals need to be outlined in great detail and be very comprehensive in structure.

Example 4.2

Company BCD has a marketing strategy on developing an export initiative to Mexico. A brief outline of the strategy reads as follows:

- BCD has an overall goal of developing export sales to Mexico over a five-year period that will lead to 25–30 million sales at the end of the fifth year.
- It will beef up the sales group and develop resources for them to enter the market.
- All sales personnel will be trained in basic Spanish and offered travel incentives to be in Mexico four to six times per annum.

A more comprehensive strategy might read as follows:

- BCD will create a five-year business plan for export sales to Mexico.
- The five-year growth plan is as follows:
  - Year 1: 900,000 of sales
  - Year 2: 1.6 million of sales

- Year 3: 3.5 million of sales
- Year 4: 4.2 million of sales
- Year 5: 5.3 million of sales
- Bob, John, and Ed will equally share these sales goals.
- They each will be required to be in Mexico once every 60–90 days, for 5 business day stays.
- We will develop a list of 500 prospects for sales calls on companies identified as potential clients.
- We have agreed to do four industry trade shows between now and this time next year. Details are to follow.
- Marketing has created draft sales brochures (attached) in both English and Spanish for your sales efforts.
- Next month we will retain the services of Kelly Raia, managing director of Dragonfly Global, who is a renowned international business consultant and who will provide 3 days of sales training on everything we need to know about selling in Mexico.

We trust that you can see that the strategy is now outlined in greater detail and significantly more comprehensive. Anyone reading it can see easily what steps are being taken and can review the entire thought process at a granular level. This comprehensive approach dramatically increases any chance of strategic planning of working out more successfully.

Keep in mind that you never know for sure who all of the audience will be.

Strategic planning is like doing engineering work; detailed and comprehensive sets the stage for excellence.

Alignment of Goals and Expectations

The alignment of goals and expectations with reality is an essential element of the strategic-planning process. I am trained to always ask when things go wrong between two parties, What were the goals and expectations of both parties? More often than not, the culprit is that what one had as goals, the other did not have as expectations. There was no alignment of the parties to be on the same page as to what each person expects from the other.

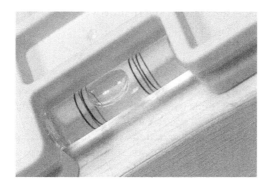

Alignment is a critical aspect of strategic planning.

There is a lot of common sense here that needs to be brought into the strategic-planning process. Make sure absolutely that everyone is on the same page and what one has as expectations are realistic and doable on the other parties' part. That these should be simple but effective is an absolute necessity to get strategic planning to be successful.

Managing a Strengths, Weakness, Opportunities, and Threats Analysis

A SWOT analysis is a standard process in many companies and with business executives to help make better decisions. It is a tool for thinking things through that utilizes some science and metrics in the process.

SWOT stands for

S: Strengths
W: Weaknesses
O: Opportunities
T: Threats

The analysis allows these four critical areas to be analyzed when making a decision: What are the strengths of the deal? What are the weaknesses of the deal? What opportunities exist, and what threats exist in this decision? All of these are great questions to ponder in the decision-making process.

Example 4.3

MNO Company is evaluating an acquisition of a competing company in China over two other potential options. The team leader on the M&A front asks each member to complete a SWOT analysis of the deal; the general consensus from the six team members reads as follows:

S: STRENGTHS

The acquisition of Ting Mao would make us the largest service provider in the Asian market. It would strengthen our presence in Shanghai, where we are weak. It would give us additional "boots on the ground" in four cities where we had all previously agreed to expand our presence. We have had access to a dozen accounts that we have had targeted for the past three years but to which we have had no success.

W: WEAKNESSES

Our investment will be over 900 million and the ROI will take nine years, two more years than our other acquisitions have taken. We will not be able to put in any trade secret or confidentiality non-compete agreements in this deal, leaving us vulnerable if any member of the senior team leaves and goes to a competitor.

Ting Mao has very old technology; integration will be arduous. They will strain cash flow. Our receivables turn every 20 days; theirs are out 60–75 days.

O: OPPORTUNITIES

With such a major foothold in China, this will allow us to move into other Asian target areas easily: South Korea, Vietnam, and Malaysia. We will gain much significant market share; we will be able to reduce our charges without reducing margins. We will make it very difficult for any of our other competitors to gain market share in China in the short run.

T: THREATS

Some of our key clients may feel intimidated by our expansion and be concerned about our customer service delivery. The M&A transition will distract several key executives for up to a year in various transitional issues.

SWOT analysis is a critical tool in strategic planning.

Will the numbers hold and clients stay once the acquisition occurs? How will the staff deal with a foreign owner? Will they stay?

The **SWOT analysis** allows a process to enter the decision-making process, forcing consideration, banter, and dialogue on the most important factors that will impact a deal, with the goal that the process will allow a more informed and well-thought-out decision to be made.

Establishment of Timelines and Action Plans

Structuring a timeline and an action plan will assist in setting up lines of accountability and responsibility to make sure that the project stays on deliverables and timing, which are typical elements of determining success.

The heart of the strategic planning is keeping everyone accountable and on schedule. The timeline and action plan are excellent management tools to make sure that happens.

Cost and Return-on-Investment Analyses

A primary reason for growing internationally is to increase revenues, enhanced margins, and opportunities for exponential growth. This will generally require some sort of financial investment. Managing the ROI is an important aspect of assuring that the initiatives have been worth pursuing. This means accomplishing a costing analysis and creating and studying financial metrics that will prove the integrity of the deal or strategy being deployed.

At some point down the road, the initiative will require an ROI analysis. Creating sensible metrics to evaluate the cost and then the return must be done. This also has a dual benefit for assessing future growth strategies and expected financial benefits, turnaround times, and anticipated ROIs.

Senior Management Buy-In

Most strategies in growing internationally will have huge costing models. Additionally, the growth strategies will put pressure on internal resources and impact multiple verticals, silos, and fiefdoms in corporations. To resolve this challenge, obtaining senior management buy-in can be a very important step in managing the process of moving forward and moving forward successfully.

Senior management will

- Provide key moral support;
- Provide additional leadership;
- Allocate proper funding;
- Help work through silo interference;
- Provide consequences to bad behavior;
- Provide benefits and incentives for success; and
- Access higher-level resources, connections, and support functions.

Initial Salvos

The strategy should include the basis to test or qualify to determine how an action will be played out. A good example is when you are considering about expanding some business development in Latin America, where prior corporate initiatives have been unsuccessful. You are anticipating lots of pushbacks from some of your colleagues and management team.

You decide to test the group by sending out a salvo.

The salvo is in the form of a 60-minute internal meeting where this subject will be discussed. You send out a memo outlining the reasons for opening up again the conversation and opportunity, reviewing the potential but addressing the concern about the past failures. You want to set up the meeting to review the opportunity and obtain everyone's constructive inputs and opinions. They willingly participate following the invitation and do create some pushback, but because

- The meeting is soft with no specific objective; it is just "discussing";
- You are valuing their input;
- You are recognizing proactively the areas of their pushback and providing solutions and options;
- You are not looking for a decision to be made; the purpose is information gathering and exploratory only; and
- You advise everyone to buy in before proceeding.

The soft approach works and you create an opportunity to test the approach to Latin America. The salvo has worked.

Implementation

A strategy works only when the implementation plan is solid. It must be as well thought out as the strategy itself. Implementation can also include transitional issues, which are part of the overall success of any global growth initiative.

Implementation needs to include the following traits:

- Inclusive of all stakeholders to assure buy-in and participation
- Quality communication with those with all vested interests, keeping everyone appraised of the implementation strategy status
- Systems for holding all team members accountable and responsible, inclusive of tracking the status; there are a lot of software programs available to assist in project management to support accountability initiatives
- Specific goals to assure that all deliverables are met and closure is put up

Problem Anticipation and Proactive Mitigation

Experts in global expansion and international business management develop a sixth sense that anticipates problems. The anticipation then allows proactive steps to be put forward to thwart the negative consequences that anticipated problems might cause.

Tweaking Period

In any strategy an allowance of time, resources, and actions needs to be contemplated for adjustments to happen. Hopefully, most of these are necessary to keep the strategy on track and on time.

Closure

The final step is to bring closure—no "loose, hanging chads." Closure involves assurance that all deliverables and expectations have been met, analysis of the job and what was done, and a discussion on what should have happened or what will happen on the next opportunity.

> Let our advance worrying become advance thinking and planning.
>
> **Winston Churchill**

5

Management Assessment Tools

Developing tools, resources, and capabilities in managing growth strategies is a critical component of any executive's tool chest to assure successful planning and execution. This chapter is an excellent tutorial on resource and tool development.

OVERVIEW

The utilization of tools and resources will many times be the dividing factor between success and failure in global growth. If it is not the dividing factor, then for sure it will determine the extent one can be successful in any initiative or transaction.

The receipt of timely and comprehensive information is a critical factor in making better and more informed decisions. I have been witness too many times to decisions made based upon bad information, old information, or personal sensibilities. These decisions lead to errors in judgment that can be expensive mistakes.

To prevent mistakes from likely occurring, the utilization of resources and tools will provide serious risk mitigation information flows that will produce better results.

TOOLS AND RESOURCE OPTIONS

The outline below lists the key areas one would look to for support in developing tools and resources:

- Industry trade publications
- Centers of influence
- Consultants
- M&A leading companies
- Financial reports
- Industry associations
- Particular conferences
- Networking

Industry Trade Publications

I recommend that personnel engaged in global expansion and M&A activities dedicate up to 10 percent of their time to reading industry-related publications. This action has the following benefits:

- It keeps you current on industry and world events that keep you informed on related business occurrences that impact decision making.
- It keeps you ahead on local, national, and world events, including political and economic, that will have potential short- and long-term impacts on your decision-making process.
- Information is gold when utilized effectively. Information must be timely, comprehensive, and informative.

Today's competitive world of communications has forced several publishers to be very effective at accomplishing these information transfer goals. On the industry front, we recommend two publications:

- *Journal of Commerce*
- *American Shipper*

For world events, the following are recommended:

- *The Economist*
- *The Wall Street Journal*

While there are dozens of good publications, the author has narrowed the choices for those with limited schedules to the four options outlined above. Reading these on a regular, consistent, and thorough basis will provide significant information flow, hopefully leading to better decision making. The key to this thought process is that one should never be so confident as not to still require increase of knowledge and industry data to make better decisions and lead more successfully.

On the subject of leadership, acquiring and being able to transfer timely knowledge is a good character trait and will make it easier for others to feel you are informed, articulate, and someone to follow. Remember: **Lead, follow, or get out of the way!**

Centers of Influence

Centers of influence are companies and people who are in the know and have access to senior executives and the strategies they are commanding. Typically, they fall into a number of job descriptions:

- Lawyers
- Accountants
- Bankers
- Financial and investment firms
- Trade association professionals

These companies and the key individuals who manage these entities typically

- Have relationships with the principals of companies expanding in the global arena;
- Additionally, they are "in the loop" of strategic plans that outline their international growth strategies and the plans to be executed;
- Have access to key decision makers;
- Are often participative in the strategic planning process, along with implementation strategies;
- Have extensive research capability for information access;
- Have offices and agents globally for local reach and knowledge; and
- Often are connected to specific industry segments with contacts and knowledge useful to make connections.

As centers of influence, they can be very successful at making important introductions, providing useful intelligence, and helping sway decision making in your favor.

Consultants

Consultants can be one of the best sources for global expansion, as well as M&A activity, for a number of reasons:

- Many tend to specialize in niches where their defined expertise may prove invaluable, particularly if they are in the areas of your anticipated needs.
- Many have geographic and demographic prowess, which is also invaluable.
- Typically, through their office and agency network, they have local facilitation, information flow, and presence that can prove very useful.

Consultants typically prove valuable in the following:

- Advice, counsel, and risk mitigation
- Implementation strategies
- Access to additional resources that are required to close a deal: lawyers, accountants, tax specialists, logistics expertise, technology resources, supply-chain partners, etc.
- Problem resolution

Consultants add cost but bring value in bringing solid information and planning capability to the benefit of the company seeking to grow internationally and/or create M&A opportunities in the global economy.

Merger and Acquisition Leading Companies

In most industries there are leading M&A companies that specialize in developing, assessing, and making M&A deals happen. For example, in West Palm Beach, Florida, resides the Ben Gordon Strategic Advisors (BGSA) Company (http://www.bgsa.com), led by Ben Gordon and his senior colleague and partner Mitchel Gordon. They specialize in supply chain, transportation, technology, energy, distribution, and related companies and have operated for more than 12 years in these spaces, helping companies execute M&A opportunities, aligned with their global growth strategies. BGSA are leaders in their respective fields and have hundreds of M&A transactions for their clients' benefit. BGSA runs a high-level executive conference every January in South Florida that brings industry leaders together for powerful information gathering, networking, and some "fun in the sun" where deals are born, made, and consummated.

Other companies such as EVE Partners, Goldman Sachs, Bain & Company, Axial, Sullivan & Cromwell, and Crowe Horwath are a few of the hundreds that enter this specialized arena of M&A activity.

Financial Reports

Staying on top of all the growth and M&A activity can be daunting. Focusing on a few reports can be very helpful in lessening the burden and at the same time keep you in the loop of essential market information, which is necessary for making better decisions. Some of these reports are the following:

IPO Monitor's reports (http://www.ipomonitor.com)
BGSA index (http://www.bgsa.com)
TransValue M&A Advisors' reports (http://www.transvaluema.com)
CapTarget's M&A research reports (http://www.captarget.com)
EVE Partners's newsletter (http://www.newsletter@evepartners.ccsend .com)
PitchBook's newsletter (http://www.pitchbook.com)

Industry Associations

Industry associations such as, but not limited to, specific industries, supply chain, Council of Supply Chain Management Professionals (CSCMP), and Institute for Supply Management (ISM) are all great options. These work specific verticals and industry segments and therefore become more targeted.

Many associations also have member benefit groups focused on M&A and global expansion opportunities. Additionally, many associations have advocacy programs that promote global expansion and develop the skill sets of international businesses as a member benefit.

Particular Conferences

There are numerous conferences with global business and expansion as subject matter that would be worth attending. Two of these are the following:

- *BGSA Supply Chain Conference 2015* (http://www.bgstrategicadvisors .com/conference2015/)
- JOC Group's *TPM 2015 Conference* (http://events.joc.com/tpm2015/)

Networking

If you are truly committed to growing globally and expanding your business in international arenas, you must become committed to spending at least 10–15 percent of your operating time in networking functions and opportunities. All the areas outlined above, associations, conferences, industry groups, etc., are areas that you need to spend time on.

> Create a definite plan for carrying out your desire and begin at once, whether you are ready or not, put this plan into action.
>
> **Napoleon Hill**

6

Anticipated Merger and Acquisition Problems

The author has developed a "laundry list" from over 30 years of M&A experience that details the anticipated M&A problems with a few case studies. The value of this chapter's focus is to provide the reader with a cautionary approach so that problems that are likely to occur can be proactively mitigated in advance.

MERGER AND ACQUISITION'S LIKELY SOURCES OF PROBLEMS

The author, with over 30 years' experience in M&A activity with companies of all sizes, has developed a very credible list of issues common to numerous merger and growth situations. Not necessarily in any order, these are the following:

- Unrealistic expectations
- Not engaging all key personnel
- No specific transition strategy
- The financial side not holding up

Unrealistic Expectations

In many of the M&A situations I have been involved in as a principal or as a consultant, a primary reason for the development of problems, issues, and challenges have to do with unrealistic expectations from one or both parties. For these issues not to become overwhelming, both parties must be open, transparent, and proactive in how they define what they are looking for and wish to accomplish in the deal being made.

In most businesses and personal situations that go awry, the culprit will always point to one or both parties having differences on what was expected. These differences come out of

1. Lack of transparency;
2. Lack of open, straightforward discussions;
3. Inability of becoming confrontational when that posture is warranted;
4. Not being truthful and afraid of addressing shortcomings upfront; and
5. Having no clear articulation of what one expects from the other or is willing to do themselves.

The fix is easy: make sure points 1–5 do not happen and conduct yourself in the opposite ways by being

- Transparent;
- Open and straightforward;
- Confrontational when warranted;
- Truthful and discussing the negatives, along with the positives; and
- Articulate.

Not Engaging All Key Personnel

Very often when we become involved in transition problems and begin to interview some of the key management and operations personnel, we quickly find out that they have been out of the loop on what is going on. They become resentful, uncooperative, and actual adversaries to the transition process, making the likelihood of success and ease much more unlikely and/or complicated. They become agents of issue and discourse and will make everyone's lives miserable, and the entire transition process becomes jeopardized.

From my experiences, I would estimate that over 80 percent of international M&A and growth transitions have disruptions and that 90 percent of these fall into the area of not engaging all the necessary key management and operations personnel in the transition process. This includes bringing them into the loop from the very beginning and to the execution and implementation stages.

Keep in mind a critical issue here: transition means change. Human beings are traditionally, historically, and by nature very resistant to change of any form. And when they believe that there are unknown risks with that change, the resistance will increase and be preventive. It is human nature to get comfortable and complacent in known circumstances. And even when change presents opportunity, resistance can be significant, disruptive, and certainly discouraging.

In my circle of influence with movers and shakers, the key and high-powered executives in international business, I conducted numerous formal and informal interviews of these senior team leaders and was very easily able to create a consensus of concerns they all clearly defined as challenges to global expansion and international M&A plans. Some of these challenges are outlined in additional chapters. But, for sure, all the executives addressed this issue of engagement of all personnel involved in the implementation. In summary, they all put forth the following recommendations:

- You have to identify who the key players are in the growth, expansion, or M&A strategy and actively engage them in the planning, business development, decision making, and execution strategies to obtain their unended and committed support.
- Even when those personnel may not be part of the end game, being transparent and upfront and rewarding positive participation will help make the deal close more successfully.

I was reminded in a few interviews of a common theme and example: In a lot of M&A deals, there will be personnel casualties. It is unlikely that you will need two CFOs, as an example. Once you have made the decision which one will survive, make everyone aware, particularly the one who will lose his or her employment. But create an open exchange. Incentivize their staying through the transition period with the following:

- Quality incentive on compensation structure during transition period
- Bonus money on end of implementation
- Positive recommendations
- Support in finding a new home
- Possible ongoing consulting work

Where there is a will, you can find a way. Being deceptive will come back to haunt you. Many interviewees advised that in early experiences they were not as upfront as they are now and experience has taught them that taking the high road is a much better path, with much better results. People facing challenges through an open, transparent, and honest dialogue will be more likely to perform as needed.

Engaging key personnel in the strategy development will allow additional insight and recommendations that might prove very viable. When the personnel participate and believe what they have to say and contribute has value, they feel appreciated and are more likely to make a positive contribution. More importantly, they are less likely to create disruption.

I think it is important to note that the experience represented by the author and all the senior executives interviewed in the construction of this book is huge. Their experiences, counsel, and advice are a culmination of making mistakes and learning the right way to grow and make deals that will stick, make money, and add value.

No Specific Transition Strategy

Chapter 8 goes into great detail on what can be done proactively to develop and execute a transition strategy that creates the best opportunity for M&A and international growth. Having said that, it is well known that many companies enter global expansion, growth, and M&A plans without developing specific strategies first. The "seat-of-the-pants" approach is what occurs and often this "cowboy" approach has merit; but more often than not, it is a recipe for failure.

A strategy will often contain all the elements for success including a strengths, weaknesses, opportunities, and threats (SWOT) analysis, which puts forward "thinking and analysis" with metrics that will then allow following a plan or strategy that affords the best opportunity for success.

SWOT is outlined in more detail in Chapter 8.

The Financial Side Not Holding Up

There are both short-term and long-term financial considerations for global growth, expansion, and M&A activity. So, what causes these issues? My interviews pointed to numerous and certain consensus on the following reasons:

1. Poor due diligence
2. Poor analysis
3. Not turning over enough stones
4. Creating false financial expectations
5. Allowing wishes to become realities

There was a consistent flow of discussion in the interviews that pointed to the above list. Many senior executives pointed to all points 1–5. They extolled that the enthusiasm in doing the deal outweighed common-sense principles in the financial evaluation process. Sometimes this was due to lack of expertise, but more importantly timing did not allow the proper process of due diligence to take place. Or personnel cut corners in making sure that all the financial metrics were made available and reviewed as thoroughly as possible. Often analysis was completed based upon hyperboles rather than hard data and facts that were readily available or that required further digging or mining.

Example 6.1

One case we discussed involved a large trucking company in the Midwest who acquired a freight forwarder in California. They believed that they needed this acquisition to expand in the global arena. This was true, but they relied upon the expertise of the principals they were acquiring to provide the analysis of their profit and loss (P&L) and balance sheets.

There were many red flags, but due to their lack of experience and their zeal to make the acquisition, they did not ask enough questions or the right questions or even had the capability to scrutinize correctly what they were being told. They felt comfortable in the management team of the freight forwarder and what they were being told. And they were being told what the forwarder knew they needed to hear to buy.

Soon after the acquisition, the numbers were not being met and the company had to add substantial additional cash flow and capital beyond what was budgeted to keep the forwarder viable. They had really needed to hire an independent consultant and advisor with specific forwarder knowledge to assess prior to the deal being closed the financials, the operation, and what they had been told. The deal could still have been closed but under a better M&A structure dealing more closely with what was real and not fiction.

This is another case study where enthusiasm, and not due diligence and proper utilization of independent expertise, led the charge. The results would have been very different and proved more favorable when due diligence, common sense, and utilization of all the available resources prevail!

You can't depend on your eyes when your imagination is out of focus.

Mark Twain

7

Problem Resolution Strategies

This chapter provides a blueprint to follow in successfully managing the anticipated and surprise problems that will pop up in any business expansion. The keys to resolution are outlined in a ten-step process.

THE TEN-STEP PROCESS FOR PROBLEM RESOLUTION

Follow this outline and you will find that the typical stresses and concerns associated with problems and conflicts will slowly dissipate. Facing problems and conflicts will be easier to deal with and the results will be much more favorable.

1. Quick assessment
2. Stopping the bleeding
3. Establishing the stakeholders
4. Better assessment
5. Responsible and timely communications
6. Creating strategy, tactics, and action plan
7. Updates and status reports
8. Tweaking
9. Summary and closure
10. Follow-up

Quick Assessment

Most problems and conflicts have an immediacy issue that you have to deal with. The best example is the following:

You are an adult supervisor at a day camp for teenagers. You walk out of the canteen and you notice a crowd gathering around two boys who are in a fistfight. Your concern in the immediacy is not to find out what the fight is about or who started it but to break it up, separate the boys, and gain control over the situation. Once that is accomplished, you can work on how it started, who is at fault, and what steps will be taken so it does not happen again. If you start the process of trying to resolve all those issues from the beginning, the potential reality is that someone could have been hurt seriously. This shows the following sequence: stop the fight then deal with all the related issues.

In business too often we do not view the immediacy of an issue and we worry about all the peripheral issues first, making the immediate damages worsen because we do not act quickly enough.

In business an example might look like this: You are a vice president (VP) of business development and have finalized a new acquisition two weeks ago. It took some nine months for the acquisition to occur from beginning to close. You created a close relationship with the senior management team at the company being acquired and worked through an array of challenges and issues in the nine-month tenure of the negotiations.

The actual transition is being handled by others in your organization at the operational level. They are in the third week of integrating the organizations, and a major issue has arisen regarding the information technology (IT) platform. Their system was better than yours, and it had been agreed that while your company was acquiring them that their IT system would be the one last standing under your company's IT management team.

It now seems that the integration is not going smoothly and there are personnel issues and the cooperation has seemed to dwindle to a whisper. The major concern is that the IT integration has to be accomplished within the next two weeks or further operational and customer service issues will be negatively consequential. This is where you have to get involved as the "savior" and get matters back on track as soon as possible (ASAP). This is where you are initially concerned not with the cause but the resolution, as timing is a critical factor here.

In your quick assessment you see that the seller's team is concerned about their job security and are putting up resistance on a number of fronts in the transition process. In this quick assessment, it leads you to that determination, which leads you to sit down with the selling IT team and review with them the strategy to integrate them into the new organization as the transitional issues are successfully managed, and you reiterate the buyer's commitment to keep them gainfully employed once the deal is accomplished.

You look into their eyes and assure them of this intent and do not leave the space until they and you feel comfortable that everyone is on the same page and understands the goals and the commitments on everyone's part.

Transitions can cause paranoia and uncertainty, particularly in personnel from the company being acquired. Managing these concerns is part of the transition process and a critical element of being proactive and engaged.

Stopping the Bleeding

Once the assessment determines that there is a serious problem that needs to be addressed now and action cannot wait, the formula requires temporary steps to stop the bleeding. In the world of emergency medicine, this concept is equivalent to triage, where a patient comes in, a quick assessment is done, and upfront temporary steps are taken to keep the patient alive, allowing more time for longer-term care. In business this can best be viewed in the following real case study.

Example 7.1

An Arkansas-based manufacturer moved certain aspects of their supply chain to China. A trial period was set up for one year. Following that year with most of the challenges addressed, the Arkansas company made more permanent manufacturing arrangements, which then immediately increased their dependency on China.

The Arkansas company had alternative manufacturing options in Reno, Nevada, and Monterey, Mexico, which accounted at that point for 60 percent of production. It was planned that two to three years down the road as much as 70 percent would be moved to the new sourcing option in China, the obvious reason being costs.

After a few months into the second year, many end-use customers began complaining and canceling orders due to quality-control issues. The sales force was beside themselves as they were losing long-term customers to competitors, and it was happening quickly.

A quick assessment determined that what the contract Chinese manufacturer was doing with the raw-material purchases impacted performance, and this needed to be altered ASAP. It would take several months for implementation.

It was then determined that the Reno and Monterey manufacturing sites, where there was tenured manufacturing success with no quality issues, would "step up to the plate" and immediately pick up the slack on processing orders until China had time to get it right.

The stopping-the-bleeding step worked immediately, and the clients were back processing orders. Four months later, China was back on line and the quality-control issues went away once raw-material purchases were managed better. The stopping-the-bleeding step, or the triage, worked.

The preceding case study documents the importance of certain intermediate steps that will help in rectifying a problem in the short term until a longer-term, more permanent solution can be found.

Establishing the Stakeholders

In the process of problem resolution, it is imperative to identify those personnel internally and externally who have a vested interest in resolving the problem and/or would be impacted by the consequences. They could be as few as one person or as many as an entire division.

In problem resolution, the stakeholders to be identified are not only those impacted by the problem but also those that can participate in the resolution process. Once identified, they need to be brought into the information flow of the problem and acknowledge the importance of the immediacy and the level of the concern.

More often than not, the stakeholders can be a very valuable asset in the problem-resolution strategy. I am always surprised by how sometimes just bringing in those with vested interests, the problem can take a different shape, both good and bad, and how these stakeholders are of immediate value to the process moving forward and being brought to a favorable close.

Mentoring is a critical element in problem resolution.

There are two additional reasons for bringing in stakeholders. Firstly, their buy-in and participation many times are critical to the action steps being successful. Secondly, as part of the entire process of management, the resolution process is part of mentoring that takes place and you have the opportunity to show and lead others to how to best handle these situations.

Better Assessment

Down the path of problem resolution, after the bleeding has been stopped, longer-term solutions will typically need to be developed. This will require additional steps and mining to better assess what happened and what solutions are available. This can be viewed as a middle step, once initial actions have been implemented or even a tweaking of the initial actions, creating better results. This is likely to be done with more thought, more time, and better analytics and even bringing enhanced resources and resolves to the table for consideration.

Responsible and Timely Communications

Effective communicating requires cooperation and everyone making a best effort.

Communicating timely and responsibly may be the most important aspect of problem resolution. It allows all parties

- A status report on what is going on;
- To know what steps are being taken;

- To know what timing is anticipated;
- Ability to communicate back concerns, suggestions, or constructive comments; and
- The announcement of the resolve and future implications, etc.

Done at the international another level of managing communication responsibilities are the following:

- Watch time zone issues.
- Be careful of language differences.
- Be aware of legal implications.
- Be sensitive to cultural differences.

Creating Strategy, Tactics, and Action Plan

The problem will get resolved in three primary active steps: strategy, tactics, and action plan.

Understanding the difference between the three steps is critical to successfully resolving issues and constructively obtaining a solution.

Strategy

The strategy will come from the assessments that are accomplished in the fact-finding, information flow, and mining that produce critical information for the analysis. The strategy is a higher-level thought process on how a problem is going to be resolved. It is usually more intellectual and thought driven and typically longer term in its goals.

Tactics

Tactics are set up to create the path on how the strategies will happen. This is where an analysis discussing various options and the anticipated results will occur. Tactics will generally identify what the identified stakeholders will do in the resolve. It will also set up a time frame for action.

Referring to the difference between strategy and tactics, one would look to how the White House interfaces with the Pentagon (Department of Defense). Policy decisions are created by the president. The Pentagon then transfers the strategy into a tactical plan of action, or more boots-on-the-ground positions. This will further move down the line to field officers, who create the steps that will resolve the specific issues at hand.

Strategy and tactics like in a chess game require focus, skill set, and diligence.

Action Plan

As an extension of tactics, the action plan provides the specific to-do list at a granular level: Who will do what? By when?

Example 7.2

Problem: Dealing with customs challenges in Brazil for the Olympics

Excel Spreadsheet Action Plan

Action	Stakeholder	Date	Status
Create committee	John	1 October	Memo sent out last week
Obtain current regulations	Sue	5 October	Currently has and is vetting
Set next meeting	Bob/Andy	27 September	Awaiting confirmation from committee members
Meet with Brazil's customs	Sue	10 October	Waiting for invitation

The action plan creates the details and the activities that will move the initiative to a resolve. The action plan becomes the deliverer of the strategy and tactics developed by the stakeholders. It takes the theory, or the intellectual thought process, and brings it into the process.

The action plan is dependent equally on the strategy and tactics developed. When it works well, it is a thing of beauty and excellence. When it fails, it can create chaos, discord, and even mayhem.

Many times strategies are developed such that it is nearly impossible to be accomplished by any tactics or actions. Strategies, tactics, and action plans must work well together and be contemplative of the other's strengths and weaknesses when creating. SWOT analysis is another great tool to utilize in creating strategies, tactics, and action plans.

Updates and Status Reports

As an extension of timely and responsible communications in problem resolution, we recommend that very timely updates and status reports be provided to all interested parties. This keeps everyone informed and on the same page. It also affords their input. As the initiative moves forward and dynamically changes, the interested parties' input and scrutiny may prove very helpful and valuable.

From years of managing numerous problems, I have found that you will seriously mitigate the circumstances when you are proactively in the face of all the interested parties with updates and status reports. Even when nothing has changed, an update will send the message that you are still actively engaged and on top of the situation. That provides a comfort level to all the interested parties and helps to keep things calm while a resolve is working.

Generally, when matters are stable we tend to be complacent with updates. And that is really the time to keep communicating and make sure everyone is aware you are still working on the resolve.

Tweaking

It will always be necessary to make adjustments to your strategies, tactics, and/or the action plan that was initially developed to resolve the problem at hand. This is as a result of

- New information coming to light;
- Various expectations changing as a result of actions taken;
- Changes in personnel's mindset as a result of progress being made in the problem-resolution strategy;
- Various changes in needs as the strategy moves forward; and
- When certain actions are not working, introducing other steps.

Tweaking needs to have consensus to assure success and must be communicated to all the team and stakeholders.

Summary and Closure

The problem-resolution strategy eventually must be brought to closure. Hopefully favorably, but whether successfully or not, there needs to be an end. If it does not work out, the end may be to shift to another strategy or another entire initiative; but the effort needs to end and steps should be taken to move forward.

A communication declaring the end is what is typically necessary to bring everyone onto the same page. If it is successful, the closure communication can include the following:

- Congratulations to all those who contributed
- Making sure that all stakeholders and senior management are aware of results
- Summary of the activity and the favorable results
- Lessons learned
- Potential laundry list of any still open items or issues that will need to be followed up on

Follow-Up

A mistake often made after a problem is resolved is that in fact the problem may have been resolved only temporarily but not necessarily in the long run. This is often found by looking at the following example, where someone deals with the symptoms and not the actual proximate cause.

Example 7.3

A person has a headache. Give him or her an aspirin. The problem is resolved, or so we think. What we have dealt with was the symptom. Why is there a headache?

Diagnosis shows that the headache comes with how that person deals with stress. When the person gets stressed, he or she often gets a headache.

Give the person an aspirin. Sometimes the effects of the headache are eliminated or reduced. You are dealing with the symptoms only and not the cause.

Show the person how to deal with stress, and the problem can truly be resolved. It may not be easy, but in the long run it is much more effective.

Example 7.4

XYZ Company is receiving from your parts division numerous complaints about the customer service and their lack of timely response on time-sensitive orders. When you analyze the issues, you determine a number of facts:

- The customer complains about the high cost of expedient shipping of time-sensitive parts that often do not arrive as scheduled.
- The customer complains about the lack of knowing what the status of time-sensitive shipments is.
- The customer complains about the difficulty of navigating the technology you have made available for communicating about, tracking and tracing, and determining part-replacement status.

In your strategy to deal with the issues above, you lower the price on the time-sensitive shipping, which the client appreciates, and you issue some credits on past activity. The client seems relieved and you move along. You also meet with the operations personnel and tell them to step up their handling of the client's needs.

After a month the problem arises again and the customer is back complaining about service and is now threatening to utilize an alternative competitor. You have an option to deal with this problem by following the outlined steps below.

THE PROBLEM-RESOLUTION PROCESS
QUICK ASSESSMENT AND STOPPING THE BLEEDING

You immediately raise the problem with all operating staff and give significant hand-holding to all of this client's shipment activities. Everyone needs to do whatever is necessary to move the shipments timely and communicate proactively with the client about the status.

You, as a senior executive, speak to the client directly and assure him or her that you are working on the problem and will bring favorable resolve. You will also communicate with the client every day to assure that the problem is being resolved.

BETTER ASSESSMENT

You assemble the team and reassess the entire problem at a very granular level. That process confirms what were previously identified:

- The customer complains about the high cost of expedient shipping of time-sensitive parts that often do not arrive as scheduled.
- The customer complains about the lack of knowing what the status of time-sensitive shipments is.
- The customer complains about the difficulty of navigating the technology you have made available for communicating about, tracking and tracing, and determining part-replacement status.

These are the issues that must be rectified and not dealt with with an "aspirin" but with an action plan that will make all these issues go away. You communicate with the client a review of the issues and restate the commitment to resolve.

MENTORING TIME!

You are not only resolving the problem at hand, but you will also be showing the team working for you how to bring this client's problem to a favorable resolve not just for the short term but for a long time. You are also soliciting the team members' inputs on the resolve, and they are participating in the steps involved with the solution(s).

ANALYSIS OF SOLUTION

The problems are restated as follows:

- The customer complains about the high cost of expedient shipping of time-sensitive parts that often do not arrive as scheduled.

If you do the job right, you can legitimately earn the revenue for a job well done. The client is paying you for getting the job done. Get the job done; earn the revenue!

- The customer complains about the lack of knowing what the status of time-sensitive shipments is.

Timely and comprehensive communications must be built into the customer service function.

- The customer complains about the difficulty of navigating the technology you have made available for communicating about, tracking and tracing, and determining part-replacement status.

You speak with a number of other clients who are successfully working with your technology and you have a very repetitive consensus that with training the system is easy to work with. This specific client has received only very minimal training on your technology.

ACTION PLAN AND TIMELINE

You create an action plan that is summarized as follows:

1. Each shipment from this client will be manually tracked and traced from origin to destination and the client updated by phone and e-mail with the status every six hours. This is discussed with the client and is an acceptable communication activity and time frame.
2. From a management perspective, you are alerted to this activity and will stay on top of your account team to assure responsiveness.

3. You implement a very comprehensive training program for your client on the use of your technology. You work with the client until they are navigating the technology easily and successfully.

4. You implement a zero-tolerance policy with the client, assuring 100 percent satisfaction with a full money refund for nonperformance as a backup measure that hopefully will not ever have to be acted on.

You meet with the client "eyeball to eyeball" and get his or her buy-in of the plan and commitment to allow an agreed time frame to make it work.

PROCESS IMPLEMENTATION

You implement the program immediately. All stakeholders are engaged and participating.

REVIEWING, ASSESSING, AND TWEAKING

Within a reasonable time frame, maybe two weeks, the action plan is assessed and tweaked if necessary. Direct communication and feedback from the customer is required here to see how they feel about the steps taken and their success. If any changes need to be made, make sure that the client and the team are on the same page and fully engaged.

MAKING SURE THAT THE PROBLEM HAS BEEN RESOLVED

Even when it appears the problem has been resolved, do not assume it has! Obtain absolute, clear, and concise words from the client that all is okay.

CREATING A FUTURE ASSURANCE MODEL

Even though the problem has been resolved, set up a structure to make sure that down the road, the fix has longevity! Set up a quarterly business review (QBR) that includes the problem as a discussion point.

CLOSURE: BRINGING IT TO AN ADVANTAGE!

Follow up down the road within a timely fashion to dialogue with the client, reiterating how the problem was dealt with and the proactive and successful actions taken to bring a favorable resolve. Utilize this problem resolution to leverage additional opportunities and certainly no less than business equity/capital.

Lack of direction, not lack of time, is the problem. We all have twenty-four-hour days.

Zig Ziglar

8

Transition Management

Once growth is achieved, there is an important transition period to make the expansion, the merger, and the acquisition successful, which is just how that new initiative is brought into the balance of the organization. No matter how strategic the growth has been, without a successful transition it will all be for naught.

This chapter outlines specific transition strategies.

THE IMPORTANCE OF A WELL-THOUGHT-OUT TRANSITION PLAN

It is critical to think out a transition plan as far in advance as possible. The transition plan moves a company from strategy and tactics into action or, in other words, from the dream to the reality, from intention to delivery. No matter how successful a growth initiative or acquisition is, the ultimate success will be determined by how we move from the intention to the action.

I have been witness to a number of great deals gone sour because the transitions went south. They tend to go south for a number of potential reasons:

- No transition plan exists.
- The plan that existed was neither robust nor comprehensive.
- Transition issues were handled with poor timing.
- The transition process lacked leadership and/or ownership.
- The transition plan did not create enough anticipation and/or expectation of potential problems.

No Transition Plan Exists

While it may be hard to believe, you could not imagine how many move forward in global growth initiatives or acquisitions without thinking through the transitional stage.

While I hate to go into politics, I will utilize what happened to the United States after taking action and militarily and seriously defeating Iraq in 2006. We won the war very quickly and soon became an occupying force with a whole slew of unanticipated issues, which we paid a very high price for in dollars, lives, and resources.

Many analysts feel that we had never thought out the consequences of the war and the aftermath of occupation until we were faced with these. Many students of the action felt that we could have better planned the occupancy (for these purposes, the transition is from a military action to an occupying action). If we had better planned this upfront, we might have handled the whole Iraq dilemma by following an entirely different course.

On the business side, I had a company in North Carolina enter a joint venture with a Bombay-domiciled Indian company for the purpose of accessing their manufacturing capabilities. They did minimal due diligence and put US$2.5 million into the deal. When they began to transition their U.S. management team into the Bombay plant, a number of issues immediately surfaced:

- They had Indian visa issues because they were temporarily displacing Indian nationals. This delayed the whole project by six to nine months.
- The entire staff spoke Hindi only, and nobody in the U.S. management team spoke Hindi; communications through translation became arduous, slowed progress, and was costly.
- The U.S. management's style conflicted very negatively with the Indian manufacturing workers.
- Many of the SOPs that were introduced by the U.S. management team were contrary to business practice in India and in some instances had bad legal ramifications.

After one year, the North Carolinian company had to renegotiate the entire deal. The initial loss was just over US$2 million. Through the learning curve, they eventually got it right but were two years behind schedule and US$2.75 million over budget. They had a hard lesson: think out the transition strategy as part of the overall deal, plan for it in advance, and do a much better job at due diligence at the front end.

The Plan That Existed Was neither Robust nor Comprehensive

I have seen a lot of transition plans that were very weak in structure, content, and diligence. I was involved with a company in New York who acquired a competitor business in Bermuda. The financials were solid; there was an agreed upon buyout formula of the earnings before interest, taxes, depreciation, and amortization (EBITDA) that was credible; and the entire buyout structure was solid for both parties.

The management of the New York company created a one-page transition document, which outlined various topics for the middle-management team to utilize in their execution strategy, given to them on the closing date of the deal.

DEF COMPANY
NEW YORK CITY

To: Ed, Mary, and Phil

Transition issues to deal with on the acquisition of XYZ Company in Hamilton, Bermuda:

- Severance packages for two owners
- Appointment of new local CEO/president
- Transition of our technology into their software
- Advising common clients

Let me know if you encounter any problems.

John B.

DEF Company, New York City

The above memo did not go deep enough and was sent without sufficient notice to deal with many of the transitional issues, which could have been easily anticipated. In this case,

- The severance packages needed to become part of the acquisition agreement and be executed simultaneously became an issue as what the XYZ owners wanted was too rich. This led to a very complicated and difficult negotiation, almost killing the deal.
- The new CEO, who was an obvious choice, should have been notified proactively and upfront. He was nervous for his job and ended up giving notice and going to a competitor, fearing he was going to be let go once the acquisition occurred.
- When it came time to deal with the technology, the software being utilized by the Bermudan company was so antiquated it was next to impossible to merge the two technologies electronically. Over 200 man-hours was needed for manual input.
- Common clients were very upset when they heard officially about the acquisition, which they had previously heard via the rumor mill. They felt as though that before the deal happened, they should have been consulted first and asked for their advice on how they felt about the deal. The largest client left with the departing CEO for his new company based upon emotional issues of not being included. This issue also stresses the point previously made in this book on the importance of timely communications in handling M&A activities.

Transition Issues Were Handled with Poor Timing

Transition issues need to be thought out and strategized as a deal is coming to fruition. Many times transitional issues need to be taken even before a deal is consummated.

I worked on a deal with a German company last year that was building a supply chain, with warehousing and distribution capability here in North America. Their strategy included the acquisition of four companies who all presented various pieces of the deal.

We determined early on that the deal would work well only if one of the CEOs from one of the acquisitions remained on to manage the entire North American operation in New York, Toronto, Atlanta, and Las Vegas. He was based in New York, but it was thought out that the corporate structure in North America would be best served out of Atlanta.

So at a point in time the deal looked like it would happen. The buyers, through me, acting as a consulting advisor to the acquisition initiative, and with all the permissions in place, began the process of talking to this CEO from the New York company. He was approached carefully, with full transparency and with good intentions to see if he was interested in running the show and would he be willing to move to Atlanta.

After two meetings, with a discussion on a tentative compensation structure with the right incentives, he agreed to the position. With him on board, it became much easier to structure the deal to close and start the transition-strategy structure with a firm leader in place. This was a quality timing issue that eventually helped to make the M&A work well.

The Transition Process Lacked Leadership and/or Ownership

Transitional management is usually a team effort. But the team must be led.

A singular owner works best at coordinating and managing a team effort at making the transition work as needed. Ownership is best led by a person with the following skill sets:

- Good sense of timing
- Good negotiation capabilities
- Knowing how to be flexible and with an innate ability to get along
- Multicultural
- Organized
- Good communicator
- Good delegator

Leading the team means making transitions run smoothly.

The Transition Plan Did Not Create Enough Anticipation and/or Expectation of Potential Problems

An in-depth analysis outlining what problems and challenges will be expected needs to be accomplished early on. This will lead to identifying potential ways of negating the problems from occurring in the first place and ways to provide mitigation actions.

From our experiences, typical problems might include the following:

- Resistance from staff
- Technology interface
- Human resource differences
- Clients' reactions
- Vendors' and suppliers' reactions
- Financials not working

Resistance from Staff

Many times resistance develops from the staff on both sides of growth, acquisition, and new business partnerships. This is typically due to fear of loss of compensation, their employment, or career opportunities.

When poor communication is a consequence of poor planning of the strategy, the staff will become paranoid and negative and with some or no reason will always contemplate the worse. That behavior is bad because it becomes endemic, spreads contagiously, and creates bad morale, all of which can kill any growth or acquisition initiative from moving forward. This is why transparent, proactive communications are usually important if you plan on maintaining staff and harmony among the troops.

Technology Interface

Technology can be a serious complication if it is not well thought out in advance.

Substantial due diligence needs to be accomplished at the front end of any growth or acquisition initiative in regards to technology. Some operating platforms are easy to integrate, others have some challenges, and some are even next to impossible.

Of course, throw enough money and/or resources at any problem and it can eventually be fixed. But usually M&A and growth strategies work when maintained within operating budgets; increased expenditures and resource mongers will kill a deal's success.

Human Resource Differences

We have been witness to numerous acquisitions that went wrong after the takeover when there were major differences in human resource and huge gaps in employee benefit plans between companies. These differences can create significant disharmony and discord between employees and management and create exposure to the deal moving forward smoothly and even successfully.

Human resource managers from both companies need to meet, outline employee benefit programs, compare similarities and differences, and then provide integration strategies to deal with these issues proactively, aggressively, and in keeping with the mantra of being fair and responsible in the approach for resolution. You may never obtain 100 percent similarity and convergence, but you need to get to acceptable levels of harmonization. Patience and articulate communication are good traits of human resource management in transitional strategies.

Human resource strategies need to be part of any global M&A or growth initiative to avoid transition issues from occurring.

Clients' Reactions

Surprises are not good for client relationships.

Clients can be very sensitive to vendor M&A and growth initiatives. Additionally, no one typically likes surprises, and clients in favored relationships usually want to be in the know.

I was involved in a large supply-chain-management company's takeover of a large competitor. They shared a very large client. They never discussed the merger with the client. The client's first notice came when it was notified in an industry publication. Thirty days later the client moved their business to another competitor. Why?

The client's strategy in maintaining the two vendors was very specific. They felt that by keeping both vendors involved equally, they would be more successful in negotiating service and pricing agreements. For over eight years, the strategy worked. The client felt very vulnerable when the two providers became one. Additionally, they were quite perturbed when neither provider whom they had a close relationship with felt comfortable enough to discuss the merger in advance and hold enough respect to elicit their opinion. At the end of the day, the client was upset because they felt they were not even considered in the merger and how they would react to the same.

I spoke with the CEOs of both companies, who, in retrospect, clearly and unanimously agreed they feared how the client would respond and took the low road of keeping it quiet until the very end. They recognize now that the high road dictated transparency and open dialogue with such a key client and comprehend now that that was their best opportunity to have saved the client, who is now lost, probably for at least a few years if not forever.

Vendors' and Suppliers' Reactions

Vendors and suppliers also need to be part of the M&A and growth strategies as they could be impacted as well. First of all, they will feel very vulnerable. Being a vendor/supplier in my own businesses over the past 35 years, I have always felt vulnerable when an M&A activity or growth initiative happens. It sometimes can work in your favor or against you. As a vendor, for sure, you are vulnerable; the vulnerability is what is threatening.

This is why we as vendors and suppliers appreciate being part of the communication chain so that we can

- Possibly add value to the growth or M&A process;
- Prepare for either increase or decrease in business flow; and
- Add content to the strategic initiative or be part of the transition process.

Vendors and suppliers are critical components of the global supply chain and should be factored into all the decision-making processes that go along with growth and business development. This will work to everyone's advantage.

Financials Not Working

This is often the most frequent problem associated with transitional initiatives in growth and M&A activities, that the anticipated numbers are not holding true. This impacts a number of areas:

- The reasons for doing the deal in the first place
- Cash flow
- Transition budgets

The numbers anticipated not showing up is one of the most frequent areas for transition and M&A failures.

Financial anticipations not being met are typically due to any of the following reasons:

- Economic or political events or circumstances not anticipated
- Fraud or misrepresentation
- Loss of business during transition
- Insufficient due diligence in the assessment stage

Economic or Political Events or Circumstances Not Anticipated

When deals are done on a global basis, both political and economic occurrences can happen quickly. Macroissues are usually present in responsible forecasting. But microissues can occur at a moment's notice and may never be anticipated. Some of these events can be devastating.

The world economic collapse in 2007 came over a period of months and was in a number of economic forecasts. The big debate then was not if it was going to happen but more of to what extent.

The political events surrounding the Islamic State of Iraq and Syria (ISIS) in the Middle East in 2014 came suddenly; and the impact on Iraq, Syria, and surrounding countries was severe. This was predicted by only a few and impacted the world and certainly that geographic area very suddenly. ISIS went from a minor concern to an international plague that the USA and their allies are now dealing with very aggressively with military, political, and economic strategies involved.

In the assessment stage of any M&A deal or growth strategy, as we advised in Chapter 1, political and economic considerations need to be entertained in both the short and long term.

We recently worked with an airfreight company based in Shanghai who was developing a huge presence in the Middle East. They were both buying and opening stations in various Middle East countries to develop an airfreight service originating from both Asia and Europe.

The implementation began in December of 2013 and moved successfully until July of 2014. When ISIS had become a more serious concern in Iraq and Syria, followed by U.S. air strikes in surrounding territories, it stopped this company's expansion plans, which were brought quickly to a halt. They had difficulty moving foreign nationals into the region for management posts and also equipment that suppliers became very sheepish about.

Economic and political events can play a big toll on global growth and M&A strategies.

Cash flow that was in excess of $3 million a month trickled down to several hundred thousand dollars. The project was put on hold in October, awaiting for the political instability to lessen before starting up operations again. Clients were disappointed and investors were all very unhappy.

Fraud or Misrepresentation

Hopefully, quality and comprehensive due diligence in the assessment process will mitigate the exposure to fraud. But, having said that, the "bad guys" can be one step ahead of auditors and analysts and fraud can be a sizable exposure.

In 1998, I participated in the acquisition by a French company of a food products company in New Jersey. The purchase price included the value of the inventories held in multiple and globally located warehouses.

The French company sent out a general maritime surveyor to view inventory balances in eleven locations, seven here in the United States and four overseas. The surveyor estimated volumes off the balance sheets and confirmed that estimated inventories were correct.

The acquisition moved forward with a 10 percent margin allowance for inventory balances, determined at once after the takeover, and a more detailed inventory was accomplished. Within 60 days of the inventory accounting, it was determined that only 1 of the 11 locations had the correct inventory; 8 of the locations were off by an average of 27 percent, and 2 were off by more than 50 percent, all reports indicating much smaller balances.

The acquisition amounted to a US$18 million transaction. The variance in the inventory accounted for $4.5 million or 25 percent loss to the acquirer. A lawsuit ensued, and criminal charges were filed and management served jail time. Both intentional fraud and a misrepresentation had occurred. The due diligence in the inventory accounting was less than stellar.

What should have happened before closing was a more robust, forensic-type inventory analysis, which would have identified the inventory issue before the deal was consummated, preventing a year's delay in the M&A, significant legal costs, and jail time.

Loss of Business during Transition

Sometimes a transition can cause major distractions in key accounts and management personnel. When distractions occur, client services will likely suffer. The suffering can cause a loss of revenue and eventually business.

People are the front line to client services. Being distracted in a transitional stage can cause problems with the potential loss of revenue, clients, and opportunities.

Time is wasted on mitigation issues.

Insufficient Due Diligence in the Assessment Stage

Due diligence is one of the most important aspects of acquisition strategies.

Due diligence is an investigation of a business or person prior to signing a contract, or is an act with a certain *standard of care*. It can be a legal obligation, but the term will more commonly apply to voluntary investigations.

A common example of due diligence in various industries is the process through which a potential acquirer evaluates a target company or its assets for an *acquisition*. The theory behind due diligence holds that performing this type of investigation contributes significantly to informed decision making by enhancing the amount and quality of information available to decision makers and by ensuring that this information is systematically used to deliberate in a reflexive manner on the decision at hand and all its costs, benefits, and risks (Wikipedia).

Due diligence includes many of the following headliner topics of scrutiny:

- Financial analysis: balance, profit and loss (P&L), general ledger, receivables/payables aging bank statements, etc.
- Interviews with key trade partners: law firms, accountants/auditors, and lead consultants
- Interviews with key clients
- Interviews with key vendors and suppliers
- Asset and liability analysis
- Insurance coverages, pending claims, and claims history
- Interviews with key management and operations and sales personnel
- Compliance status and trade-compliance controls
- Technology system, platform, and integration capabilities

Before we review each of these areas in greater detail, a few guidelines need to be established:

- The review is typically done in stages. You do not go from 0 to 90 in 4.6 seconds. The process may be to go from 0 to 90 in 120 days. You start slowly with a cursory review, leading to full forensics when the time is appropriate in the growth or M&A process.
- Due diligence must be done with sensitivity, politeness, patience, and respect for the other party irrespective of what you find and uncover.

- Many times, based on initial findings, additional unexpected steps will be required to learn what you need to.
- Many times the process will have you become more liberal in your approach as the review is affirming all that has been discussed, or become more conservative as the review is identifying misrepresentations or new issues are surfacing and requiring additional and more serious inquiry.
- The inquiry process may have you go down new, unanticipated paths or directions or turning over additional stones.
- This is detailed, comprehensive, and patient work.

When warranted ... all this additional scrutiny ... is "good stuff"!

Financial Analysis: Balance, P&L, General Ledger, Receivables/Payables Aging Bank Statements, etc. This must be detailed and thorough. Financial analysis must be accomplished by those experts with analytical and forensic skill sets. Every stone must be turned and reviewed until all of the information on the financials is understood and explained and a determination of how it is being weighed is made. This will require access to company finance directors, controllers, and personnel responsible for the financial condition of the company, including external trade professionals. Typically significant banter will take place between the analyst and the CFO and principals to explain what is being found in the financial review.

Interviews with Key Trade Partners: Law Firms, Accountants/Auditors, and Lead Consultants   This group of trade professionals will have the "inside track" and "heartbeat" of the company and could offer significant insight into the "soul" of the company.

Information gathering and mining is an important component of the analysis process. These resources of this group of trade professionals can provide a good sense about the company or the growth opportunity from legal, compliance, operating, and financial perspectives. Often their insight could be very useful in the evaluation process and in making critical decisions regarding the growth or M&A opportunity. Their skill sets also can help shape the direction and the course you follow.

Interviews with Key Clients   There are two primary reasons to interview key clients:

1. They will advise on how they feel about the growth or M&A activity.
2. They can provide insightful and important information to be utilized in the decision-making process.

Approaching clients could be a very delicate concern, so the timing and approach has to be well thought out. The consequences of doing this step incorrectly could be severe, with loss of revenue and a client as the most extreme. Additionally, the cooperation of all vested interests with full transparency needs to be part of how these interviews are handled.

Interviews are an important due diligence step.

Interviews with Key Vendors and Suppliers   As was discussed earlier in this chapter, vendors and suppliers in favor need to be part of the information mining and discovery process. They will have a vested interest in cooperating as they have a lot to lose or gain in maintaining the relationship within the new company or structure. Hopefully, they view this mining as an opportunity to be cooperative and make a favorable impression.

Developing an intimate relationship with key vendors and suppliers will also be important in any transition and ongoing business relationship. In some business models a vendor and the relationship with that vendor can be the most critical component that makes the model work. And in some industries quality vendors are hard to come by and must be treated as a partner. In an expansion mode, they must be intertwined in the decision-making process, as if they are a key employee.

Asset and Liability Analysis   Obtaining a thorough and complete listing of all assets and liabilities, beyond and in detail as to what may be available in a balance sheet schedule, is very important. This list tells you a few things:

1. How organized the company is
2. How much detail is there at the level they are operating in
3. Exactly what they have as assets so that a contemporary and realistic appraisal can be accomplished
4. In determining liabilities, the track record and potential exposures, which help determine strategy for growth or M&A

Insurance Coverages, Pending Claims, and Claims History

Insurance is a necessary evil in business, but when managed correctly, it can be a real asset. This area is often missed until an insurance claim pops up. But it needs to be accomplished at the front end to

- Identify what exposures exist;
- Determine how insurance is being handled; and
- Create any necessary contingent liabilities plan.

This area will require analysis by insurance professionals and those with an ability to apply that insurance knowledge with sound business decision making.

Areas in insurance requiring scrutiny are as follows:

- Casualty and liability
- Product liability
- Cybersecurity products/data breach
- Property
- Marine
- Directors and officers liability (D&O)
- Fidelity
- Bonds
- Employee benefits
- Pensions
- 401(k)
- Workers' compensation
- Umbrella
- Excess
- Automobile
- Errors and omissions (E&O)
- Political risk
- Credit (receivables)

The following is an overview of specific insurances for corporations and businesses.

1. **General liability insurance:** Every business, even if home based, needs to have liability insurance. The policy provides both defense and damages if you, your employees, or your products or services cause or are alleged to have caused bodily injury or property damage to a third party.
2. **Property insurance:** If you own your building or have business personal property, including office equipment, computers, inventory, or tools, you should consider purchasing a policy that will protect you if you have a fire, vandalism, theft, smoke damage, etc. You may also want to consider business-interruption/loss-of-earning insurance as part of the policy to protect your earnings if the business is unable to operate.

3. **Business owner's policy (BOP):** Business owner policy packages are all the coverage a business owner would need. Often, BOPs will include business-interruption insurance, property insurance, vehicle coverage, liability insurance, and crime insurance. Based on your company's specific needs, you can alter what is included in a BOP. Typically, a business owner will save money by choosing a BOP because the bundle of services often costs less than the total cost of all the individual coverages.

4. **Commercial auto insurance:** Commercial auto insurance protects a company's vehicles. You can protect vehicles that carry employees, products, or equipment. With commercial auto insurance you can insure your work cars, sport-utility vehicles (SUVs), vans, and trucks from damage and collisions. If you do not have company vehicles but employees drive their own cars on company business, you should have nonowned auto liability insurance to protect the company in case the employee does not have insurance or has inadequate coverage. Many times the nonowned auto liability insurance can be added to the BOP policy.

5. **Workers' compensation:** Workers' compensation provides insurance to employees who are injured on the job. This type of insurance provides wage replacement and medical benefits to those who are injured while working. In exchange for these benefits, the employee gives up his rights to sue his employer for the incident. As a business owner, it is very important to have workers' compensation insurance because it protects yourself and your company from legal complications. State laws will vary, but all require you to have workers' compensation if you have W-2 employees. Penalties for noncompliance can be very stiff.

6. **Professional liability insurance (E&O):** This type of insurance is also known as errors and omissions insurance. The policy provides defense and damages for failure to render or improperly rendering professional services. Your general liability policy does not provide this protection, so it is important to understand the difference. Professional liability insurance is applicable for any professional firm including lawyers, accountants, consultants, notaries, real-estate agents, insurance agents, hair salons, and technology providers, to name a few.

7. **Directors and officers liability insurance:** This type of insurance protects the directors and officers of a company against their actions

that affect the profitability or operations of the company. If a director or an officer of your company, as a direct result of their actions on the job, finds him or herself in a legal situation, this type of insurance can cover costs or damages lost as a result of a lawsuit.

8. **Cyber/data breach:** If the business stores sensitive or nonpublic information about employees or clients on their computers or servers or in paper files, they are responsible for protecting that information. If a breach occurs either electronically or with a paper file, a data breach policy will provide protection against the loss.

9. **Homeowner's insurance:** Homeowner's insurance is one of the most important kinds of insurance you need. This type of insurance can protect against damage to the home and against damage to items inside the home. Additionally, this type of insurance may protect you from accidents that happen at home or may have occurred due to actions of your own.

10. **Renter's insurance:** Renter's insurance is a subset of homeowner's insurance that applies only to those who rent their home. The coverage protects against damage to the physical property, contents of the property, and personal injury within the home.

11. **Life insurance:** Life insurance protects an individual against death. If you have life insurance, the insurer pays a certain amount of money to a beneficiary upon your death. You pay a premium in exchange for the payment of benefits to the beneficiary. This type of insurance is very important because it allows for peace of mind. Having life insurance allows you to know that your loved ones will not be burdened financially upon your death.

12. **Personal and business automobile insurance:** Another very important type of insurance is auto insurance. Automobile insurance covers all road vehicles (trucks, cars, motorcycles, etc.). Auto insurance has a dual function, protecting against both physical damage and bodily injury resulting from a crash and also against any liability that might arise from the collision.

13. **Personal and business umbrella insurance:** You may want some additional coverage on top of insurance policies that you already have. This is where personal umbrella insurance comes into play.

This type of insurance is an extension of an already existing insurance policy and covers beyond the regular policy. This insurance can cover different kinds of claims, including homeowner's or auto insurance. Generally, it is sold in increments of $1 million and is used only when liability on other policies has been exhausted.

14. **Marine cargo:** This provides protection for goods in transit that move both domestically and internationally. Covers import and export exposures, along with sales between domestic entities.
15. **Political risk:** This covers the exposures in the international arena where government intervention can cause financial risk or loss.
16. **Receivables insurance:** This covers the risks of receivables not being paid by customers under commercial legitimate obligations.

Interviews with Key Management and Operations and Sales Personnel This is another one of those areas fraught with concern on timing and approach. Additionally, it requires full transparency and cooperation among all vested interests. This area can be of high value in obtaining hidden and inside information that might not normally be available in the due diligence process. It also allows you to obtain a "sense" of the staff and management who you will be working with, down the road.

Establishing rapport with key salespeople is also very important. They have the outreach to the customer, which can prove very valuable whenever change is happening.

Compliance Status and Trade-Compliance Controls In most companies today compliance can be a full-time position and in others where someone has ownership as part of their overall job description. Compliance will tell you how well a company is doing in meeting regulatory requirements and keeping out of trouble. In certain industries, such as, but not limited to,

- Pharma;
- Food;
- Chemicals;
- Cosmetics; and
- Defense,

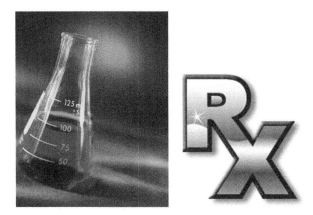

compliance can be a very critical factor in how well a company is doing. Compliance can mirror in these industries the company's ability to grow, gain sustainability, and earn revenue.

Technology System, Platform, and Integration Capabilities   Technology is now a critical aspect of any business. In evaluating any growth or M&A activity, technology must be factored in early.

Technology can quickly become a very expensive part of any growth or M&A deal, and in order to make sure that the deal can work successfully, this area needs to be mined and explored in great detail and with determined diligence.

Technology on a global basis presents major challenges in growth and M&A activities.

Software, hardware, operating systems, and cloud-based data storage all are some of the concerns when integrating technology from one company to another.

THE TRANSITION MANAGEMENT PROCESS

1. Beginning the transition process early on
2. Establishing a transition worksheet
3. Communications and meeting(s) structure
4. Testing of the process
5. Keeping close tabs on the process
6. Personalization of the process

Inspiration is the windfall from hard work and focus. Muses are too unreliable to keep on the payroll.

Helen Hanson

9

Legal and Regulatory Considerations

Throughout this book we discuss the importance of paying attention to legal and regulatory considerations on both the microlevel and the macrolevel. This chapter provides a basic outline to list and understand the basic regulations we need to pay attention to. This chapter was dependent upon the input of a counsel with 30-year-plus experience in global supply chain, M&A, and transportation regulations, Richard Furman, a good friend and colleague of the author.

OVERVIEW

Regulation and compliance with the laws on global supply chains is now a very integral part of any growth or M&A strategies. In most corporations, the general counsel's office would have this primary responsibility. However, the complexities of global trade and international business dictate that all executives and managers have a basic working knowledge of legal and regulatory factors involved in their business models.

In the past 30 years of global business activities, the events of 9/11 had the biggest impact on global supply chain compliance issues, which are outlined in detail in the next chapter.

The 9/11 Event

The events of 9/11 impacted global supply chains in a way unprecedented in our most recent economic and political history. 9/11 raised the vulnerabilities corporations, face in managing the complexities of global trade. This means that any growth or M&A opportunities in the global arena must contemplate the impact that the 9/11 legacy has on the decision making of

- Whom to work with;
- Whom to partner with;
- Whom to merge with;
- Whom to acquire; and
- Whom to associate with as clients, suppliers, vendors, channel partners, etc.

The consequences of not bringing 9/11 factors into the growth and M&A equation could lead to

- Fines and penalties;
- Inability to make deals happen internationally;
- Ineffective or inefficient supply chains;
- More costly logistics; and
- A lot of time wasted in dealing with haunting regulatory matters that interrupt daily operations.

Do not be "behind the eight ball" in proactively dealing with the supply chain consequences of 9/11.

Companies are impacted in various verticals operating the company:

- Legal
- Finance
- Manufacturing
- Warehousing and distribution
- Freight management and logistics
- Customer service
- Sales and business development
- Operations
- Purchasing

Going global requires a lot of internal reach into a company, coordinating all the stakeholders and vested interests to get it right!

The critical verticals in the company most impacted by the events of 9/11 are those that have to move goods and services from one country to another. Typically, these encompass purchasing, sales, supply-chain, and international-operations personnel.

The events of 9/11 put an onus on companies who move goods *and* services to and from the United States to do the following:

- Consider trade compliance and global security as priorities in moving freight to and from the United States.
- Bring some additional costs into the landed cost modeling referenced in Chapter 2.

  Some of these costs are

  - Security surcharges from transportation carriers;
  - Security surcharges from various port authorities and cargo handlers;
  - Increased documentation costs;
  - Technology enhancements;
  - Creation and adaptation of internal SOPs and business process changes;
  - Raising the bar of due diligence, reasonable care and supervision, and control in the global supply chain; and
  - Engagement processes that will need to be executed.
- Create a new job description in most major companies engaged in international business, that of the global trade compliance manager.

This became a shared responsibility in some companies and in others its own distinct vertical reporting into compliance, legal, supply chain, or global logistics.

The events of 9/11 created over 120 pieces of legislation and/or regulatory changes that impacted global operations at the time of the regulatory execution until this current time frame. A partial list of some of these regulatory and legislative changes follows:

- Customs trade partnership against terrorism

Customs-Trade
Partnership Against Terrorism

- USA Patriot Act
- *9/11 Commission Report* recommendations
- Department of Homeland Security
- Customs Border and Protection
- Transportation Security Administration
- Trade Act of 2002
- Security and Accountability for Every (SAFE) Port Act
- 24-Hour Advance Manifest Rule
- Federal Food, Drug, and Cosmetics Act and Food Safety Modernization Act (FSMA)
- International Ship and Port Facility Security (ISPS) Code
- Maritime Transportation Security Act

Some rules enacted were made into laws; others became business process changes; all were designed to make our borders and trade more secure and trade complaint.

U.S. STATUTES AND REGULATIONS GOVERNING EXPORT SHIPPING AND TRADE

Introduction

The smooth and profitable operation of any enterprise depends not only on the conduct of its fundamental business purpose but also on avoiding or minimizing potential external pitfalls. Some pitfalls are beyond the control of a company, and these are often unforeseeable, such as natural disasters or accidents. Other potential difficulties are foreseeable and within the ability of a company to address proactively.

Lack of awareness of and failure to comply with laws and regulations of the United States that govern export shipping is one potential source of problems. If ignored or not carefully attended to, the result could be interference in the movement of goods and additional costs, including potential penalties and sanctions. Therefore, every company, whether a supply-chain services company or an exporter, can and should endeavor to maintain the highest standard of compliance with such statutes and regulations.

The purpose of this chapter is to identify and outline statutes and regulations that can affect the business interests of the reader. It is intended to alert the reader to importance of the laws and regulations discussed, so that the reader may seek more detailed information and guidance; this chapter should not be relied upon as legal advice or opinion.

Our focus will be the following:

1. The Carriage of Goods by Sea Act (COGSA), governing international ocean shipping
2. The Warsaw and Montreal Conventions, governing international air transport*
3. The Export Administration Regulations, governing export licensing of commercial goods
4. The International Traffic in Arms Regulations
5. The Foreign Assets Control Regulations

---

* While the transport statutes discussed are the laws of the land, they are usually supplemented or, where permitted, modified by tariffs and similar rules and conditions issued by carriers. As ocean carriers and non-vessel-operating common carriers (NVOCCs or NVOs) (described infra) are subject to licensing and regulation by the Federal Maritime Commission, responsible for enforcing U.S. maritime statutes, the ability of carriers and NVOs to modify COGSA is basically limited to entering into service agreements with shippers. However, the statutory limitation of liability, suit time bar, and certain other provisions cannot be reduced but can be increased. Similarly, air carriers and indirect air carriers (also described infra) often maintain tariffs, rules and terms, and conditions in addition to those imposed by law under the air-transport statutes of the United States. However, the regulation of air transport does not include oversight or approval of the carriers' tariffs rules and terms, as in the case of ocean carriers and NVOs. Therefore, air carriers and indirect air carriers can to a greater degree contract out of the air-transport statutes that govern them as discussed below, although limitations of liability suit time bars and some other key terms cannot be decreased.

6. Foreign Corrupt Practices Act
7. Automated Export System*

This chapter is not exhaustive, either as to the substance of any of the laws or regulations discussed or as to all potential statutes and regulations that might come into play as part of an export shipping transaction; for example, many laws and regulations that are unique to certain classes of merchandise will not be addressed. It is incumbent on the reader, therefore, to obtain more detailed information on the laws and rules discussed, together with other statutes and regulations that may impact the conduct of their business and/or the merchandise they handle or sell. Furthermore, this chapter will not discuss any of the myriad of foreign laws and regulations that must also be taken into consideration and complied with. All shippers or shipping agents of goods to foreign destinations are well advised to be conversant with the import and related laws of the foreign countries with which they trade to avoid adverse consequences for noncompliance.

The International Shipping Laws of the United States†

The Carriage of Goods by Sea Act‡

COGSA is the law that governs transportation of cargo to and from ports of the United States, whether or not expressly incorporated in the terms

---

* The agencies that administer the regulations discussed in this chapter are the U.S. Customs and Border Protection, the United States Department of Commerce's Bureau of Industry and Security, the U.S. Department of State's Office of Defense Trade Controls, the Bureau of Census, the Department of Justice, and the Securities and Exchange Commission. All have websites with substantial online information and guidance, as well as phone, fax, and e-mail details for divisions that can be contacted for advice and rulings on compliance with their regulations. The shipping statutes are best understood through advice from a knowledgeable transportation intermediary or attorney expert in cargo-transport laws and regulations.

† Copies of the statutes outlined below are attached as appendices to this chapter for the benefit of the reader interested in knowing the full details of the provisions discussed and those to which no reference was made.

‡ There are actually two COGSA statutes on the books at present. As a result of an agreement among most of the world's maritime nations, a uniform set of rules, intended to supplant the multiplicity of national statutes governing ocean transport, such as U.S. COGSA, was agreed to some years ago and known familiarly as the Rotterdam Rules. In 2006 Congress adopted these new rules, apparently under the belief that they would become universally accepted in relatively short order. That has not been the case; therefore, for the moment the Rotterdam Rules are not effective. So U.S. COGSA, as discussed in this chapter, is still the law of the land but shares the statute books with the U.S. codification of the Rotterdam Rules. Presumably, at some point in the future the Rotterdam Rules will supplant COGSA as the only U.S. statute governing carriage of goods by water, but at this juncture no one can reasonably predict when.

of the bill of lading* or other form of shipping terms.† However, it is most common for COGSA to be incorporated by reference in the terms and conditions of the back of its bill of lading, which a carrier‡ must issue in connection with a shipment.§ Such a term is known as a clause paramount.

Absent shipping terms on the face of the bill of lading that extend the time of the shipment are covered by the bill of lading, i.e., door to door, door to port, or port to door. COGSA is deemed to be applicable to a shipment rail to rail, meaning from the time the cargo crosses the rail when the vessel is being loaded to the time the cargo crosses the rail when being discharged. However, under circumstances where the carrier uses contractors or agents, such as truckers, stevedores, and warehousemen, prior or subsequent to the loading, carriage, and unloading of the cargo, COGSA is generally deemed to also govern the shipment.

As a consequence, most carrier bills of lading have what is known as the Himalaya clause. This term expressly extends the bill of lading terms and conditions, including the clause paramount, to any agent or subcontractor engaged by the carrier.¶ The significance of the provision is that it can

---

* A bill of lading, whether issued for ocean, air, or surface transport is considered a contract, usually referred to as a contract of carriage. In the case of ocean shipping, the bill of lading is required by regulation to be part of a tariff carrier's obligation to electronically maintain and make available to the shipping public upon request. As such it is a quasipublic record, and as a general proposition a shipper is deemed to know and be bound by its terms, whether or not it actually receives a copy of the bill of lading before, during, or after the shipment. Such knowledge can also be imputed based on a course of dealing with the carrier, especially where the shipper routinely receives a copy of the bill of lading in connection with prior shipments.

† Cargo shipping within the territorial waters of the United States, including to and from Puerto Rico and Hawaii, is governed by the Harter Act. For all practical purposes the provisions of the Harter Act regarding liability of the carrier, limitation of the carrier's liability, and related terms are the same or similar to those discussed regarding COGSA.

‡ Any reference in the chapter to "carrier" or "carriers" includes NVOCCs. COGSA also governs NVOCCs, as they operate in all respects like an ocean carrier but do not own and operate vessels. Since many, if not most, regular shippers utilize the services of NVOCCs, everything discussed regarding COGSA applies equally to both NVOs and carriers. An NVOCC should not be confused with an ocean freight forwarder, even though an NVO frequently provides many of the same services. An ocean freight forwarder is strictly a middleman that arranges for the carriage of a shipper's goods by a carrier and provides other services on behalf of the shipper related to the booking, carriage, and export clearance of the shipment, while an NVOCC is a carrier.

§ It is not uncommon for a bill of lading not to be issued or to be issued at a later date and at the time of shipment or for an express bill of lading (a nonnegotiable bill of lading sent by fax or other electronic means) to be used in connection with a shipment. It is well settled that as long as the bill of lading would have been issued in the ordinary course of business, it serves as a contract of carriage governing the relationship of the shipper and the carrier.

¶ To be on the safe side, most bills of lading spell out certain key terms that would otherwise be incorporated by reference under the clause paramount, such as the limitation of liability, the right of the shipper to declare a value for carriage, and limitation on suit time, just in case for some reason COGSA is deemed not to cover the shipment.

foreclose a claimant from pursuing a claim against a carrier's agent or sub-contractor for an amount greater than the carrier's limitation of liability.

Among the terms of COGSA that should be of particular concern are those relating to the limitation of a carrier's liability for loss, damage, or delay to the goods in transit; the means for increasing the amount of the carrier's liability; the time within which a claim for loss or damage needs to be made; and a limitation on the time within which suit needs to be commenced if a claim is denied.

COGSA provides that in the absence of a declaration of a higher value for carriage by the shipper, the carrier's liability will be limited to $500 per package or customary shipping unit* or the actual value of the loss, whichever is less. A provision in a bill of lading that purports to set a lower limitation of liability is ineffective.

As the calculation of the amount of a potential recovery based on the statutory limitation is predicated on the number of packages or customary shipping unit, it should not be surprising that there has been, and continues to be, ongoing litigation as to what constitutes a package. Before the advent of containerized shipping, the issue was of far less significance. Once the use of containers started to develop, the debate centered on whether the container, which might be loaded with numerous packages, was the "package" for COGSA purposes or the actual packages in the container should be the basis for determining the number of packages. The carriers argued that as most containers were loaded and sealed by the shipper, they had no way of knowing how many individual packages were loaded in a container and therefore should not be imputed with knowledge of the contents of the containers by having accepted responsibility for them when loading them on the vessel. Over time this issue was resolved by the courts based on the fact that most bills of lading issued by carriers listed not only the number of containers accepted by the carrier for transport but also the number of packages in the containers. It is now accepted that the limitation of liability for loss or damage to goods covered by a bill of lading is the number detailed as having been loaded in the container, whether or not the carrier was able to verify the count at the time it accepted the container for shipment. Therefore, the knowledgeable shipper or shipper's export agent should ensure that any bill of lading that

---

* Generally, a customary shipping unit is not a package as the term is generally or familiarly understood. So, for example, an automobile, a truck, or a piece of machinery is a shipping unit in and of itself. Likewise, fungible goods such as liquids or grains, transported in bulk on a vessel, are customary shipping units.

covers the transport of the shipper's goods states the number of packages in the container.

The debate as to what is a package continues, however, as the manner in which goods are packed has evolved. For example, there is divided opinion in the courts as to whether the COGSA limitation of liability for palletized cargo should be calculated by the number of pallets listed on the bill of lading or the number of packages on the palette. Some courts take the position that if the palette is shrink-wrapped with black or opaque plastic such that it cannot be determined by observation as to how many packages are on the palette, the carrier may treat the palette as the package for COGSA purposes; but if the shrink-wrap is clear, the number of packages on the palette will be used to calculate the limitation of liability. Other courts do not recognize the palette as a potential package under any circumstances. While some shippers prefer black or similar wrapping that obstructs the ability to view the packages on a palette, for security and possibly other reasons, all things being equal, given the divided opinion, it would be best to err on the side of caution when shipping palletized goods and use clear shrink-wrap.

In addition to the foregoing, there are other package debates that arise with some regularity, due to the nature of the goods or ambiguities in the description of the shipment. It behooves the wise shipper or its forwarding agent, therefore, to be alert to the possibility that the issue of to how the calculation of the carrier's COGSA limitation of liability may affect its right of recovery for loss or damage in circumstances other than those where the shipment consists of traditional packages, cartons, crates, etc.

To enable the opportunity to recover a sum of the actual value of a loss or damage to a shipment, COGSA provides that the shipper may declare a higher value for carriage, rather than rely on the statutory limitation of liability, in consideration of a supplemental charge for the carrier's assumption of the greater risk.* It is fairly common for carriers to charge a significant amount for the right to make excess declaration of value for carriage. This has the effect of discouraging shippers from making a declaration of value for carriage.

---

* As a rule, most carrier bills of lading do not have a space on the front of the bill of lading for noting a declaration of value for carriage. Therefore, the declaration needs to be made with the carrier when booking the shipment or in the terms of a service agreement, which frequent or volume shippers increasingly use to spell special rates and understandings with carriers, in consideration of commitments to use the carrier for tendering a certain volume of shipping.

It is important to understand, however, that a declaration of value does not create a guarantee that in the event of a loss or damage, the claimant will receive the amount declared. The declaration is not insurance, guaranteeing a recovery of the loss as if it is covered by an insurance policy, and the fee for the declaration is not a premium for an insured risk. Therefore, in the event of a claim for loss or damage, it is incumbent on the claimant to prove the value of the loss or damage to the shipment. If there is no such proof or it is insufficient to sustain the full claim, no recovery based on a declaration of value will result, despite the supplemental payment in consideration of the declaration.

In the face of the foregoing circumstances, it is more customary, probably overwhelmingly so, for shippers to maintain their own cargo policies of insurance or to purchase such insurance from their freight forwarder or even an NVOCC. As a general proposition, insurance is less costly than a declaration of value and, assuming the loss is covered by the policy, there is a much better probability of a recovery within the policy limits.

Both COGSA and the customary bill of lading have terms containing time limits within which claims must be filed and how the claims must be submitted. However, failure to comply with such terms will not result in the claim being denied, although it can have consequences on the ability to recover certain costs should the claim be litigated and the claimant prevails.

Should a claim be denied or not satisfied to the extent that the claimant believes it is entitled, COGSA requires that suit be commenced within one year of the date of delivery of the shipment or in the event of nondelivery, when the shipment could have been delivered.* It is important to take careful note of the timing of when the shipment arrived at the port or was delivered to ensure a healthy margin of time within which to file an action, so as to avoid unwittingly exceeding the one-year time bar. It is an issue that frequently arises and is easily avoided.

Two possible issues need to be kept in mind that are not part of COGSA but are necessary to know when complying with the COGSA one-year suit time bar. First, there is almost nothing in COGSA that addresses the causes of action that may be alleged against a carrier by a

---

* Determining when a shipment could have been delivered is a fact specific to any given case and there are no objective criteria that can be universally applied. As a result, this can often be an issue, especially when there appears to be an 11th-hour filing of a suit, as the carrier will endeavor to assert that it is untimely.

shipper. In most instances claims will be predicated on the same issues and principles of law that are common to everyday commercial litigation, such as breach of contract and negligence. However, in the United States and some other maritime countries, there are also traditional admiralty causes of action. Of particular note is the concept of material deviation.

Historically, deviation meant geographic diversion of a vessel from its stated route for purposes other than the safety of passengers, crew, and goods or similar necessity. Often such geographic deviation resulted from the master of the vessel putting into a port in order to try and find additional freight to increase the profitability of a voyage. If a vessel casualty occurred or the vessel failed to arrive in a timely fashion because of the deviation, the vessel owners and the master would not have the ability to limit their liability or assert any of the traditional, and later statutory, defenses that they could otherwise rely on, and they would be fully liable for any claimed loss.

As shipping and technology of vessels and ocean transport evolved, deviation has been interpreted as applying to a wide variety of circumstances other than geographic deviation. Consequently, placing a container below or on deck, contrary to an agreement to stow the container in one location or the other, or failure to place perishable goods in a refrigerated container or properly maintaining the temperature of goods in a refrigerated container can be considered a deviation, among many other possibilities.

Second, most equipment-operating carriers and many, if not most, NVOCCs have forum selection and choice of law terms in their bills of lading. The terms specify where a case must be filed and which jurisdiction's law will govern the issues raised by the case. In the absence of concern on the part of the court as to whether a designated jurisdiction's procedures and laws are reasonable and fair, such as in North Korea, for example, courts will almost universally enforce such forum and law clauses.

One must be mindful of the enforceability such provisions and the consequence. For example, most of the Japanese, Chinese, and South Korean carriers require that they be sued in their home countries, subject to their national legal standards. Therefore, consideration needs to be given to the possible risks and added costs of pursuing an action halfway across the world against the carriers, many of which are owned by their governments, under alien practice and procedure.

The Warsaw and Montreal Conventions*

At present, there are two principal regimes in effect in the United States that govern the international transport of goods by air, the Warsaw Convention and the Montreal Convention.† As explained below, this duality of existence is a consequence of the manner in which the conventions are adopted by the countries that are signatories to them.

The Warsaw Convention was enacted following World War II. Due to the exponential growth in passenger and cargo air carriage, it was made the subject of a number of amendments needed to respond to the evolving air-transport industry and the world economy. Over time it was recognized that something of a patchwork had developed. Therefore, the international community came together to agree on a new convention that would better address current passenger and cargo air transport. The result preserved what was good from Warsaw and implemented more modern concepts and standards. The result is the Montreal Convention.

The reason for the concurrent existence of the Warsaw and Montreal Conventions is the fact that for one or the other to govern in a given case, for our purposes an air cargo transaction, both the country from which the shipment originates and the country to which the shipment is being sent must have fully adopted one or the other of the conventions. So, for example, if a shipment is sent from the United States, which has adopted Montreal, to a foreign country that that has also adopted Montreal, then Montreal would govern. If the shipment is sent to a country that has yet to adopt Montreal but observes Warsaw, then Warsaw would govern as both the United States and the destination country adopted Warsaw.‡ This distinction is important since although many of the terms of both statutes are the same in substance, there are differences that can affect the rights of the parties to the shipping transaction.

The foregoing circumstance is due to the fact that the political process for adopting Montreal in many, if not most, countries can take a considerable amount of time for a variety of reasons. As a consequence,

---

* The Warsaw and Montreal Conventions are two separate statutes. However, the specific terms that are outlined are the same in both. Therefore, the two conventions are being discussed jointly. However, there are differences that should be understood. Both documents are not lengthy and a read of them for familiarity would be worth the effort. Copies can be found in the appendices.

† Although both the Warsaw and the Montreal Conventions are international treaties, when Congress voted to adopt them they became the laws of the land. Therefore, for purposes of this discussion they are considered statutes of the United States and enforced as such.

‡ If both countries have adopted both conventions, then Montreal would prevail.

since the convention was signed in 1999 and became effective in 2003,* only 108 countries of the 191 countries in the world today have adopted Montreal.

As in the case of COGSA, Warsaw and Montreal contain provisions that govern the rights and duties of the shipper and the carrier with respect to the carriage of cargo.[†]

Air carriers issue air waybills, whose faces are recognizably similar to the waybills issued by ocean carriers, as they serve the same purpose of setting forth the details of the who, what, when, and where of the shipment they are issued to cover for transport. The air waybills also contain terms and conditions on the reverse, some of which are similar to those one would find on the back of an ocean bill of lading, such as, for example, the right to exercise a lien on the goods described on the front of the bill of lading or air waybill; others are unique to air carriages. Just as in the case of the ocean bill of lading, the air waybill is considered a contract of carriage and is binding as such on the shipper and the carrier.

Similar to ocean bills of lading, air waybills usually incorporate by reference the statutes or conventions that govern air transport. Since either Warsaw or Montreal may apply in a given case, as a rule they are both incorporated by reference to indirect air carrier and airline waybills. In addition, since air transport is more widespread geographically and the same air waybill can be used in locations within other countries and regions, many air waybills incorporate air treaties, conventions, or statutes unique to such other locations so as to be enforceable when and if a shipment is subject to their provisions.

Also similar to ocean bills of lading, air waybills will spell out certain key terms that are part of Warsaw and Montreal. Such terms generally cover the limitation of liability, times within which claims must be filed and their form, and a suit time bar. If for some reason the statutory terms are found not to cover the shipment, the written ones, as a matter of simple contract, will preserve the carrier's right to enforce them.

---

* At least 30 countries had to accede to the convention before it could become effective.
† In air carriage there are service companies that operate just like NVOCCs, referred to variously as indirect air carriers or air freight forwarders. Just like an NVOCC, an indirect air carrier issues an air waybill in its own name but does not own or operate any transport equipment. However, similarly to an NVO, an indirect air carrier is considered an "airline" and is subject to Warsaw/Montreal just like an equipment operating airline. Therefore, all references to a "carrier," "carriers," "air carriers," or "airline" should be read as including indirect air carriers.

The period of carriage of goods under cover of an air waybill is from airport to airport. This period however has flex time built into it by Warsaw/Montreal. In the language of both Warsaw and Montreal, in part, "the period of carriage by air does not extend to any carriage … performed outside an airport. If, however, such carriage takes place in the performance of a contract for carriage by air, for the purpose of loading, delivery or transshipment, any damage is presumed, subject to proof to the contrary, to have been the result of an event which took place during the carriage by air." Montreal has added language that makes it clear that substituted modes of transport used by the carrier to perform the contract of carriage, even if without the consent of the consignor, is deemed to be within the period of carriage by air. In addition, while equipment-operating air carriers most often issue air waybills governing a shipment only on an airport-to-airport basis, it is not uncommon for an indirect air carrier's waybill to be door to airport, door to door, etc., on the face of the air waybill, thus extending the coverage of the air waybill's contract of carriage terms to such carriage.

Although a great deal of air cargo is shipped in containers, familiarly known as a unit load device (ULD), this circumstance has never been any issue of consequence in connection with calculation of a carrier's limitation of liability for cargo claims, as in the case of ocean containers. In air carriage it is the weight of the shipment that is the key factor, not the quantity of goods in the container. However, it is still incumbent on the claimant to satisfactorily prove what was in the ULD, and the value of the loss, when submitting a claim.

As in the case of COGSA, Warsaw and Montreal both provide the air carrier with authority to limit its liability. In the absence of a declared value for carriage, a carrier's liability is limited to 19 special drawing rights (SDRs). The carrier's maximum liability is based on the weight of the entire shipment if the damaged cargo affects the value of the other cargo covered by the same air waybill. The claimant is entitled to recover only the actual value of the loss or damage if it is less than the amount of the limitation, or the limitation if it is less than the actual value.

An SDR is treated like any other currency, derived from a "basket" of national currencies, managed by the International Monetary Fund (IMF). Since an SDR is a fluctuating currency and is traded like any national currency, on any given day it can have a different exchange rate. Its daily exchange rate in dollars can be determined by reference to the IMF's website; it is also listed among the daily exchange rates published by some newspapers, such as the *New York Times*. Therefore, it is wise to keep track of the exchange rate to determine if and to what extent the limitation may affect the amount of a recovery for a claim. This will also aid in assessing whether to declare a value for carriage or secure insurance to cover the shipment.

All air waybills have a box on the front of the air waybill in which to enter the declaration value for carriage. Absent the declaration being endorsed on the front of the air waybill in the space provided unless the result of the fault of the carrier, the shipper will have no right to claim a greater amount of loss or damage than the statutory limitation of liability. Failure of a carrier to issue an air waybill will not deprive the carrier of its right to limit its liability or other benefits under provided by Warsaw/Montreal.*

As in the case of COGSA, a declaration of value is not a guarantee of payment in the event of a loss or damage. The declaration is not insurance, which would provide a recovery if the loss is one covered by the insurance policy; and the fee for the declaration is not a premium for an insured risk. Therefore, in the event of a claim for loss or damage it is incumbent on the claimant to prove the value of the loss or damage. If there is no such proof or it is insufficient to sustain the full claim, no recovery based on declaration of value will result, despite the supplemental payment in consideration of being able to make the declaration. Moreover, if the value of the claim as proven is less than the declared value, the claimant may recover only that amount. Concomitantly, if

---

* Formally this was not the case. In its original form Warsaw required a physical bill of lading be issued to the shipper and that certain particulars be on the face of the bill of lading. Failure to comply with those terms would void the right of the carrier to assert its limitation of liability. The change was the result of an amendment to Warsaw known as Montreal Protocol No. 4 (MP-4). MP-4 also changed the amount of the limitation of liability from $9.07 per pound or $20 per kilo, which was a fixed amount that did not adjust over time. Instead, the limitation was initially set at 17 SDRs per kilo, with the proviso that it would be subject to review and revision every five years. The current limitation of 19 SDRs is the result of the most recent adjustment of the limitation. MP-4 also did away with certain circumstances that would void a carrier's limitation and other rights under Warsaw, such as willful misconduct. Notably, under both Warsaw, as amended by MP-4, and Montreal, the limitation of liability is considered unbreakable, despite the fact that there is saving language in both statutes that would set aside the limitation of liability if it is proved that damage resulting from an act or omission of the carrier, its servants, or agents has been done with intent to cause damage or recklessly and with knowledge that the damage would probably result. It should also be noted that the limitation of liability is extended by both statutes to the servants and agents of a carrier.

the value of the claim as proven is more than the declaration, the declaration acts as a limitation of liability and is a cap on the recovery.

The airline has the right to charge a supplemental fee for a declared value for carriage. It is often costly and as a consequence it is most common for shippers not to declare a value for carriage and obtain insurance instead, either from the carrier or under its own cargo policy.

In the event of a claim, Warsaw/Montreal have specific time limits within which claims must be filed. In the case of damage, the claim must be made within 7 days from receipt of the cargo by the claimant. In the case of delay the complaint must be made at the latest within 21 days from the date at which the cargo is placed at the disposal of the claimant. Both the forgoing time limits are often longer in the terms of most air carrier waybills.

The issue as to what the date is at which the cargo was placed at the disposal of the claimant has led to some litigation. As a general rule, once the goods are made available to the claimant for receipt, usually by a notice to the claimant or its customs clearance agent, the time limit will begin running. Circumstances vary, however, so it is not a hard and fast standard. Unlike COGSA, however, failure to file a timely claim, in proper form and substance, will permit the carrier to deny the claim and will forever bar the claim from suit or any other means of obtaining a recovery.

Should a claim be denied, Warsaw/Montreal provides a two-year limitation of time within which suit must be commenced against the carrier. Under Warsaw, the suit time begins to run from the date on which the carriage stopped. A determination as to when carriage stopped can sometimes be difficult, depending on the facts and circumstances of the particular shipment. Therefore, under the Montreal suit, in an effort to avoid disputes over when suit time begins to run, suit time is calculated from the date of arrival at the destination, or from the date on which the aircraft ought to have arrived, or from the date on which the carriage stopped. One may be forgiven from thinking that the Montreal standard perhaps creates even more ambiguity than that of Warsaw.

Unlike suits for ocean loss or damage claims, air carrier waybills do not usually have a choice of law and forum selection clauses. This is due to the fact that Warsaw and Montreal have provisions that stipulate where an action may be brought "at the option of the plaintiff, in the territory of one of the signatories to the conventions, either within the jurisdiction where the carrier is ordinarily resident, or has its principal place of business, or has a location where the contract of carriage was made, or in a court at the place of destination."

U.S. Export Trade Controls

Exporting is a privilege, not a right. In order to exercise that right and avoid having it revoked, it is incumbent on exporters to comply with a number of regulations administered by various agencies of the United States, depending on the nature of the export commodity and the underlying trade transaction.

Among the regulations that can affect export trade most regularly are the Export Administration Regulations (EAR), enforced by the United States Department of Commerce's (DOC) Bureau of Industry and Security (BIS); the International Traffic in Arms Regulations (ITAR), enforced by the United States Department of State's Office of Defense Trade Controls (ODTC); the Foreign Assets Control Regulations (FAC), enforced by the United States Department of the Treasury's Office of Foreign Assets Control (OFAC); and the Foreign Corrupt Practices Act (FCPA), overseen jointly by the Department of Justice and the Securities and Exchange Commission. In addition, the U.S. Customs and Border Protection (CBP) is involved in enforcement of the referenced regulations and those of other agencies relating to commodities and the activities of exporters and importers, as goods pass through its hands when entering and leaving the United States.

The referenced regulations are substantial and at times complex. Therefore, what follows is an overview of the purposes and scope of the controls the regulations are intended to exercise over export shipping. Consequently, reference to the regulations and the agencies that enforce them as to if and how they may apply to an export transaction is strongly urged.

Moreover, one should never rely on prior study of the regulations or prior advice from an administrative agency, in connection with subsequent transactions, as the rules are regularly updated and amended. What was correct in one instance may not be acceptable in a subsequent situation. As the saying goes, ignorance of the law is no excuse and one is presumed to know the law and comply with it. Inadvertent noncompliance, let alone intentional noncompliance, will not avoid a potentially serious sanction, although in the former instance it may be less severe than the latter unless the perpetrator has a record of chronic inadvertence.

The Export Administration Regulations

The EAR is intended to serve the national security, foreign policy, non-proliferation of weapons of mass destruction, and other interests of the United States.

All exports of commodities from the United States are subject to licensing.* The overwhelming percentage of commodities may be exported under one or another of general licenses, which means a formal application for a valid export license need not be submitted and approved before the goods may be exported. Certain classes of commodities may not be exported, however, without first obtaining a valid export license from BIS.

As a consequence, a significant portion of the EAR is dedicated to providing rules on how to determine if a particular commodity needs to be the subject of an application for a valid license, the types of licenses that can be applied for, the license application process, and, inevitably, the penalty and sanctions that will be imposed if a license is not obtained when it should have been.

The EAR is primarily intended to control certain exports and reexport of commercial commodities and the activities of exporters and their export agents, such as freight forwarders. In addition, the EAR oversees compliance with antiboycott laws, which prohibit furthering or supporting boycotts maintained by foreign states against countries friendly to the United States, such the Arab boycott of Israel.

The issue of whether or not an antiboycott statute is in danger of being violated often comes up in transactions involving letters of credit. There may be a provision in the letter of credit restricting the seller/exporter from engaging in trade with a country that is the object of the boycott, or a myriad of other possible provisos, many of which are often very subtly and seemingly innocuous such that if these are complied with would place the seller/exporter in a position of liability, most often inadvertently, for an antiboycott violation. The EAR has an extensive set of examples of what is or is not an antiboycott provision that may be found in a letter of credit, sales order or confirmation, sales agreement, and other possible documents representing the terms of performance of the sale and export transaction.

The bottom-line advice is that when and if an export seller encounters any language in any document from a foreign purchaser/consignee that

---

* Various other U.S. agencies have licensing authority for different exports. For example, nuclear exports are subject to oversight by the Nuclear Regulatory Commission and the Departments of Energy and Commerce, and trade embargoes and sanctions/transactions are addressed by the Department of the Treasury.

references any third country, the seller/export should seek guidance from BIS without hesitation.

Some provisions are broadly interpreted to apply to transactions outside the United States or activities other than exports in addition to exports and export activities within the United States. The EAR also applies to dual-use commodities. Often this applies to exports of what normally would be considered purely civilian goods, with both civil and military, terrorism, and potential weapons of mass destruction's capabilities, as well as commodities exclusively used for military purposes, that do not warrant control under the International Traffic in Arms Regulations, as outlined further on in this chapter.

In addition to the foregoing, the EAR governs exports of technology and software. Technological information and software can be considered an export even if it is merely disclosed through a demonstration, oral briefing, or electronic transmission. In fact, the definition of what is an export is the subject of some lengthy explanation in the EAR and important to be familiar with, as it is very broad and not limited in the least to just physical shipment of a commodity out of the United States. There is also a lengthy list of what is not considered an export.

The EAR is as user friendly as any government regulation can possibly be, which is not to say that it cannot be confusing at times or downright obtuse. However, the process of understanding and complying with the EAR is helped by the fact that within the regulations there are flowcharts* and step-by-step instructions to assess whether an export requires a validated license and if that is not sufficient, phone and mail contacts within the agency where more guidance can be obtained.

The most direct means of making an initial determination of whether or not a commodity can be exported under a general license or requires a validated license begins with reference to the Commerce Control List (CCL), which is part of the EAR. The CCL lists almost all commodities requiring a validated license. It is not exhaustive though, as the concerns outlined above that the EAR is intended to address sometimes result in products being restricted or denied from being exported due to current foreign policy or other considerations not spelled out in the EAR.

---

* The EAR has a "decision tree" as a supplement to part 732 of the EAR, intended to make it easy for an exporter to make a determination as to whether or not a commodity will require an application for a valid export license. It takes a bit of coaching by reference to the EAR to understand its use, but all things considered it is fairly user friendly.

The CCL is not a mere list of commodities. It is quite detailed as to the specifications, quantities, value, the basis for the restriction or prohibition requiring a license, and other factors that would apply for a validated license. If a commodity on the list does not fall within the criteria for that product, so to necessitate obtaining a validated license, then the commodity may be exported without a validated license.

Of course, nothing is ever quite that simple, and the EAR spells out guidelines for determining if an export is subject to prohibitions that would preclude or restrict the export being made. The process begins with a determination by the exporter of five facts, which should be addressed as questions, as follows:

1. Classification of the item: The classification of the item on the Commerce Control List, as discussed above.
2. Destination: The country of ultimate destination for an export or reexport. The EAR contains a country chart that classifies to which countries controlled commodities can be sent, subject to some restrictions, and those to which all but very limited classes of goods can be sent, such as, for example, Cuba, Iran, or North Korea.
3. End user, meaning the ultimate end user: The EAR lists persons to which exports to are not permitted or are subject to limitations.
4. End use: The ultimate end use of the exported commodity.
5. Conduct: Conduct such as contracting, financing, and freight forwarding in support of a proliferation project.

The answers to the foregoing are needed to assess if the export is covered by any of the ten general prohibitions to exporting:

1. Export and reexport of controlled items to listed countries
2. Reexport and export from abroad of foreign-made items incorporating more than a de minimis amount of controlled U.S. content
3. Reexport and export from abroad of foreign-produced direct products of U.S. technology and software
4. Engaging in actions prohibited by a denial order
5. Export or reexport to prohibited end uses or end users
6. Export or reexport to embargoed destinations
7. Support of proliferation activities
8. In transit shipments and items to be unladen from vessels or aircraft

9. Violation of any order, terms, and conditions
10. Proceeding with transactions with knowledge that a violation has occurred or is about to occur

Ultimately, it is the responsibility of the shipper, and its forwarding agent, to ensure that commodities are not improperly exported, consistent with foregoing guidelines and other controls detailed in the EAR.

The International Traffic in Arms Regulations

The ITAR are the regulations written to enforce the Arms Export Control Act, which is intended to control the export* and import of defense articles,[†] technical data,[‡] and defense services.[§] The regulations are administered by the United States Department of State's ODTC.

---

* Export means sending or taking a defense article out of the United States in any manner except by mere travel outside of the United States by a person whose personal knowledge includes technical data; or transferring registration, control, or ownership to a foreign person of any aircraft, vessel, or satellite covered by the U.S. Munitions List, whether in the United States or abroad; or disclosing (including oral or visual disclosure) or transferring in the United States any defense article to an embassy, any agency, or subdivision of a foreign government (e.g., diplomatic missions); or disclosing (including oral or visual disclosure) or transferring technical data to a foreign person, whether in the United States or abroad; or performing a defense service on behalf of, or for the benefit of, a foreign person, whether in the United States or abroad. A launch vehicle or payload will not, merely by reason of it having being launched, be considered an export for purposes of this subchapter. However, for certain limited purposes spelled out in the ITAR, any sale, transfer, or proposal to sell or transfer defense articles or defense services may be considered an export.

[†] A defense article means any item or technical data covered by the U.S. Munitions List in the ITAR. The term includes technical data recorded or stored in any physical form, models, mock-ups, or other items that reveal technical data directly relating to items on the Munitions List. It does not include basic marketing information on function or purpose or general system descriptions.

[‡] Technical data means information other than software that is required for the design, development, production, manufacture, assembly, operation, repair, testing, maintenance, or modification of defense articles. The foregoing includes information in the form of blueprints, drawings, photographs, plans, instructions, or documentation; classified information relating to defense articles and defense services on the Munitions List and commodities in the "600-series" items controlled by the CCL; information covered by an invention secrecy order; or software that includes but is not limited to the system functional design, logic flow, algorithms, application programs, operating systems, and support software for design, implementation, test, operation, diagnosis, and repair.

[§] Defense services means the furnishing of assistance (including training) to foreign persons, whether in the United States or abroad, in the design, development, engineering, manufacture, production, assembly, testing, repair, maintenance, modification, operation, demilitarization, destruction, processing, or use of defense articles; the furnishing to foreign persons of any technical data controlled under this subchapter, whether in the United States or abroad; or military training of foreign units and forces, regular and irregular, including formal or informal instruction of foreign persons in the United States or abroad or by correspondence courses, technical, educational, or information publications and media of all kinds, training aid, orientation, training exercise, and military advice.

A license issued by the ODTC for export or import of a commodity subject to the ITAR may be issued only to a U.S. person,* subject to a few limited exceptions.†

The ITAR is a large set of rules, but its core is the United States Munitions List and the procedures for obtaining a license from the ODTC for manufacture, export, or import of defense articles or technical data subject to control under the Munitions List commodities or rendering of defense services. Most everything else in the ITAR focuses on identifying whether or not a commodity requires a license, the types of licenses available, and the process for obtaining a license.

The Munitions List serves a similar purpose as the CCL in the EAR, by specifying what commodities or classes of goods are subject to export licensing by the ODTC. Moreover, while both the ITAR and the EAR provide authority and discretion to the agencies that enforce them to go beyond the express items listed on the CCL and Munitions List, the ODTC, as an agency of the Department of State, has far more broad discretion to co-opt oversight of an export of any commodity, no matter how seemingly innocuous, civil, and commercial it appears, if it perceives that the export might be used for military, paramilitary, police, terrorist, or similar enterprise. It can and will hold up or refuse to allow the exportation of goods to places, people, or entities for foreign policy reasons, as current circumstances may dictate, regardless of the fact that the same or similar export had been licensed on a previous occasion.

The Munitions List is organized by categories that contain subparagraphs that define enumerated defense articles. The ITAR instructs a prospective exporter to first review the general characteristics of its commodity to guide it in determining which category on the Munitions List the commodity falls within. Once the appropriate category is identified, the exporter is then advised to match the particular characteristics and

---

* *U.S. person* means a person who is a lawful permanent resident as defined of the United States or who is a protected individual as defined. It also means any corporation, business association, partnership, society, trust, or any other entity, organization, or group that is incorporated to do business in the United States. It also includes any governmental (federal, state, or local) entity. It does not include any foreign person as defined elsewhere in the ITAR.

† (i) A foreign government entity in the United States may receive a license or other approval (often this is intended to cover foreign military sales by the United States to the foreign government); (ii) a foreign person, as defined in the ITAR, may receive a reexport or retransfer approval for goods shipped to the person under an ITAR license issued in the United States to a U.S. person that shipped the goods to the foreign person; and (iii) a foreign person may receive prior approval for brokering activities, meaning acting as an intermediary arranging for the sale of commodities subject to the ITAR, rather than being a manufacturer, exporter, or importer of the commodities.

functions of its commodity to the specific entry that covers its commodity within the appropriate category.

There are 21 categories, beginning with firearms, close-assault weapons, and combat shotguns, covering along the way commodities such as ammunition, aircraft, naval vessels, missiles, explosives, and a host of other potentially lethal items or those associated with their use, and ending with a catchall category covering articles, technical data, and defense services not otherwise enumerated in the 20 preceding more specific categories.

While the detailed subparagraphs are numerous, they may not always precisely or clearly address a commodity, especially when one considers the fast pace of changing technology and design that continuously evolves existing defense articles and the creation of new ones. Therefore, as in the case of items listed on the CCL, it is unwise to make any assumptions as to whether or not a particular commodity is subject to ITAR licensing, and inquiry with OCTC is always a wise precaution if there is any doubt or question. Failing to ensure an export that should have been licensed in ignorance of the law, as in the case of compliance with the EAR or any other regulations for that matter, is no excuse and the sanctions that can and will be imposed can range from the painful to the draconian.

ITAR requires that any person who engages in the United States in the business of manufacturing or exporting or temporarily importing defense articles, or furnishing defense services, is required to register with the Office of Defense Trade Controls. Even engaging in only one, isolated manufacturing, export of temporary import of a defense article or furnishing defense service, requires registration. Even a manufacturer that does not engage in exporting, importing, etc., must also register.

There are exceptions to the registration requirement, but for the overwhelming percentage of those who must comply with the ITAR, those exceptions do not apply. Registration requires submission of a registration statement, the specifics of which are spelled out in the ITAR. While the registration process is not complex or overly cumbersome, registration is not a mere formality. The ODTC will examine the prospective registrant for any possible reason that might require denying it the right to manufacture, export, or import defense articles or technical data or provide defense services. Registration can take time as well. So a registrant should not wait until the last instance to register. If a registration is not submitted well in advance of the time a license may be needed, the registrant risks delays in the ability to obtain the license in time to meet manufacturing or shipping commitments.

Once approved, however, the registrant must not only comply with the ITAR, as well as other regulations that may have a bearing on its activities, but also thereafter update the information provided as part of the registration statement as and when changes in the information occur. The registrant must also comply with certain record-keeping requirements spelled out in the ITAR in connection with all ITAR-related activities, all of which are spelled out in the ITAR.

The Foreign Assets Control Regulations

The Foreign Assets Control Regulations (FACR) is enforced by the U.S. Department of the Treasury's OFAC. The mission of OFAC and the object of the FACR is to administer and enforce economic trade sanctions based on U.S. foreign policy and national security goals against targeted foreign countries and regimes, terrorists, international narcotic traffickers, those engaged in activities related to the proliferation of weapons of mass destruction,* and other threats to the national security, foreign policy, or economy of the United States.

OFAC oversees a number of different sanctions programs. The sanctions can be either comprehensive or selective, using the blocking of assets and trade restriction to accomplish foreign policy and national security. Currently, the following sanctions programs are being administered by OFAC:

- Iran sanctions
- Ukraine-related sanctions
- Syria sanctions
- Counterterrorism sanctions
- Counternarcotics sanctions
- Cuba sanctions
- Other sanctions programs, several of which were established by the United Nations (UN), which the United States as a member state acts in compliance with

---

* This is a good example of how the regulations of more than one agency may have to be known and complied with in connection with export trade, in this instance the ITAR and FACR, as well as, in appropriate circumstances, the regulations of the Nuclear Regulatory Commission and possibly other agencies, depending on the nature of the commodity. There is also an agency of the Department of Defense, the Defense Security Service, which administers and implements the defense portion of the National Industrial Security Program (NISP). Exporters of security information are subject to compliance with the National Industrial Security Program Operating Manual (NISPOM), which provides standards for the protection of classified information released or disclosed to industry in connection with classified contracts under the NISP.

As in the case of the EAR and ITAR, OFAC has a licensing authority that also must be complied with in order to export or import those commodities that may be traded with, or end up in, a country or territory subject to sanctions.

The takeaway on compliance with the FACR, as well as the EAR and the ITAR, is to make sure before engaging in an export that it is not destined to end up, directly or indirectly, in a country subject to a sanctions program, the list of which is subject to change and amendment on an ongoing basis.

The U.S. Foreign Corrupt Practices Act

The title says it all: The FCPA of the United States is intended to prohibit issuers* and their directors, employees, stockholders, or agents; domestic concerns†; and certain persons and entities other than issuers and domestic concerns and entities while in the territory of the United States from engaging in bribery and other forms of corrupt practices in order to influence foreign government officials so as to secure economic or other advantage in dealings with the foreign country, by offering to pay, paying, promising to pay, or authorizing the payment of money or anything of value (even charitable contributions may in certain circumstances violate the prohibitions of the FCPA) to a foreign official in order to influence any act or decision of the foreign official in his or her official capacity or to secure any other improper advantage in order to obtain or retain business. The FCPA is enforced by the U.S. Department of Justice (DOJ) and the Securities and Exchange Commission (SEC).

The FCPA has two main components, antibribery provisions and accounting provisions. Both sections of the act consist of detailed rules that describe what actions are prohibited by the FCPA and what conduct is subject to exception from the FCPA's prohibitions and define key terms used by the prohibitions.

The antibribery provisions prohibit individuals and businesses from bribing foreign government officials in order to obtain or retain business.

---

* A company is an issuer under the FCPA if it has a class of securities registered under the Exchange Act.

† A domestic concern is any individual who is a citizen, national, or resident of the United States or any corporation, partnership, association, joint-stock company, business trust, unincorporated organization, or sole proprietorship that is organized under the laws of the United States or its states, territories, possessions, or commonwealths or that has its principal place of business in the United States officers, directors, employees, agents, or stockholders acting on behalf of a domestic concern, including foreign nationals or companies, are also subject to the FCPA.

The accounting provisions impose certain record keeping and internal control requirements on issuers of stocks subject to SEC supervision, impose certain record keeping and internal control requirements on issuers, and prohibit individuals and companies from knowingly falsifying an issuer's books and records or circumventing or failing to implement an issuer's system of internal controls.

Additional sections of the FCPA spell the sanctions for violation, "resolutions," whistleblower provisions and protections, and DOJ opinion procedures.

Sanctions can include criminal prosecution and civil and criminal financial penalties.* Criminal penalties levied against officers, directors, employees, stockholders, and agents of companies may not be paid by their employer or principal. In addition, under federal guidelines governing procurement, an individual or company can be debarred (meaning barred or suspended) from doing business with the federal government. Additionally, multilateral development banks, like the World Bank, have the ability to debar companies and individuals for corrupt practices.

Resolutions of violations handled by the DOJ include possible criminal prosecution, plea arrangements, deferred prosecution agreements, nonprosecution agreements, and declinations. Resolutions of claims handled by the SEC include civil injunctive actions and remedies, civil administrative actions and remedies, deferred prosecution agreements, nonprosecution agreements, and termination letters and declinations.

Automated Export System

The Automated Export System (AES) is a joint venture between the U.S. CBP, the Foreign Trade Division of the Bureau of Census and the Bureau of Industry and Security (both part of the Department of Commerce), and the Office of Defense Trade Controls, as well as other federal agencies.

---

* For antibribery violations by individuals, the civil penalty can be up to $10,000, and a criminal fine can be up to $250,000 with imprisonment of up to five years. For antibribery violations by entities, the civil fine can be up to $10,000 and the criminal fine, up to $2 million. In both the foregoing instances, under authority of a statute known as the Alternative Fines Act, the fine may be increased to twice the gross financial gain or loss resulting from the corrupt payment. For accounting violations by an individual, the civil penalty can be up to $100,000 and a criminal violation penalty can be up to $5 million or twice the gain or loss caused by the violation and imprisonment of up to 20 years. Accounting penalties by entities can incur a civil penalty of up to $500,000 and a criminal penalty of up to $25 million or twice the gain or loss caused by the violation.

AES is the means by which information on an exportation must be filed with the U.S. government before a commodity may be exported.

Formerly such filings were done by submitting a document known as a shippers export declaration (SED) to CBP at the time the export shipment was tendered to the export carrier, along with the other shipping and commercial documents necessary to be tendered to the carrier, such as the carrier's bill of lading. AES now accomplishes the same thing electronically. In the days when the export data were submitted on the SED, its primary purpose was to provide the Bureau of Census with statistical information used to monitor the balance of trade and for other purposes. In addition, the SED was used to monitor whether or not a valid export license for goods subject to the EAR and ITAR had been obtained. AES also serves the foregoing goals and, in addition, is part of the network of procedures utilized for cargo security purposes.

AES filing can be done by the exporter but most commonly it is done by the exporter's forwarding agent or similar transportation intermediary. In either case both the exporter and the intermediary are responsible for the accuracy of the filed information, and both can and will be penalized for even inadvertent, let alone intentional, mistakes, such as the wrong value, the wrong classification of the goods, the wrong port of export or destination, and the wrong consignee or end user, along with many other specifics required to be disclosed as part of the AES filing.

Penalties, if incurred, can be mitigated and occasionally canceled, based on guidelines published by CBP, which administers the imposition of penalties. The determination of how severe the penalty will be is made in large measure on mitigating and aggravating factors listed in the guidelines. However, the guidelines are just that, and other circumstances and facts can be considered by CBP, beyond those listed.

Although primarily administered by CBP, the details as to what an AES filing must accurately contain are set forth in the Foreign Trade Regulations (FTR), enforced by the Bureau of Census. As in the case of the other regulations outlined in this chapter, the FTR is too detailed to be addressed as an overview.

It is incumbent on the shipper and export agent of the exporting shipper to understand what is required by the FTR, especially as to the definitions of some of the data elements that must be submitted as part of an AES filing. The meaning of some of the terms of art are not necessarily susceptible to common-sense understanding, nor can even common words and phrases be read as carrying their most commonly understood intent.

A shipper will not necessarily be exonerated from responsibility by arguing it relied on the advice and guidance of its export agent for the correctness of an AES filing, nor will the export agent necessarily be free from liability for arguing that it relied on the accuracy of the information provided by the exporter for use in making the AES filing. Each is independently responsible to ensure its participation in the process is compliant and should take steps to ensure the other is holding up its end in the process.

> Regulations must be continually "tested" to determine their boundaries and limits. This will result in better regulations.

> **Thomas A. Cook**

10

Trade-Compliance Issues in Global Expansion and Mergers and Acquisitions Activities

As part of the due-diligence process in global expansion along with mergers and acquisitions, companies must not overlook the trade-compliance profile of the new business partner. In recent years the Export Administration Regulations, the Office of Foreign Assets Control Regulations, the International Traffic in Arms Regulations, customs regulations, and the Foreign Corrupt Practices Act have all played a role in enforcing successor liability.

TRADE COMPLIANCE

Global supply chains require companies to be familiar with the rules and regulations of the various government agencies throughout all countries in which that supply chain operates. Trade-compliance requirements are country specific and may also be commodity driven. For example, an export shipment of salted butter may not require an export license to be shipped but will require an import license and approval from a food and drug or the health department prior to importation. An import shipment of remote-control cars may not require a license to import but will require Federal Communications Commission (FCC) approval at the time of import.

Frequently, trade compliance is looked at after the acquisition has been completed by the business-development acquisition team. In these instances a company may be in for a rude awakening as they discover there are duties owed to CBP and/or export violations to be disclosed to the Bureau of Industry and Security (BIS).

In many instances, the financial team working with the company prior to acquisition may be able to ascertain a considerable amount of information regarding compliance if they are trained to ask the right questions and have an understanding of trade compliance.

Managing trade compliance within a company is a detailed process that requires the cooperation of overlapping departments including shipping, logistics, finance, purchasing, sales, and legal. This process may be onerous on its own without the added disadvantage of not being familiar with the processes, commodities, sales destinations, and vendor agreements of a new acquisition. That said, the most basic trade requirements are the same for all companies, whether they are importing screws and food products or exporting coal and aircraft parts.

When compliance violations are found in a company, massive amounts of time by internal personnel or the expense of hiring outside assistance to determine if the compliance issue is endemic or a one-time incident may be necessary.

EXPORT TRADE COMPLIANCE BASICS

In the United States, there are several government agencies involved in the export process. Within the Department of Commerce there are BIS and the Bureau of Census. The Office of Foreign Assets Controls (OFAC) is part of the Department of Treasury. Companies that deal with items on the United States Munitions List (USML) will also fall under the jurisdiction of the Department of State's Office of Defense Trade Controls (ODTC). The Department of Homeland Security's CBP is also involved in the enforcement of export regulations.

The Export Administration Regulations (EAR) are the rules by which the BIS regulates and controls the export of goods from the United States.

The EAR also controls certain activities such as the transfer of information to foreign nationals or engaging in restrictive trade boycotts not sanctioned by the United States. Companies that export from the United States are required to comply with these regulations and must have a process for managing their exports and international activities such as an export management compliance program. The export management compliance program becomes the game plan for staying compliant and avoiding export violations.

Export Management Compliance Program

As previously mentioned, the core elements of an effective export management compliance program are the same for all companies regardless of the commodities and services they are shipping and providing. However, there are additional steps that must be taken for those companies who are engaged in commodities that are controlled for export due to the type of commodity and/or for transactions with those companies and countries that are listed on the various denial lists or companies that are domiciled in an embargoed country or restricted country.

The basic elements of an export management compliance program will minimally include

1. Senior management commitment
2. Identification of risks in the current export program
3. Formal written manual
4. Training and awareness
5. Screening of business partners, customers, financial institutions, and supply-chain partners
6. Record-keeping requirements
7. Periodic auditing and monitoring
8. System for reporting violations and handling compliance issues
9. System for implementing corrective actions where a compliance issue is indicated
10. Partnering with knowledgeable and compliant service providers

Senior Management Commitment

Managing compliance requires senior management support. Compliance touches many silos within a company, which, in turn, requires managing delicate relationships such as between sales and shipping. Managing compliance may delay a shipment for a day or so while stones are turned to ensure that the customer is not the Jones Company that is indicated on the Denied Parties List. Senior management's support of compliance efforts allows compliance measures to be successfully implemented within the supply chain. The lack of senior management support will be taken by anyone as a chance to skirt the compliance program because if the management does not care, then why should he or she care.

In the due-diligence process of mergers and acquisitions, it is simple enough to get a feel if a company has any compliance on its radar by a few key indicators such as the mission statement touching on compliance and/or regulatory matters; the company website including links to government regulatory sites; and the company website listing harmonized tariff numbers and/or export control classification numbers (ECCNs). Any of these listed on a website does not ensure that compliance exists within the organization but it does indicate that the company has minimally dabbled in compliance.

Identification of Risks in the Current Export Program

There are a few quick and dirty questions the responses to which can identify potential risks in the company's export profile. Are there products subject to the Commerce Control List (CCL) or USML? What industries are our customers involved with? Where are our customers located? Do we have routed export transactions? Do we utilize any software programs for screening our customers and service providers? Blank stares or hemming and hawing will indicate that these basic compliance measures are not in place.

If a company is exporting, they are subject to export controls. Identifying the potential risks in the export supply chain is key to determining what level of compliance should be in place and where the potential for fires exist within the supply chain.

For those companies that state they have domestic sales only, there are additional questions that need to be asked such as, Do any of the ship-to/bill-to details indicate a location in a foreign country? Are we using FedEx, UPS, or a trucker to move the goods to a border location? Are we shipping the goods to a freight forwarder's warehouse? Each of these situations would indicate the goods will be moving internationally and subject to the export regulations. A written manual maps out the scope of the company's compliance program. Responsible parties within the organization identify the documentary requirements specific to the company's transactions, sample documents, etc. The manual becomes the go-to resource, whether in hard copy or posted on the company intranet. The ability to obtain a copy of this document is priceless as it may indicate the program to be robust and dynamic or a carbon copy lifted from an Internet site. Either outcome will provide a good feel for the company's level of compliance.

Training and Awareness

In recent years, many companies under budget restraints have reduced training within the organization. A good compliance program provides personnel with the training to understand the importance of compliance as well as to provide a forum for vibrant discussions on new business opportunities and existing customer issues.

Training can be in the form of webinars, outside forums, or a monthly lunch-and-learn update. Training may also be piggybacked with other meetings that are being held within a department, such as a quarterly sales meeting. All training should be documented as to who attended as well as the content of the training and materials provided.

Asking general questions about company training in regards to Occupational Safety and Health Administration (OSHA) or any human resources training can easily include compliance training.

Screening of Business Partners, Customers, Financial Institutions, and Supply-Chain Partners

As previously mentioned, identification of risks in the supply chain must include how the company screens its business partners. The U.S. government maintains lists of companies, individuals, and countries that U.S. companies may not do business with or require the prior authorization of the U.S. government in order to do business with. The key lists include

- Department of Commerce—Denied Parties List, Unverified List, and Entity List;

- Department of State—Debarred List and Nonproliferation Sanctions; and
- Department of Treasury—Office of Foreign Assets Control, Specially Designated Nationals List, and Sanctions Evaders List.

This area of due diligence could be tested during the financial-soundness-testing portion of the acquisition by the accounting team responsible.

Record-Keeping Requirements

Record-keeping requirements under the Export Administration Regulations and Foreign Trade Regulations are for five years from the date of export. Under the International Traffic in Arms Regulations (ITAR), the ODTC requires records to be kept for five years from the date of expiration of the export license.

All companies engaged in export activity must keep records including, but not limited to, memoranda, notes, correspondence, contracts, financial records, restrictive trade practice or boycott documents, electronic export information records, and corresponding documentation.

Record keeping should also include correspondence with the BIS or any other government agency in regard to requested information, warning letters, and/or issued penalty notices.

Periodic Auditing and Monitoring

Many companies have implemented compliance programs that limp along and have lost momentum once the initial training and awareness have taken place. Compliance programs are repetitive and personnel get into a groove of working within the program without much enthusiasm. This can set up the environment for a compliance program becoming lax and ineffective.

Periodic monitoring of shipments and a regularly scheduled audit keeps everyone on their toes. The ability to monitor the AES*Direct* monthly compliance report issued by the Bureau of Census, for example, ensures that the trade-compliance manager as the AES account administrator is seeing the monthly picture if not the daily filings. Managing by exception and pulling those files that have a "verify" message, for example, is a great tool for monitoring. Regularly scheduled audits of records should include pulling a few test files to see if the records are in place for everything from the customer's purchase order to the Electronic Export Information (EEI) copy and actual payment. Once again, this area of concern could be included as part of the diligence by the financial team as part of their questions.

System for Reporting Violations and Handling Compliance Issues

As part of the periodic auditing process, it is likely a problem will be uncovered. Depending on the nature and extent of the problem, it may be necessary to report the problem to the responsible government agency. Within the company, there may be reporting up to senior management or the legal department. Regardless of how the company is structured, make certain to involve management prior to any government reporting.

Each government agency has a different mechanism and even different requirements for disclosure. The Bureau of Census requires a company to make a correction to the EEI filing once that error is discovered. BIS encourages voluntary disclosure but as of this writing, voluntary disclosure is not a requirement. While the majority of voluntary disclosures made to the BIS result in a warning letter and no monetary penalty, that is not always the case, as we will see farther along in this chapter. In many instances, it is possible to perform an Internet search to determine if a company has had BIS or OFAC violations as these agencies make a point of publicizing violations.

System for Implementing Corrective Actions

As part of the reporting of the violation, the company will provide a plan of corrective actions as part of the disclosure. Once the dust settles, the plan must be implemented. Many corrective action plans will include retraining, review of actions, and a section of compliance manual covering the area where the violation took place, interview of personnel, and rehashing the gory details to avoid future violations.

In the due-diligence process, asking for the answer to, "Well, what happened after the violation took place?" is important. If a reprimand was issued and everyone feels relieved, is there another chapter covering the next steps that were followed? Additionally, revisiting the issue by reviewing documentation and the actual parties involved in the violation will provide transparency and allow the trade-compliance manager to get to the heart of the current view of compliance in the new company.

Partnering with Knowledgeable and Compliant Service Providers

Most companies work with a freight forwarder to handle their export transactions. The freight forwarder will prepare export documentation and arrange bookings with the air/ocean/rail carriers and truckers. By default, these companies consider their freight forwarder to be experts and heavily rely on the forwarder's expertise at moving the freight as well as compliance with regulations.

In most penalty cases, the actual shipper is held responsible even if the actions of the freight forwarder caused the violation. Therefore, all shippers must confirm that their freight forwarder is knowledgeable, has their own internal compliance program in place, and trains their personnel to follow the rules and regulations.

In making an acquisition, the company should obtain a list of the service providers being used and those companies should be interviewed to determine the level of compliance within that business partner's organizational structure. A compliant exporter aligns himself with a compliant forwarder.

Additional Note for Those Companies Engaged in Exports under the International Traffic in Arms

Companies that are acquired and merging with a new parent that have licenses under the prior company's name must ensure that they amend licenses and agreement with the ODTC. If the company is a new U.S. registrant, a list of open licenses and agreements should be provided to ODTC to make the necessary name changes. Failure to properly transfer over licenses and/or make necessary name changes by becoming a new registrant may result in freight delays, seizures, and monetary penalties.

SUCCESSOR LIABILITY AND EXPORT VIOLATIONS

Sigma-Aldrich: Unlicensed exports made by the acquired company that took place prior to acquisition; penalty: $1.7 million (Bureau of Industry and Security)

Qioptiq: Unlicensed exports made by the acquired company that took place prior to acquisition; penalty: $25 million (Office of Defense Trade Controls)

Sirchie Fingerprint: Violation of denial order made by company acquired that took place prior to acquisition; penalty: $12.6 million (Bureau of Industry and Security)

Example 10.1

Gator Enterprises is a computer software service that has decided to grow its business by moving into products complementary to the services they offer to their clients. The software designed by Gator Enterprises monitors gauges, actuators, and valves. Gator Enterprises has many customers in the construction industry and has determined a niche market for reselling these types of valves. Gator Enterprises closes a deal with Red Chair Valves, a valve manufacturer.

Red Chair's product line is diverse and includes items such as check valves for basement pumps and valves that are used in construction drilling. Gator Enterprises is excited about this expansion into new territory and, following due diligence on the acquisition side, moves ahead into selling their software services to Red Chair's customer base as well as selling valves to the Gator Enterprises' customer base.

Gator Enterprises has a sales manager who has fielded questions regarding export compliance in the past. The company is knowledgeable about screening potential customers through the various government denied party lists, and the company has a list of countries that are embargoed and to which Gator Enterprises refuses to sell.

The challenge is that Red Chair has items they are now beginning to sell internationally. Some of the valve types are controlled for export. The sales manager has stumbled upon this while reading an export-compliance blog post and recognizes that their new acquisition has this issue.

The sales manager proceeds to perform a review of the Commerce Control List along with technical support from the Red Chair design staff. While the Department of Commerce permits a company to self-classify their products, the sales manager is not familiar enough with Red Chair and its product team and decides to reach out to the BIS for assistance. The sales manager registers for the Simplified Network Application Process (SNAP) on the BIS website. Through SNAP, the sales manager verifies that the determinations made by the Red Chair design staff were correct. The sales manager now implements a compliance plan to manage these new products. The compliance plan includes

- Training staff on export controls and restrictions on the specific controlled products;
- Creating a freight forwarder letter of instruction for use by shipping as a compliance tool to supervise the actions of the freight forwarder;

- Review and update of the Gator Enterprises compliance manual to include the new product line; and
- Senior management rollout to bring management up to date on changes that have been made and to obtain budget approval for training for the following year.

IMPORT TRADE COMPLIANCE BASICS

The CBP is part of the Department of Homeland Security. CBP has responsibilities for border control, immigration, border security, agricultural protection, and enforcement of the customs regulations. Any shipment being imported into the United States is subject to the customs clearance process and the payment of duties and taxes. Additional government agency requirements may be required depending on the nature of the commodity being imported.

Import Compliance Management Program

Importers are required to exercise reasonable care and supervision and control over the import process. Many importers hire a customs broker to handle the customs clearance and entry submission to CBP on their behalf. Unfortunately, many importers judge the performance of their customs broker by the success and expeditious delivery of the import shipment. This faith in the broker's expertise usually results in an ignorance of the rules and regulations by which the importer is held accountable.

CBP makes available many valuable resources to the import trade community. Among these resources are the informed compliance publications. In reviewing the listing of the informed compliance publications, importers will have a good idea of what the basic elements of their import compliance management program should include. In addition to the informed compliance publications, an importer can access the Focused Assessment Pre-Assessment Survey to better understand the expectations of CBP in the event the company is challenged on its import process.

Similarly as with diligence in ascertaining export-compliance levels, companies looking to acquire a company with imports as part of its profile need to establish the levels of compliance with CBP regulations and other government agency requirements.

Corporate Structure

CBP is very interested in how risk on import shipments is assessed, including the frequency of assessments, changes made due to assessments, and who has the overall responsibility on these matters. Where compliance sits internally in an organization can determine how seriously compliance is taken such as being a corporate function versus being a fallback responsibility on the receiving manager.

The setting for the compliance culture within a company is dictated by how management views compliance with the customs regulations. Is there a dedicated group that manages the import process together? For example, does the purchasing department work with business development or are import decisions made independently without following any guidelines? Is there a working compliance manual for personnel to follow? These factors add up to the corporate view of compliance and the overall level of import compliance within the company.

Invoices

In addition to its many other responsibilities and functions, CBP is a revenue agency that protects the financial well-being of the United States. The manner in which import shipments are valued is one of the key elements to the entry process as we will see in the next section. CBP does not examine each and every shipment that is imported into the United States.

CBP relies on the commercial invoice that is the heart of the transaction; this invoice details many facts about the import transaction. The invoice is so key to the import process that the failure of an importer to present a proper invoice is a violation of the basic bond requirement, and the failure of a broker to correct the importer is a lack of reasonable care on the part of the broker.

Invoices must be in English and must include the following:

1. Probable port of entry
2. Name and address of importer of record
3. Name and address of ultimate consignee if known at the time of import and if different from the importer of record
4. Name and address of the manufacturer and shipper
5. Description of merchandise, with the name of each item known
6. Unit price of the merchandise

7. Currency of sale
8. Country of origin for each item
9. Statement of use in the United States (if applicable)
10. Discounts from price and rebates offered between buyer and seller
11. Values of assists including tools, molds, dies, and engineering work (performed outside the United States) and provided to the manufacturer to assist in producing the imported items
12. Packing list
13. Endorsement by the person who prepared the invoice

The acquiring company should request a sample entry package and purchase order as well as copies of the correspondence on a typical import shipment to review whether invoices appear to be in line with the transaction prior to performing a full import review.

Valuation

Importers tend to rely on the invoice value as the correct value for CBP without understanding the actual valuation methods that CBP requires importers to use. Further to this, many import brokers are also not clear on how valuation has been determined by the importer. A customs broker reviewing an import invoice may not be aware of other factors that have been negotiated between the importing company's purchasing team and the foreign shipper such as assists.

Customs requires importers to declare the free-on-board (FOB)/free-carrier (FCA) value on the entry summary. This means that customs is looking for the cost of goods and the inland freight costs to bring the goods to the port of departure. Should an importer purchase on a carrier paid to (CPT) or carriage and insurance paid to (CIP) basis, the importer can deduct the prepaid freight and insurance from the value on the invoice and declare the FOB/FCA value to CBP. If not included as part of the invoice value, packing charges are also dutiable. As CBP is concerned with the value of the goods at the FOB/FCA point, the importer must make certain that they are declaring a proper value and using a proper method of valuation.

The understanding of valuation concepts by the company being acquired may not be where it should be or may have been incorrectly interpreted by the broker working with the importer. In either case, the financial group handling the preacquisition work can ask about assists and valuation methods.

Harmonized Tariff Classification

Customs around the world utilizes the harmonized tariff system (HTS) as the method for describing imports. Additionally, trade statistics are collected through the information submitted via entry declarations. The ten-digit number describes the product and is one of the factors in determining the correct amount of duty and taxes payable to customs in addition to the country of origin.

HTS numbers are not identical throughout the world. A vendor in Japan must follow the applicable rules of interpretation for Japan. The importer in the United States must follow the applicable U.S. rules of interpretation when making their entry declaration.

Many importers rely on their brokers to determine their tariff classifications without input from the importer. This is a lack of reasonable care on the part of the importer as they need to be a part of the process. The importer should make drawings and full-blown product descriptions and have someone available to answer questions from the broker regarding tariff classification. The broker should exercise reasonable care and work with the importer to come to a mutual decision that the correct number is being used and have the importer sign off on the classification. This classification process should also be documented.

HTS numbers should be maintained as part of the importer's product database and updated as the importer is advised of any changes to the HTS by the broker. Once a year, the HTS numbers should be reviewed against the new HTS numbers posted by CBP in January.

As previously mentioned, HTS numbers and the county of origin dictate the tariff rate. In some instances, there may be additional duties owed as a result of trade protection legislation. These duties are called antidumping duties (ADDs). ADD cases may take several years to be sorted out until a final duty rate is decided by the Court of International Trade (CIT). There have been several well-publicized cases of successor liability in which the company acquiring the importer was required to pay the additional duties owed for imports that took place prior to the acquisition.

Country of Origin

There are many misunderstood ideas regarding the declaration of country of origin. In addition to the country of origin requirement on an import invoice, most imported products are required to be marked, with the country of origin permanently marked indicating the country of origin to the ultimate purchaser.

Importers should include marking requirements as part of their purchase agreement. Customs states that the marking must be legible, in English, and visible to the person in the United States who will receive the item in the form in which it was imported.

Containers of articles excepted from marking must be marked with the name of the country of origin of the article unless the container is also "excepted" from marking. CBP regulations contain a listing of items exempted from marking. While the item itself is exempted from marking, the outermost container in which the article reaches the ultimate purchaser is required to be marked. The items include screws, bolts, nuts, and washers, among other items on the J list.

Determination as to the country of item is generally accepted as substantial transformation, but there are exceptions to this rule for certain commodities. Other exceptions to this rule include the various free-trade agreements in which the United States participates. Products being imported under preferential duty treatment must meet an applicable rule of origin in order to avoid penalties. The due-diligence process should include questions as to country of origin determinations and participation in any free-trade agreement (FTA).

Record Keeping

Records are required to be kept for five years from the date of import. Record-keeping requirements are extensive and can be found in detail on the (a)(1)(a) list. Some of the records that must be included are the purchase order, invoices, bills of lading, customs entry documentation, communications, broker letter of instructions, and supplier payments.

Hard-copy records must be retrievable for 30 days. Electronic records may be kept provided CBP has approved the importer's method of storage. Many importers make the mistake of assuming that their broker has the documents required under the record-keeping requirements. However, brokers are not privy to the internal documents an importer must retain and in the event that the importer severs ties with their broker, the importer will no longer have access to the broker's records. Brokers are required to keep their records in accordance with the requirements for brokers, not for importers. Importers should retain their own records.

In requesting import documentation from the company being required, it will become evident pretty quickly if the company is correctly managing their record keeping.

Internal Controls and Supervision

An importer is not required to use a broker to handle their customs clearance. An importer is permitted to handle their own clearance and transmit entries to CBP if they choose to do so. Many companies choose to work with a customs broker as they have the electronic systems for dialoguing with CBP. Customs brokers are considered experts and have a core skill set that the importer may not have.

In choosing a broker, the importer must be diligent in choosing their partner. The importer should visit the broker's office and meet the personnel handling import shipments. These personnel will be handling import transactions. Whether they are seasoned entry personnel with knowledge of customs regulations or are data-entry clerks makes a difference in using the broker as a resource.

The importer should provide the broker with copies of their purchase orders for recommendations from the broker to streamline the clearance process and for the broker to understand if there are any other values that should be added to the declared entry value such as assists.

Power-of-attorney documents provided to a broker should be dated in order to require the broker to follow up on a yearly basis with the importer to understand if there have been changes in the inbound supply chain. Importers should require their brokers to provide their Importer Security Filing (ISF) report cards, obtain ACE reports, and use their broker as a resource.

The importer is ultimately responsible for the declarations made by their broker. Due diligence by the acquisition team should request the number of brokers being used and conversations with those brokerage offices should take place to ensure the brokers are operating in an environment conducive to compliance which funnels down into a compliant resource for the importer.

Example 10.2

Flying High Imports purchases Sky Pie. Sky Pie is a small kite manufacturer that imports the materials used to manufacture its products. As part of the integration process, Flying High Imports has its trade-compliance manager meet with the responsible parties for imports at the Sky Pie's offices. Sky Pie is a small company and the purchasing manager wears the hat of issuing tariff classifications and managing the import process, in addition to many other day-to-day responsibilities.

The trade-compliance manager has a brief conversation with the purchasing manager to schedule a review of what has been done by Sky Pie prior to Flying High's acquisition of Sky Pie. Included in this conversation is the request for purchasing agreements, import entries, vendor payments, etc.

Upon arrival at Sky Pie, the trade-compliance manager meets with the purchasing manager and is walked through the import process, including the assignment of HTS classification numbers. The purchasing manager advises that they have always used the HTS numbers provided by the foreign shipper in China. The purchasing manager has not used their broker, a customs consultant, or a customs attorney for assistance nor have they requested any binding rulings from CBP.

The trade-compliance manager accesses the International Trade Commission database and the Customs Ruling Online Search System and determines that incorrect HTS numbers have been used and have been submitted to CBP on over 50 import entries in the past two years. The incorrect HTS numbers are at a lower duty rate, resulting in roughly $20,000 in duties owed. In addition, the trade-compliance manager is uncomfortable that there may be additional valuation and country-of-origin issues on the component materials as well as supplemental items imported and sold by Sky Pie.

SUCCESSOR LIABILITY AND IMPORT VIOLATIONS

Ataka America: Antidumping duties underpaid for wire rope: $189,000. Adaptive Engineering: Unpaid duties, $6.8 million.

CORE ELEMENTS OF AN EFFECTIVE EXPORT MANAGEMENT AND COMPLIANCE PROGRAM

1. Management commitment: Senior management must establish written export-compliance standards for the organization, commit sufficient resources for the export-compliance program, and ensure that

appropriate senior organizational official(s) are designated with the overall responsibility for the export-compliance program to ensure adherence to export control laws and regulations.

2. Continuous risk assessment of the export program.
3. Formal written export management and compliance program: Effective implementation and adherence to written policies and operational procedures.
4. Ongoing compliance training and awareness.
5. Preexport/post-export compliance security and screening: Screening of employees, contractors, customers, products, and transactions and implementation of compliance safeguards throughout the export life cycle including product development, jurisdiction, classification, sales, license decisions, supply chain, servicing channels, and post-shipment activity.
6. Adherence to record-keeping regulatory requirements.
7. Internal and external compliance monitoring and periodic audits.
8. Maintaining a program for handling compliance problems, including reporting export violations.
9. Completing appropriate corrective actions in response to export violations.

FOCUSED ASSESSMENT PRE-ASSESSMENT SURVEY QUESTIONNAIRE

The purpose of this document is to obtain information from the importer about its import operations over compliance with CBP laws and regulations. The contents of the Pre-Assessment Survey Questionnaire (PASQ) will be tailored based on the auditors' analysis of the importer's import activity and the audit team's initial assessment of the potential risks for each of the audit areas that was identified in the preliminary assessment of risk (PAR). Auditors may adapt or modify this document as needed or may develop alternate formats. Auditors may also request copies of documentation in conjunction with the PASQ.

PRE-ASSESSMENT SURVEY QUESTIONNAIRE

Instructions to the Importer for Completing the PASQ

Please respond to all questions. The information you provide will assist us in focusing on the specific risks relative to your imported merchandise and the processes/procedures used to mitigate the risk of being noncompliant with CBP laws and regulations. In addition, your responses will help us to identify the individuals that are responsible for performing the procedures and the types of documentation that will be available for us to review.

The audit team will review your responses and prepare supplemental questions that will be discussed with your personnel to further our understanding of your processes and procedures. This PASQ file is a word document that may be filled in with your responses and returned to the auditors either as a word or portable document format (pdf) file. We request that your complete response be provided to us by [insert date] so we may prepare our questions prior to the Entrance Conference.

- Point of Contact Information
- Name(s) of the person(s) preparing the form:
- If there are multiple preparers, you may identify a single person that can be contacted to obtain clarification of the responses.
- Title(s):
- Phone Number(s):
- E-mail address(s):

Section 1—Information about [name of importers]'s organization and policy and procedures pertaining to CBP activities

1.1   Describe the company's mission statement, code of ethics/conduct, and company's objectives.

1.1.1   How is the mission statement, code of ethics/conduct, and company's objectives disseminated within the organization?

1.2   Who is responsible for assessing the risks to achieving the company's objectives? *Indicate if there is a subgroup or individual responsible for assessing the risk for being noncompliant with CBP laws and regulations.*

1.2.1   Describe how the risk assessment is accomplished. *Indicate, for example, when/ how often the risk assessment is performed, what information is used, what thresholds/tolerances the company considers to be acceptable.*

1.2.2   When was the last risk assessment performed? *Describe any significant changes that were made as a result of the risk assessment.*

1.3   Who, within your company, has overall responsibility for ensuring compliance with CBP laws and regulations?
- Indicate if there is an import function or department and describe the chain of command (e.g., identify who they report to).
- Alternately, your company may entrust compliance to a customs broker, customs consultant, or other outside agent. Identify them and indicate who within your company (i.e., individuals or groups) is/are responsible for interacting with the broker, consultant, or other outside agent (i.e., providing information to them and monitoring their work).

1.3.1   If there is an import function or department, provide the following information:
- How is it staffed? Indicate if an individual is assigned as the manager and identify the number of employees that report to them.
- How long has the manager been assigned to his or her position?
- What are the responsibilities of the manager and how are they accountable? Indicate if they are responsible for providing weekly activity reports and describe any performance measures.

1.3.2   If compliance has been entrusted to a customs broker, customs consultant, or other outside agent (i.e., no import department per se), provide the following information:
- How long has the company engaged the current broker, consultant, or other outside agent?
- Describe the processes used to communicate information and to monitor their work. *Indicate if there is a written contract or agreement.*

1.4   Who is responsible for developing and maintaining the written policies and procedures used to ensure compliance with CBP laws and regulations?
- How often are the written policies and procedures updated?

Section 2—Information about the valuation of imported merchandise

2.1   What basis of appraisement is used for the value of imported merchandise?

2.2   Who is responsible for transacting with the foreign vendors? *Identify all individuals or groups/departments that are responsible.*

2.2.1   Describe how transactions are negotiated with foreign vendors. *Describe all processes used and the conditions that apply.*

2.2.2   Describe the terms of sale used. *If there are different terms of sale, explain the conditions when each is used.*

2.2.3   If applicable, describe the terms/conditions when discounts or rebates are made.

2.2.4   If applicable, describe any additional expenses such as management fees or engineering services that are separately billed by the foreign vendors.

2.2.5   What documentation shows the terms of sale and prices (e.g., contracts, distribution, and other similar agreements, invoices, purchase orders, bills of lading, proof of payment, correspondence between the parties, and company reports or catalogs/brochures)?

2.3   Describe the accounting procedures for recording purchases and payments.
- What accounts are used to record purchases of foreign merchandise? *Identify or provide a list of vendor codes.*
- What accounts are used to record payments made to foreign vendors? Explain the methods of payments used (e.g., wire transfer, letters of credit).

2.4   If applicable, what accounting data/reports are provided to the import function or department? *Indicate how often data/reports are provided (e.g., quarterly reports of price adjustments for purchases from foreign vendors).*

For risk pertaining to related party transactions

2.5   Describe the nature of the relationship between your company and the related foreign vendor/seller. *Indicate if your company is the exclusive U.S. importer.*

2.5.1   Describe any financial arrangements (e.g., loans, financial assistance, and expense reimbursement) between your company and the foreign vendor/seller.

2.5.2   If applicable, explain the terms and conditions of goods sold to your company on consignment.

2.5.3   Describe how prices between your company and the foreign vendor/seller/manufacturer are determined. *Identify all sources of data used and explain the accounting methodology or computational formulas where appropriate. If transaction value is used, indicate if your company supports circumstances of sale or test values.* If applicable, provide the following information:

- Describe when price adjustments are made.
- Identify any additional expenses such as management fees or engineering services that are separately billed to your company.

2.5.2   Explain how transactions are accounted for. *Indicate if your company maintains its own accounting books and records.*

2.5.2.1   What intercompany accounts are used?

For risk pertaining to statutory additions

2.6   Assists

2.6.1   If applicable, describe the type of assists that are provided to the foreign vendors for free or at a reduced cost (e.g., tooling, hangtags, art or design work).

2.6.2   Who decides (or determines) that the assists will be provided? *Identify all individuals or groups/departments that are involved in the decision.*

- When is it decided that the assists will be provided?
- What accounts are used to record the costs of the assists?

2.6.3   Describe the procedures used to ensure that the costs of the assists are included in the values declared to CBP. *Indicate who decides how the actual cost of the assist will be apportioned to the imported items and explain how the apportioned cost is tracked.*

2.7   Packing

2.7.1   If applicable, describe the type of packing (i.e., labor or materials), containers (exclusive of instruments of international traffic), and coverings of whatever nature that is separately paid to the vendor to put the imported merchandise in condition ready for shipment to the United States.

2.7.2   Who decides (or determines) that the cost of packing will be separately charged? *Identify all individuals or groups/departments that are involved in the decision.*

- When is it decided that the cost of packing will be separately charged?
- What accounts are used to record the costs of packing, containers, and coverings?

2.7.3   Describe the procedures used to ensure that the cost of the packing is included in the values declared to CBP.

2.8   Commissions

2.8.1   If applicable, describe the terms of sale with foreign vendors that require your company to separately pay for "selling agent" commissions. *Identify the vendors.*

2.8.2   Who decides (or determines) that "selling agent" commissions will be paid directly to the intermediary?
- When is it decided that the "selling agent" commissions will be paid directly to the intermediary?
- What accounts are used to record the payment of these commissions?

2.8.3   Describe the procedures used to ensure that these commissions are included in the values declared to CBP.

2.9   Royalty and License Fees

2.9.1   If applicable, describe the terms of sale with foreign vendors that require your company to pay, directly or indirectly, any royalty or license fee related to the imported merchandise as a condition of the sale of the imported merchandise for exportation to the United States. *Identify the vendors.*

2.9.2   Who decides (or determines) that royalty or license fees will be paid as a condition of the sale?
- When is it decided that royalty or license fees will be paid as a condition of the sale?
- What accounts are used to record the payment of the royalty or license fees related to imported merchandise?

2.9.3   What procedures ensure that royalty or license fees are included in the values declared to CBP?

2.10   Proceeds of any subsequent resale, disposal, or use

2.10.1   If applicable, describe any agreements with the foreign vendors where the proceeds of any subsequent resale, disposal, or use of the imported merchandise accrue directly or indirectly to the foreign vendor. *Identify the vendors.*

2.10.2   Who decides (or determines) that the proceeds of any subsequent resale, disposal, or use of the imported merchandise will accrue directly or indirectly to the foreign vendor?
- When is it decided that the proceeds of any subsequent resale, disposal, or use of the imported merchandise will accrue directly or indirectly to the foreign vendor?
- What accounts are used to record the payment of these proceeds?

2.10.3   Describe the procedures used to ensure that proceeds of any subsequent resale, disposal, or use of the imported merchandise accruing directly or indirectly to the foreign vendor are included in the values declared to CBP.

Section 3—Information about the classification of imported merchandise

3.1   Who is responsible for determining how imported merchandise is classified? *Identify all individuals or groups that are responsible.*

3.1.1   What records and other information (e.g., product specifications, engineering drawings, physical items, laboratory analyses, etc.) are used to determine the classification of merchandise?

3.2   Does your company have a classification database?

3.2.1   If there is a classification database, do you archive previous versions of it? *Indicate how long previous versions are retained.*

3.2.2   If there is a classification database, is a copy provided to the broker? *Indicate how it is provided to the broker.*

3.2.3   If there is a classification database, what procedures ensure that the information in the database is accurate?

Section 4—Information about special classification provisions HTSUS 9801

4.1   Describe the type of merchandise that is imported under HTSUS 9801.

4.2   Who decides (or determines) that products of the United States will be returned after having been exported? *Identify all individuals or groups/ departments that are involved in the process.*

   • When is it determined that products will be returned after having been exported?
   • What documentation/records are maintained for the exported items?

4.3   Describe the procedures that ensure the exported items have not been advanced in value or improved in condition by any manufacturing process or other means while abroad.

4.4   Describe the procedures that ensure that drawback has not been claimed for the exported items.

Section 5—Information about special classification provisions HTSUS 9802

5.1   Describe the type of merchandise that is imported under HTSUS 9802.

5.2   What documentation/records are maintained for the exported items?

5.3   **For items imported under HTSUS 9802.00.40/9802.00.50:** What documentation/records support the cost or value of the repair?

5.4   Describe the procedures or means (e.g., unique identifiers) used to ensure that the articles exported for repair or alterations are the same articles being re-imported.

5.5   **For items imported under HTSUS 9802.00.40/9802.00.50:** Describe the procedures that ensure the foreign operation (e.g., repair or alteration process) does not result in the exported item becoming a commercially different article with new properties and characteristics.

5.6   Describe the procedures that ensure that drawback has not been claimed for the exported items.

Section 6—Information about GSP/FTA

6.1   If applicable, identify the name and MIDs for all of the foreign vendors from whom items are imported under GSP/FTA.

6.2   Describe any agreements with unrelated foreign vendors. *Indicate if the unrelated vendors are required to provide cost and production records to CBP or are legally prevented from releasing the records.*

6.3   Describe the procedures used to ensure that the origin of articles imported under GSP (or FTA) is wholly the growth, product, or manufacture of the BDC (or FTA country). *Identify who performs the procedures and when/how often the procedures are performed.*

6.3.2   What documentation/records are verified? *Indicate if copies of the documentation/records are retained on file or may be obtained upon request.*

6.4   Describe the procedures used to ensure the cost or value of the material produced in the BDC (or FTA country), plus the direct processing cost, is not less than 35 percent of the appraised value of the articles at the time of entry into the United States. *Identify all individuals/groups that perform the procedures and when/how often the procedures are performed.*

6.4.1   What documentation/records are verified? *Indicate if copies of the documentation/records are retained on file or may be obtained upon request.*

6.5   What documentation is maintained on file showing that the articles are shipped directly from the BDC (or FTA country) to the United States without passing through the territory of any other country, or if passing through the territory of any other country, that the articles did not enter the retail commerce of the other country?

Section 7—Information about NAFTA

7.1   Who is responsible for maintaining the certificates of origin from NAFTA vendors?

7.2   Describe the procedures used to ensure that imported items are eligible for NAFTA.

Section 8—Information about AD/CVD

8.1   Who decides (or determines) that items may be subject to AD/CVD? *Indicate when and how often items are reviewed.*

8.1.1   What information is used to determine whether items may be subject to AD/CVD? *Identify all individuals or groups/departments that provide information as well as the documentation/records used.*

8.2   Describe the procedures used to ensure that the correct (true) country of origin is identified for items subject to AD/CVD.

8.3   Describe the procedures used to ensure that the correct AD/CVD case numbers are identified on the entry.

Section 9—Information about IPR

9.1   Identify all imported items for which your company has authorizations from the holders of IPR such as trade names, trademarks, or copyrights. *Describe the item and indicate the type of IPR.*

9.2   Who decides (or determines) that an imported item may have IPR belonging to other entities? *Indicate when and how often items are reviewed.*

- When is it decided that an imported item may have IPR belonging to other entities?
- What information is used to determine that the items have IPR belonging to other entities? Identify all individuals or groups/departments that provide information as well as the documentation/records used.

9.3   Describe the procedures used to ensure there is a valid authorization/ agreement between your company and the owner of the trade name, trademark, copyright or patent prior to the importation of the items.

9.4   What accounts are used to record royalties, proceeds, and indirect payments related to the use of the IPR?

REQUEST FOR DOCUMENTATION

DATE OF REQUEST:

RESPONSE DUE:

SUBJECT: *When submitted in conjunction with the PASQ, the subject matter may be "Information about the organization and policies and procedures relative to compliance with CBP laws and regulations."*

Item no.	Description of Documentation
1	A copy of the organizational chart, if there is one.
2	A copy of written policies and procedures used to ensure compliance with CBP laws and regulations (e.g., an Import Compliance Manual).
3	A copy of the GL working trial balance for the period ending [xxxx] and description of accounts used.
4	A copy of written accounting procedures for recording purchases and payments.

From CBP Informed Compliance Publication: Reasonable Care General Questions for All Transactions:

1. If you have not retained an expert to assist you in complying with customs requirements, do you have access to the Customs Regulations (Title 19 of the Code of Federal Regulations), the Harmonized Tariff Schedule of the United States, and the GPO publication Customs Bulletin and Decisions? Do you have access to the Customs Internet Website, Customs Bulletin Board, or other research service to permit you to establish reliable procedures and facilitate compliance with customs laws and regulations?

2. Has a responsible and knowledgeable individual within your organization reviewed the customs documentation prepared by you or your expert to ensure that it is full, complete, and

accurate? If that documentation was prepared outside your own organization, do you have a reliable system in place to ensure that you receive copies of the information as submitted to U.S. Customs and Border Protection; that it is reviewed for accuracy; and that U.S. Customs and Border Protection is timely apprised of any needed corrections?

3. If you use an expert to assist you in complying with customs requirements, have you discussed your importations in advance with that person and have you provided that person with full, complete, and accurate information about the import transactions?

4. Are identical transactions or merchandise handled differently at different ports or U.S. Customs and Border Protection offices within the same port? If so, have you brought this to the attention of the appropriate U.S. Customs and Border Protection officials?

QUESTIONS ARRANGED BY TOPIC:

Merchandise Description and Tariff Classification

Basic Question: Do you know or have you established a reliable procedure or program to ensure that you know what you ordered, where it was made, and what it is made of?

1. Have you provided or established reliable procedures to ensure you provide a complete and accurate description of your merchandise to U.S. Customs and Border Protection in accordance with 19 U.S.C. 1481? (Also, see 19 CFR 141.87 and 19 CFR 141.89 for special merchandise description requirements.)

2. Have you provided or established reliable procedures to ensure you provide a correct tariff classification of your merchandise to U.S. Customs and Border Protection in accordance with 19 U.S.C. 1484?

3. Have you obtained a customs "ruling" regarding the description of the merchandise or its tariff classification (see 19 CFR Part 177), and if so, have you established reliable procedures to ensure that you have followed the ruling and brought it to U.S. Customs and Border Protection's attention?

4. Where merchandise description or tariff classification information is not immediately available, have you

established a reliable procedure for providing that information, and is the procedure being followed?

5. Have you participated in a customs pre-classification of your merchandise relating to proper merchandise description and classification?

6. Have you consulted the tariff schedules, customs informed compliance publications, court cases, and/or customs rulings to assist you in describing and classifying the merchandise?

7. Have you consulted with a customs "expert" (e.g., lawyer, customs broker, accountant, or customs consultant) to assist in the description and/or classification of the merchandise?

8. If you are claiming a conditionally free or special tariff classification/provision for your merchandise (e.g., GSP, HTS Item 9802, NAFTA, etc.), how have you verified that the merchandise qualifies for such status? Have you obtained or developed reliable procedures to obtain any required or necessary documentation to support the claim? If making a NAFTA preference claim, do you already have a NAFTA certificate of origin in your possession?

9. Is the nature of your merchandise such that a laboratory analysis or other specialized procedure is suggested to assist in proper description and classification?

10. Have you developed a reliable program or procedure to maintain and produce any required customs entry documentation and supporting information?

Valuation

Basic Questions: Do you know or have you established reliable procedures to know the price actually paid or payable for your merchandise? Do you know the terms of sale; whether there will be rebates, tie-ins, indirect costs, additional payments; whether assists were provided, commissions or royalties paid? Are amounts actual or estimated? Are you and the supplier related parties?

1. Have you provided or established reliable procedures to provide U.S. Customs and Border Protection with a proper declared value for your merchandise in accordance with 19 U.S.C. 1484 and 19 U.S.C. 1401a?

2. Have you obtained a customs "ruling" regarding the valuation of the merchandise (see 19 CFR Part 177), and if so, have you established reliable procedures to ensure that you have followed the ruling and brought it to U.S. customs and Border Protection attention?

3. Have you consulted the customs valuation laws and regulations, customs Valuation Encyclopedia, customs informed compliance publications, court cases, and customs rulings to assist you in valuing merchandise?

4. Have you consulted with a customs "expert" (e.g., lawyer, accountant, customs broker, customs consultant) to assist in the valuation of the merchandise?

5. If you purchased the merchandise from a "related" seller, have you established procedures to ensure that you have reported that fact upon entry and taken measures or established reliable procedures to ensure that value reported to U.S. Customs and Border Protection meets one of the "related party" tests?

6. Have you taken measures or established reliable procedures to ensure that all of the legally required costs or payments associated with the imported merchandise have been reported to U.S. Customs and Border Protection (e.g., assists, all commissions, indirect payments or rebates, royalties, etc.)?

7. If you are declaring a value based on a transaction in which you were/are not the buyer, have you substantiated that the transaction is a bona fide sale at arm's length and that the merchandise was clearly destined to the United States at the time of sale?

8. If you are claiming a conditionally free or special tariff classification/provision for your merchandise (e.g., GSP, HTS Item 9802, NAFTA, etc.), have you established a reliable system or program to ensure that you reported the required value information and obtained any required or necessary documentation to support the claim?

9. Have you established a reliable program or procedure to produce any required entry documentation and supporting information?

Country of Origin/Marking/Quota

Basic Question: Have you taken reliable measures to ascertain the correct country of origin for the imported merchandise?

1. Have you established reliable procedures to ensure that you report the correct country of origin on customs entry documents?

2. Have you established reliable procedures to verify or ensure that the merchandise is properly marked upon entry with the correct country of origin (if required) in accordance with 19 U.S.C. 1304 and any other applicable special marking requirement (watches, gold, textile labeling, etc.)?

3. Have you obtained a customs "ruling" regarding the proper marking and country of origin of the merchandise (see 19 CFR Part 177), and if so, have you established reliable procedures to ensure that you followed the ruling and brought it to U.S. Customs and Border Protection's attention?

4. Have you consulted with a customs "expert" (e.g., lawyer, accountant, customs broker, customs consultant) regarding the correct country of origin/proper marking of your merchandise?

5. Have you taken reliable and adequate measures to communicate customs country of origin marking requirements to your foreign supplier prior to importation of your merchandise?

6. If you are claiming a change in the origin of the merchandise or claiming that the goods are of U.S. origin, have you taken required measures to substantiate your claim (e.g., Do you have U.S. milling certificates or manufacturer's affidavits attesting to the production in the U.S.)?

7. If you are importing textiles or apparel, have you developed reliable procedures to ensure that you have ascertained the correct country of origin in accordance with 19 U.S.C. 3592 (Section 334, Pub. Law 103-465) and assured yourself that no illegal transshipment or false or fraudulent practices were involved?

8. Do you know how your goods are made from raw materials to finished goods, by whom and where?

9. Have you checked with U.S. Customs and Border Protection and developed a reliable procedure or system to ensure that the quota category is correct?

10. Have you checked or developed reliable procedures to check the Status Report on Current Import Quotas (Restraint Levels) issued by U.S. Customs and Border Protection to determine if your goods are subject to a quota category which has part categories?

11. Have you taken reliable measures to ensure that you have obtained the correct visas for your goods if they are subject to visa categories?

12. In the case of textile articles, have you prepared or developed a reliable program to prepare the proper country declaration for each entry, i.e., a single country declaration (if wholly obtained/produced) or a multi-country declaration (if raw materials from one country were produced into goods in a second)?

13. Have you established a reliable maintenance program or procedure to ensure you can produce any required entry documentation and supporting information, including any required certificates of origin?

Intellectual Property Rights

Basic Question: Have you determined or established a reliable procedure to permit you to determine whether your merchandise or its packaging bear or use any trademarks or copyrighted matter or are patented and, if so, that you have a legal right to import those items into, and/or use those items in, the U.S.?

1. If you are importing goods or packaging bearing a trademark registered in the U.S., have you checked or established a reliable procedure to ensure that it is genuine and not restricted from importation under the gray-market or parallel import requirements of U.S. law (see 19 CFR 133.21), or that you have permission from the trademark holder to import such merchandise?

2. If you are importing goods or packaging which consist of, or contain registered copyrighted material, have you checked or established a reliable procedure to ensure that it is authorized and genuine? If you are importing sound

recordings of live performances, were the recordings authorized?

3. Have you checked or developed a reliable procedure to see if your merchandise is subject to an International Trade Commission or court ordered exclusion order?

4. Have you established a reliable procedure to ensure that you maintain and can produce any required entry documentation and supporting information?

Miscellaneous Questions

1. Have you taken measures or developed reliable procedures to ensure that your merchandise complies with other agency requirements (e.g., FDA, EPA/DOT, CPSC, FTC, Agriculture, etc.) prior to or upon entry, including the procurement of any necessary licenses or permits?

2. Have you taken measures or developed reliable procedures to check to see if your goods are subject to a Commerce Department dumping or countervailing duty investigation or determination, and if so, have you complied or developed reliable procedures to ensure compliance with customs reporting requirements upon entry (e.g., 19 CFR 141.61)?

3. Is your merchandise subject to quota/visa requirements, and if so, have you provided or developed a reliable procedure to provide a correct visa for the goods upon entry?

4. Have you taken reliable measures to ensure and verify that you are filing the correct type of customs entry (e.g., TIB, T&E, consumption entry, mail entry, etc.), as well as ensure that you have the right to make entry under the customs regulations?

We have included a great business-development outline with the BIS Self-Assessment Tool Kit profiled in the Appendix C.

Stressing output is the key to improving productivity, while looking to increase activity can result in just the opposite.

Paul Gaugin

11

Best Practices in Global Expansion

This chapter provides a ten-step overview for corporate executives to follow that both highlights and emphasizes all the points made in the previous chapters. It is an excellent overview of the book laid out in an easy and concise structure for the reader to utilize in any growth or expansion initiative.

OVERVIEW

There is a road map that companies and the executives in charge can follow for effective global expansion, growth, and successful M&A activities. All the preceding chapters provide a granular view of all the decision-making components of getting global expansion right.

The following ten steps make the structure of **best practices**:

1. Strategic alignment and premerger/pregrowth initiative

   All the parties who will be engaged in the global expansion, international growth, or M&A activity have to create scenarios that work for all parties to the transaction. Making these work means that there is benefit to all parties, creating win-win deals. This can be strategic or financial alignment that provides leverage and benefit to all the interests.

   Experienced international business-development experts set the stage for their growth and M&A strategies. They develop a prestrategy that allows them to plan and forecast anticipated
   - Events;
   - Timelines;
   - Costs;
   - Team participants; and
   - Team assignments.

   The preplanning will go a long way at dealing with the array of challenges that will raise their "ugly heads" throughout the entire initiative from preplanning to close and implementation.

2. Team structure

   When approaching the alignment process, it is best to work in a team structure, with a host of vested parties and stakeholders who all will have a stake in the growth initiative or be impacted by the event.

   The team can include both internal and external interests. Internally, the team includes management representing the following:
   - Sales
   - Purchasing and/or sourcing
   - Operations
   - Manufacturing
   - Finance
   - Legal
   - Compliance
   - Supply chain
   - Human resources
   - Corporate
   - IT

Externally, the team could also include the following:

- Legal support
- Consultants
- Accounting, audit, and forensics

Assembling the team and providing team leadership, sometimes referred to as project management, will determine the success of any global growth initiative.

Assemble a team of growth and M&A technicians and stakeholders who work together assessing all the options, utilizing their skill sets and previous experiences.

3. Assessing the options

International business as we have described in all the preceding chapters is fraught with risks. Determining how these risks play into your choices will help frame your options. Assessing the options and weighing the risks, challenges, and mitigating steps are all parts of the necessary thought process that has to be part of the strategic thinking in international business development.

I have too many times been witness to great M&A acquisitions and international growth strategies going awry, all due to lack of proper assessment in weighing all the options. Typically, leadership gets fixed on one way of dealing with the challenges or only one way in approaching the circumstances at hand; and if they opened their eyes more, turned more stones over, and viewed additional options, they would be in a much better place in the deal than they were now.

Assessing options is part of the due diligence process outlined in number 6.

4. Creating a tactical action plan

Creating the plan for the team to follow requires diligent leadership with business-development skill sets.

The tactical action plan becomes the implementation strategy to make concepts and wishes become reality. It creates a blueprint for the executioners to follow to make the deliverables happen.

The action plan additionally
- Sets the short-term strategies and goals;
- Keeps everyone on target;
- Sets up lines of responsibility and accountability; and
- Provides specific actions, steps, and structure to make things happen.

Action plans need to contain the structure and disciplines to
- Assure the taking of the high road when the road splits;
- Assure the maintenance of your reputation;
- Keep the targets or strategic visions on mark;
- Communicate the plan status to all necessary parties, timely and comprehensively; and
- Assure that the deal creates value.

5. Develop resources

An international business with great opportunity, as we outlined in Chapter 1, has significant risks and challenges. When a company decides to grow internationally or create global M&A opportunities, a good best practice is to find strategic partners who can provide comprehensive support. These resources come in the names of attorneys, consultants, accountants, IT specialists, and international business development experts. They have expertise in international business through the following:

- Prior experience
- Access to internal specialized subject matter expertise
- Network of international offices and agents
- Specific knowledge of where to gets answers
- Relationships with government and private resources
- Networking capability
- Help to create value in the deal

6. Due diligence personified

Due diligence is a very important aspect of business strategy.

Due diligence is defined as "the process of carefully examining something or someone, especially before agreeing to buy it or employ him or her, or before advising someone else to buy it or employ him or her."

In global business development, growth and M&A activity, the success of the deal is totally dependent upon the degree of due diligence applied.

Our experience going back over 30 years demonstrated in almost every international business initiative that went wrong that someone had not accomplished the due diligence required.

Exercising due diligence is being **prudent**, **wise**, and **thorough**. I firmly believe that everyone would agree that the three attributes—prudence, wisdom, and thoroughness—are good under any circumstance.

It is important to note that there are a dozen or so software programs available that provide due-diligence metrics, questionnaires, and technology solutions for M&A activity.

7. Execution and integration strategy

Execution is doing and implementing. Integration strategy is making sure while executing that

- The intended plan is working; and
- There is successful interface, integration, and functioning among all the parties in the growth, development, or M&A activity (this mirrors alignment issues).

Integration and alignment makes the deal successful:

- Internal workings are meshing.
- Everyone is on the same page.
- When tweaking is occurring, everyone is participating and becoming realigned.

Often execution and implementation becomes part of the pre-strategy-planning process discussed in number 1 above. When this is done at the initial stage, it becomes a best practice that has real value when the time occurs for actual action and implementation.

What is best practice? It is the way that shows results every time. It is the benchmark, referring to being best in class and leading the field.

8. Reassessment

No business-development plan or growth strategy typically works as initially planned. What normally occurs is that the strategy and tactics have to be modified to meet changes that will occur in the normal course of business relations over time.

I was involved with a manufacturer based in California who had made arrangements to build a components plant in Indonesia. After 11 months of visits, revisits, attorneys, bankers, and consultants, a deal was structured and committed to a contract with a local company in Jakarta.

Three months into the construction of the plant, they ran into a political problem that was slowing down the construction process. Although they had obtained permits from the local government, an election was held and a new party took over in the province with domicile over those contract permits. The local counsel utilized had relationships with the prior administration and not the new incumbent party. This put the whole deal in jeopardy.

After a significant number of meetings and financial commitments to help the local economy, the construction got back on track, but now nine months behind schedule. Projects costs exceeded US$1.8 million, and delays caused various consequential financial concerns. The original strategy and business model had to be tweaked because of local politics, which in overseas markets can become very influential in deciding how decisions are made locally.

The company in California had to end up hiring additional local workers, more than what had been planned, and had to help build a few training centers to help the locals train in the necessary skill sets to work in the plant. All of these were unanticipated but were successfully dealt with over time.

In tandem with this issue, concerns over the Foreign Corrupt Practices Act (FCPA), which we cover in various chapters and sections in this book. Through the U.S. counsel, this was also successfully navigated but added to the legal cost.

Tweaking and modification down the road need to be anticipated and financial allowances accounted for. You may not know what specific tweaking(s) or modifications will occur, but anticipate them generically. Some project managers will add amounts from 3% to as much as 15% in budgeting unanticipated events that will cause additional cost.

9. Compliance

Compliance needs to become part of any international business development, global growth, or M&A initiatives. Compliance is needed in all aspects of business that we have to deal with in the United States and in all the local markets we are dealing with in the various countries and cities we are doing our initiatives with or in.

Areas such as, but not limited to, the following require compliance:
- Customs
- Export control
- Foreign Corrupt Practices Act (FCPA)

- Federal Maritime Commission (FMC)
- Department of Transportation (DOT)
- Hazardous materials
- United States Department of Agriculture (USDA) and Food and Drug Administration (FDA)
- Occupational Safety and Health Administration (OSHA)

Customs officials work on goods coming through the border.

10. Closure and postmerger/postgrowth initiative

Plans need to be considered for bringing the global initiative to close. Professionals who operate in this world sometimes refer to this step as postmerger or postproject review. It creates a discussion and debate that

- Makes sure what issues are left and, if so, how they are being handled or managed successfully;
- Aligns expectations with what really happened or deliverables with targets; and
- Opens transparency and dialogue with all the deals channel partners, eliciting information on how they feel on what has happened and recommendations for going forward.

This step is key to understanding why a deal, from an appearance perspective, may be finalized, but if expectations of all vested interests are not met, the deal is not closed.

No cheering can be done until a checklist is completed, bringing complete closure to an international business development initiative.

Postdebate sets the stage for satisfied business partners and establishing a good reputation, which opens the door for the next opportunity.

Though the world is huge, a bad reputation rings loud as does a good reputation in opening doors, lowering costs, and for ease of deal making and favorable results.

Timothy Sloan

Appendices

Our business is really simple. When you look at a deal and its structure looks like an octopus or spider, just don't do it.

Timothy Sloan

Appendix A: Customs-Trade Partnership against Terrorism Overview*

AGAINST TERRORISM

C-TPAT seeks to safeguard the world's vibrant trade industry from terrorists, maintaining the economic health of the United States and its neighbors. The partnership develops and adopts measures that add security but do not have a chilling effect on trade, a difficult balancing act.

A Growing Partnership

Begun in November 2001 with just seven major importers as members, as of June 2011, the partnership has grown. Today, more than 10,000 certified partners that span the gamut of the trade community have been accepted into the program. These include U.S. importers; U.S./Canada highway carriers; U.S./Mexico highway carriers; rail and sea carriers; licensed U.S. customs brokers; U.S. marine port authority/terminal operators; U.S. freight consolidators; ocean transportation intermediaries and nonoperating common carriers; Mexican and Canadian manufacturers; and Mexican long-haul carriers. These 10,000-plus companies account for over 50% (by value) of what is imported into the United States.

---

* From U.S. Customs.

Extending the Zone of U.S. Border Security

By extending the United States' zone of security to the point of origin, the customs-trade partnership allows for better risk assessment and targeting, freeing CBP to allocate inspectional resources to more questionable shipments.

The partnership establishes clear supply-chain security criteria for members to meet and in return provides incentives and benefits like expedited processing. A corollary is to extend the partnership antiterrorism principles globally through cooperation and coordination with the international community. Back in 2005, the World Customs Organization adopted the Framework of Standards to Secure and Facilitate Global Trade, which compliments and globalizes CBP's and the partnership's cargo security efforts.

How the Partnership Works

When they join the antiterror partnership, companies sign an agreement to work with CBP to protect the supply chain, identify security gaps, and implement specific security measures and best practices. Additionally, partners provide CBP with a security profile outlining the specific security measures the company has in place. Applicants must address a broad range of security topics and present security profiles that list action plans to align security throughout their supply chain.

C-TPAT members are considered low risk and are therefore less likely to be examined. This designation is based on a company's past compliance history, security profile, and the validation of a sample international supply chain.

An Emerging Focus: Mutual Recognition Arrangements

CBP has numerous mutual recognition arrangements with other countries. The goal of these arrangements is to link the various international industry partnership programs so that together they create a unified and sustainable security posture that can assist in securing and facilitating global cargo trade.

The goal of aligning partnership programs is to create a system whereby all participants in an international trade transaction are approved by the customs function as observing specified standards in the secure handling of goods and relevant information. C-TPAT signed its first mutual recognition arrangement with New Zealand in June 2007, and since that time signed similar arrangements with Korea, Japan, Jordan, and Canada.

Goals 1 and 2: Ensure that C-TPAT partners improve the security of their supply chains pursuant to C-TPAT security criteria while providing incentives and benefits to include expedited processing of C-TPAT shipments to C-TPAT partners.

To better secure and facilitate the flow of goods into the United States, CBP will ensure that existing and new C-TPAT partners fulfill their commitments by verifying that agreed upon security measures have been implemented. CBP will also work with its C-TPAT partners to further finalize minimum applicable supply-chain security criteria and security best practices. CBP will send teams of supply-chain specialists around the globe to visit members, their vendors, and vendors' plants to validate that supply-chain security meets C-TPAT minimum security criteria and best practices and that procedures used are reliable, accurate, and effective and meet the agreed-upon security standards. CBP will continue providing tools and creating incentives for the private sector to join C-TPAT, which is a prerequisite for the Free and Secure Trade (FAST) program and other CBP-expedited processing programs.

CBP's goals—to ensure that C-TPAT partners improve security of their supply chains while providing incentives and benefits to C-TPAT partners—includes nine key objectives:

Goal 1
1. Certify security profiles and security information provided by C-TPAT partners.
2. Enhance validation selection approach using risk factors, and expand the scope and volume of C-TPAT validations.
3. Formalize the requirements for C-TPAT self-policing tool, and implement the process for the submission of the C-TPAT periodic self-assessment.
4. Require participants to engage and leverage all business partners within their supply chains.

Goal 2
1. Develop the C-TPAT secure communication platform.
2. Conduct antiterrorism training seminars and targeted outreach for certified partners and the trade community.

3. Share information and security best practices with the membership.
4. Develop minimum security criteria, especially applying security measures applicable to point of origin and point of stuffing and having smarter, more secure cargo containers.
5. Provide expedited processing benefits to C-TPAT partners.

Goal 3: Internationalize the core principles of C-TPAT through cooperation and coordination with the international community.

C-TPAT builds upon relationships with all segments of the supply chain, both foreign and domestic, to secure the entire supply chain of goods entering the United States. More broadly, it is in the interest of the United States, and the protection of global trade more generally, to internationalize C-TPAT's core principles to the possible extent. This assures greater overall security of global trade, while also facilitating trade from the United States to other nations. Thus, internationalizing C-TPAT will promote supply-chain security and facilitate global trade moving to and between all nations. C-TPAT engages many facets of the international trade community and will continue partnering with these multinational corporations. In addition, C-TPAT will develop global security standards while working with other nations and their customs administrations, the international law enforcement community, international organizations, and the international trade community.

CBP's goal—to internationalize C-TPAT through cooperation and coordination with the international community—includes four key objectives:

1. Partner with the international trade community to help secure global supply chains.
2. Partner with individual customs administrations to improve the coordination of mutual antiterrorism efforts.
3. Support the work of the World Customs Organization (WCO) to develop a WCO-sponsored framework to secure and facilitate global trade that recognizes customs–private sector partnerships.
4. Coordinate with international organizations to improve the security and integrity requirements of their membership.

Goal 4: Support other CBP security and facilitation initiatives.

There are a number of programs and initiatives, within CBP and the Department of Homeland Security (DHS), that C-TPAT supports either directly or indirectly. CBP will continue to assist programs and initiatives that help secure and speed the flow of goods into our country.

CBP's goal—to support CBP and DHS security initiatives—includes four key objectives:

1. Support the implementation and expansion of the FAST program.
2. Support the development and implementation of a more secure and smarter container.
3. Support and complement CBP's Container Security Initiative.
4. Support other CBP and DHS antiterrorism initiatives.

Goal 5: Improve the administration of the C-TPAT program.

C-TPAT will continue building a strong, modern management infrastructure. This includes effective utilization of human resources, training, information technology, financial management, and performance measures.

CBP's goal—to modernize and expand the C-TPAT program—includes all the enhancements outlined above.

Appendix B: Harmonized Tariff Schedule of the United States*

1. World Import/Export HS Code	4. China Import/Export HS Code	7. Japan Import/Export HS Code
2. Germany Import/ Export HS Code	5. France Import/Export HS Code	8. India Import/Export HS Code
3. Spanish Import/Export HS Code	6. Russia Import/Export HS Code	9. Korea Import/Export HS Code

Home | Harmonized Tariff Schedule Code Database by Chapter, Harmonized Tariff Schedule of the United States

France HS code
China HS code
Japan HS code
USA HS code
Germany HS code
Russia HS code
Spanish HS code
India HS code
Korea HS code

---

* From http://htscodes.org/ and U.S. Census.

Harmonized Tariff Schedule Code Database by Chapter, Harmonized Tariff Schedule of the United States

Harmonized Tariff Schedule	HTS Code	Heading	HTS Code Notes
01 Live animals	HTS Code 01	0101–0106	Live animals
02 Meat and edible meat offal	HTS Code 02	0201–0210	Meat and edible meat offal
03 Fish and crustaceans, molluscs, and other aquatic invertebrates	HTS Code 03	0301–0307	Fish and crustaceans, molluscs, and other aquatic invertebrates
04 Dairy produce; birds' eggs; natural honey; edible products of animal origin, not elsewhere specified or included	HTS Code 04	0401–0410	Dairy produce; birds' eggs; natural honey; edible products of animal origin, not elsewhere specified or included
05 Products of animal origin, not elsewhere specified or included	HTS Code 05	0501–0511	Products of animal origin, not elsewhere specified or included
06 Live trees and other plants; bulbs, roots, and the like; cut flowers and ornamental foliage	HTS Code 06	0601–0604	Live trees and other plants; bulbs, roots, and the like; cut flowers and ornamental foliage
07 Edible vegetables and certain roots and tubers	HTS Code 07	0701–0714	Edible vegetables and certain roots and tubers
08 Edible fruit and nuts; peel of citrus fruit or melons	HTS Code 08	0801–0814	Edible fruit and nuts; peel of citrus fruit or melons
09 Coffee, tea, mate, and spices	HTS Code 09	0901–0910	Coffee, tea, mate, and spices
10 Cereals	HTS Code 10	1001–1008	Cereals
11 Products of the milling industry; malt; starches; inulin; wheat gluten	HTS Code 11	1101–1109	Products of the milling industry; malt; starches; inulin; wheat gluten
12 Oil seeds and oleaginous fruits; miscellaneous grains, seeds, and fruit; industrial or medicinal plants; straw and fodder	HTS Code 12	1201–1214	Oil seeds and oleaginous fruits; miscellaneous grains, seeds and fruit; industrial or medicinal plants; straw and fodder
13 Lac; gums, resins and other vegetable saps and extracts	HTS Code 13	1301–1302	Lac; gums, resins, and other vegetable saps and extracts

(Continued)

Harmonized Tariff Schedule Code Database by Chapter, Harmonized Tariff Schedule of the United States (Continued)

Harmonized Tariff Schedule	HTS Code	Heading	HTS Code Notes
14 Vegetable plaiting materials; vegetable products not elsewhere specified or included	HTS Code 14	1401–1404	Vegetable plaiting materials; vegetable products not elsewhere specified or included
15 Animal or vegetable fats and oils and their cleavage products; prepared edible fats; animal or vegetable waxes	HTS Code 15	1501–1522	Animal or vegetable fats and oils and their cleavage products; prepared edible fats; animal or vegetable waxes
16 Preparations of meat, of fish, or of crustaceans, molluscs, or other aquatic invertebrates	HTS Code 16	1601–1605	Preparations of meat, of fish, or of crustaceans, molluscs, or other aquatic invertebrates
17 Sugars and sugar confectionery	HTS Code 17	1701–1704	Sugars and sugar confectionery
18 Cocoa and cocoa preparations	HTS Code 18	1801–1806	Cocoa and cocoa preparations
19 Preparations of cereals, flour, starch, or milk; pastrycooks' products	HTS Code 19	1901–1905	Preparations of cereals, flour, starch, or milk; pastrycooks' products
20 Preparations of vegetables, fruit, nuts, or other parts of plants	HTS Code 20	2001–2009	Preparations of vegetables, fruit, nuts, or other parts of plants
21 Miscellaneous edible preparations	HTS Code 21	2101–2106	Miscellaneous edible preparations
22 Beverages, spirits, and vinegar	HTS Code 22	2201–2209	Beverages, spirits, and vinegar
23 Residues and waste from the food industries; prepared animal fodder	HTS Code 23	2301–2309	Residues and waste from the food industries; prepared animal fodder
24 Tobacco and manufactured tobacco substitutes	HTS Code 24	2401–2403	Tobacco and manufactured tobacco substitutes
25 Salt; sulphur; earths and stone; plastering materials, lime, and cement	HTS Code 25	2501–2530	Salt; sulphur; earths and stone; plastering materials, lime, and cement
26 Ores, slag, and ash	HTS Code 26	2601–2621	Ores, slag, and ash

(Continued)

Harmonized Tariff Schedule Code Database by Chapter, Harmonized Tariff Schedule of the United States (Continued)

Harmonized Tariff Schedule	HTS Code	Heading	HTS Code Notes
27 Mineral fuels, mineral oils, and products of their distillation; bituminous substances; mineral waxes	HTS Code 27	2701–2715	Mineral fuels, mineral oils and products of their distillation; bituminous substances; mineral waxes
28 Inorganic chemicals; organic or inorganic compounds of precious metals, of rare-earth metals, of radioactive elements	HTS Code 28	2801–2853	Inorganic chemicals; organic or inorganic compounds of precious metals, of rare-earth metals, of radioactive elements or of isotopes
29 Organic chemicals	HTS Code 29	2901–2942	Organic chemicals
30 Pharmaceutical products	HTS Code 30	3001–3006	Pharmaceutical products
31 Fertilizers	HTS Code 31	3101–3105	Fertilizers
32 Tanning or dyeing extracts; tannins and their derivatives; dyes, pigments, and other coloring matter; paints paints and varnishes; putty and other mastics; inks	HTS Code 32	3201–3215	Tanning or dyeing extracts; tannins and their derivatives; dyes, pigments and other coloring matter; paints and varnishes; putty and other mastics; inks
33 Essential oils and resinoids; perfumery, cosmetic or toilet preparations	HTS Code 33	3301–3307	Essential oils and resinoids; perfumery, cosmetic or toilet preparations
34 Soap, organic surface-active agents, washing preparations, lubricating preparations, artificial waxes, prepared waxes, polishing or scouring preparations, candles and similar articles, modelling pastes, "dentalwaxes," and dental preparations with a basis of plaster	HTS Code 34	3401–3407	Soap, organic surface-active agents, washing preparations, lubricating preparations, artificial waxes, prepared waxes, polishing or scouring preparations, candles and similar articles, modelling pastes, "dentalwaxes," and dental preparations with a basis of plaster
35 Albuminoidal substances; modified starches; glues; enzymes	HTS Code 35	3501–3507	Albuminoidal substances; modified starches; glues; enzymes

(Continued)

Harmonized Tariff Schedule Code Database by Chapter, Harmonized Tariff Schedule of the United States (Continued)

Harmonized Tariff Schedule	HTS Code	Heading	HTS Code Notes
36 Explosives; pyrotechnic products; matches; pyrophoric alloys; certain combustible preparations	HTS Code 36	3601–3606	Explosives; pyrotechnic products; matches; pyrophoric alloys; certain combustible preparations
37 Photographic or cinematographic goods	HTS Code 37	3701–3707	Photographic or cinematographic goods
38 Miscellaneous chemical products	HTS Code 38	3801–3825	Miscellaneous chemical products
39 Plastics and articles thereof	HTS Code 39	3901–3926	Plastics and articles thereof
40 Rubber and articles thereof	HTS Code 40	4001–4017	Rubber and articles thereof
41 Raw hides and skins (other than fur skins) and leather	HTS Code 41	4101–4115	Raw hides and skins (other than fur skins) and leather
42 Articles of leather; saddlery and harness; travel goods, handbags and similar containers; articles of animal gut	HTS Code 42	4201–4206	Articles of leather; saddlery and harness; travel goods, handbags and similar containers; articles of animal gut (other than silk-worm gut)
43 Fur skins and artificial fur; manufactures thereof	HTS Code 43	4301–4304	Fur skins and artificial fur; manufactures thereof
44 Wood and articles of wood; wood charcoal	HTS Code 44	4401–4421	Wood and articles of wood; wood charcoal
45 Cork and articles of cork	HTS Code 45	4501–4504	Cork and articles of cork
46 Manufactures of straw, of esparto, or of other plaiting materials; basketware and wickerwork	HTS Code 46	4601–4602	Manufactures of straw, of esparto, or of other plaiting materials; basketware and wickerwork
47 Pulp of wood or of other fibrous cellulosic material; waste and scrap paper or paperboard	HTS Code 47	4701–4707	Pulp of wood or of other fibrous cellulosic material; waste and scrap paper or paperboard
48 Paper and paperboard; articles of paper pulp, of paper, or of paperboard	HTS Code 48	4801–4823	Paper and paperboard; articles of paper pulp, of paper, or of paperboard

(Continued)

Harmonized Tariff Schedule Code Database by Chapter, Harmonized Tariff Schedule of the United States (Continued)

Harmonized Tariff Schedule	HTS Code	Heading	HTS Code Notes
49 Printed books, newspapers, pictures, and other products of the printing industry; manuscripts, typescripts and plans	HTS Code 49	4901–4911	Printed books, newspapers, pictures, and other products of the printing industry; manuscripts, typescripts and plans
50 Silk	HTS Code 50	5001–5007	Silk
51 Wool, fine or coarse animal hair; horsehair yarn, and woven fabric	HTS Code 51	5101–5113	Wool, fine or coarse animal hair; horsehair yarn, and woven fabric
52 Cotton	HTS Code 52	5201–5212	Cotton
53 Other vegetable textile fibers; paper yarn and woven fabrics of paper yarn	HTS Code 53	5301–5311	Other vegetable textile fibers; paper yarn and woven fabrics of paper yarn
54 Sewing thread of man-made filaments, whether or not put up for retail sale	HTS Code 54	5401–5408	Sewing thread of man-made filaments, whether or not put up for retail sale
55 Man-made staple fibers	HTS Code 55	5501–5516	Man-made staple fibers
56 Wadding, felt and nonwovens; special yarns; twine, cordage, ropes, and cables and articles thereof	HTS Code 56	5601–5609	Wadding, felt and nonwovens; special yarns; twine, cordage, ropes, and cables and articles thereof
57 Carpets and other textile floor coverings	HTS Code 57	5701–5705	Carpets and other textile floor coverings
58 Special woven fabrics; tufted textile fabrics; lace; tapestries; trimmings; embroidery	HTS Code 58	5801–5811	Special woven fabrics; tufted textile fabrics; lace; tapestries; trimmings; embroidery
59 Impregnated, coated, covered, or laminated textile fabrics; textile articles of a kind suitable for industrial use	HTS Code 59	5901–5911	Impregnated, coated, covered, or laminated textile fabrics; textile articles of a kind suitable for industrial use
60 Knitted or crocheted fabrics	HTS Code 60	6001–6006	Knitted or crocheted fabrics

(Continued)

Harmonized Tariff Schedule Code Database by Chapter, Harmonized Tariff Schedule of the United States (Continued)

Harmonized Tariff Schedule	HTS Code	Heading	HTS Code Notes
61 Articles of apparel and clothing accessories, knitted or crocheted	HTS Code 61	6101–6117	Articles of apparel and clothing accessories, knitted or crocheted
62 Articles of apparel and clothing accessories, not knitted or crocheted	HTS Code 62	6201–6217	Articles of apparel and clothing accessories, not knitted or crocheted
63 Other made up textile articles; sets; worn clothing and worn textile articles; rags	HTS Code 63	6301–6310	Other made up textile articles; sets; worn clothing and worn textile articles; rags
64 Footwear, gaiters, and the like; parts of such articles	HTS Code 64	6401–6406	Footwear, gaiters, and the like; parts of such articles
65 Headgear and parts thereof	HTS Code 65	6501–6507	Headgear and parts thereof
66 Umbrellas, sun umbrellas, walking-sticks, seat-sticks, whips, riding-crops, and parts thereof	HTS Code 66	6601–6603	Umbrellas, sun umbrellas, walking-sticks, seat-sticks, whips, riding-crops, and parts thereof
67 Prepared feathers and down and articles made of feathers or of down; artificial flowers; articles of human hair	HTS Code 67	6701–6704	Prepared feathers and down and articles made of feathers or of down; artificial flowers; articles of human hair
68 Articles of stone, plaster, cement, asbestos, mica, or similar materials	HTS Code 68	6801–6815	Articles of stone, plaster, cement, asbestos, mica, or similar materials
69 Ceramic products	HTS Code 69	6901–6914	Ceramic products
70 Glass and glassware	HTS Code 70	7001–7020	Glass and glassware
71 Natural or cultured pearls, precious or semi-precious stones, precious metals, metals clad with precious metal, and articles thereof; imitation jewelery; coin	HTS Code 71	7101–7118	Natural or cultured pearls, precious or semi-precious stones, precious metals, metals clad with precious metal, and articles thereof; imitation jewelery; coin
72 Iron and steel	HTS Code 72	7201–7229	Iron and steel
73 Articles of iron or steel	HTS Code 73	7301–7326	Articles of iron or steel

(Continued)

Harmonized Tariff Schedule Code Database by Chapter, Harmonized Tariff Schedule of the United States (Continued)

Harmonized Tariff Schedule	HTS Code	Heading	HTS Code Notes
74 Copper and articles thereof	HTS Code 74	7401–7419	Copper and articles thereof
75 Nickel and articles thereof	HTS Code 75	7501–7508	Nickel and articles thereof
76 Aluminium and articles thereof	HTS Code 76	7601–7616	Aluminium and articles thereof
78 Lead and articles thereof	HTS Code 78	7801–7806	Lead and articles thereof
79 Zinc and articles thereof	HTS Code 79	7901–7907	Zinc and articles thereof
80 Tin and articles thereof	HTS Code 80	8001–8007	Tin and articles thereof
81 Other base metals; cermets; articles thereof	HTS Code 81	8101–8113	Other base metals; cermets; articles thereof
82 Tools, implements, cutlery, spoons and forks, of base metal; parts thereof of base metal	HTS Code 82	8201–8215	Tools, implements, cutlery, spoons and forks, of base metal; parts thereof of base metal
83 Miscellaneous articles of base metal	HTS Code 83	8301–8311	Miscellaneous articles of base metal
84 Nuclear reactors, boilers, machinery and mechanical appliances; parts thereof	HTS Code 84	8401–8487	Nuclear reactors, boilers, machinery and mechanical appliances; parts thereof
85 Electrical machinery and equipment and parts thereof; sound recorders and reproducers, television image and sound recorders and reproducers, and parts and accessories of such articles	HTS Code 85	8501–8548	Electrical machinery and equipment and parts thereof; sound recorders and reproducers, television image and sound recorders and reproducers, and parts and accessories of such articles
86 Railway or tramway locomotives, rolling-stock and parts thereof; railway or tramway track fixtures and fittings and parts thereof; mechanical (including electro-mechanical) traffic signaling equipment of all kinds	HTS Code 86	8601–8609	Railway or tramway locomotives, rolling-stock and parts thereof; railway or tramway track fixtures and fittings and parts thereof; mechanical (including electro-mechanical) traffic signaling equipment of all kinds

(Continued)

Harmonized Tariff Schedule Code Database by Chapter, Harmonized Tariff Schedule of the United States (Continued)

Harmonized Tariff Schedule	HTS Code	Heading	HTS Code Notes
87 Vehicles other than railway or tramway rolling-stock, and parts and accessories thereof	HTS Code 87	8701–8716	Vehicles other than railway or tramway rolling-stock, and parts and accessories thereof
88 Aircraft, spacecraft, and parts thereof	HTS Code 88	8801–8805	Aircraft, spacecraft, and parts thereof
89 Ships, boats, and floating structures	HTS Code 89	8901–8908	Ships, boats, and floating structures
90 Optical, photographic, cinematographic, measuring, checking, precision, medical, or surgical instruments and apparatus; parts and accessories thereof	HTS Code 90	9001–9033	Optical, photographic, cinematographic, measuring, checking, precision, medical, or surgical instruments and apparatus; parts and accessories thereof
91 Clocks and watches and parts thereof	HTS Code 91	9101–9114	Clocks and watches and parts thereof
92 Musical instruments; parts and accessories of such articles	HTS Code 92	9201–9209	Musical instruments; parts and accessories of such articles
93 Arms and ammunition; parts and accessories thereof	HTS Code 93	9301–9307	Arms and ammunition; parts and accessories thereof
94 Furniture; bedding, mattresses, mattress supports, cushions, and similar stuffed furnishings; lamps and lighting fittings, not elsewhere specified or included; illuminated signs, illuminated name-plates and the like; prefabricated buildings	HTS Code 94	9401–9406	Furniture; bedding, mattresses, mattress supports, cushions, and similar stuffed furnishings; lamps and lighting fittings, not elsewhere specified or included; illuminated signs, illuminated name-plates and the like; prefabricated buildings
95 Toys, games, and sports requisites; parts and accessories thereof	HTS Code 95	9501–9508	Toys, games, and sports requisites; parts and accessories thereof
96 Miscellaneous manufactured articles	HTS Code 96	9601–9618	Miscellaneous manufactured articles
97 Works of art, collectors' pieces, and antiques	HTS Code 97	9701–9706	Works of art, collectors' pieces, and antiques

Appendix C: Export Management and Compliance Program.* Audit Module: Self-Assessment Tool

July, 2011

INTRODUCTION

This is a tool created for exporters to aid in the development of an Export Management and Compliance Program. It may be used to create a new program or to assess whether internal controls have been implemented within an existing program with the purpose of eliminating common vulnerabilities found in export compliance programs. Each company has unique export activities and export programs; therefore, this is an example to build upon and does not include ALL Export Administration Regulations restrictions and prohibitions.

This tool is a combination of best compliance practices implemented by U.S. companies, auditing practices, and Export Administration Regulations requirements.

METHODOLOGY

An effective EMCP consists of many processes that connect and intersect. The connections and intersections must be planned, and then, clear directions must be given to those who are to follow the rules of the program. Without maps (instructions), chances are that personnel will all go in their own directions, leaving them vulnerable to getting lost on the way

---

* From Export Management and Compliance Division, Office of Exporter Services, Bureau of Industry and Security, U.S. Department of Commerce (http://www.bis.doc.gov).

and chancing that key connections are missed, resulting in violations of the intended rules of the program. To use this self-assessment, first look to see if your program includes written instructions that create the connections and intersections needed to maintain compliance.

Within the self-assessment columns, "Y/N/U" stands for Yes/No/Uncertain or Indeterminate.

PRE-AUDIT CHECKLIST

- Identify business units and personnel to be audited.
- Send e-mail notification to affected parties.
- Develop a tracking log for document requests.
- Prepare audit templates such as interview questions, transactional review checklist, audit report format, etc.
- Each business unit should provide their written procedures related to export compliance before the audit.
- Personnel at all levels of the organization, management and staff, should be interviewed to compare written procedures with actual business practices.
- Identify gaps and inconsistencies.

POST-AUDIT CHECKLIST

- Write draft audit report.
  - Executive Summary [Purpose, Methodology, Key Findings]
  - Findings and Recommendations [Organize in Priority Order]
  - Appendices [Interview List, Document List, Process Charts]
- Conduct post-audit briefing for affected business units to discuss audit findings and recommendations. Provide draft report. This is an opportunity for business units to address inaccuracies in report.
- Obtain commitment from business units for corrective action. Include in audit report.
- Brief executive management on audit findings and recommendations.
- Track corrective actions. Within the year, audit corrective actions.

ELEMENT 1: Management Commitment	Y	N	U	Initials _____ Date _____ Comments
Is management commitment communicated on an ongoing basis by: Company publications? Company awareness posters? Daily operating procedures? Other means, e.g., bulletin boards, in meetings, etc.?				
Does management issue a formal Management Commitment Statement that communicates clear commitment to export controls?				
Is the formal Statement distributed to all employees and contractors?				
Who is responsible for distribution of the Statement?				
Is there a distribution list of those who should receive the Statement?				
What method of communication is used (letter, email, intranet, etc.)?				
Does the distribution of the Statement include employee signed receipt and personal commitment to comply?				
Is the formal Statement from current senior management communicated in a manner consistent with management priority correspondence?				
Does the formal Statement explain why corporate commitment is important from your company's perspective?				
Does the formal Statement contain a policy statement that no sales will be made contrary to the Export Administration Regulations?				
Does the formal Statement convey the dual-use risk of the items to be exported?				
Does the formal Statement emphasize End-Use/ End-User prohibitions?				
Proliferation activities of concerns: • Nuclear? • Certain Rocket Systems and Unmanned Air Vehicles? • Chemical and Biological Weapons?				
Does the formal Statement contain a description of penalties applied in instances of compliance failure? • Imposed by the Department of Commerce? • Imposed by your company?				

	Y	N	U	Initials _____ Date _____ Comments
ELEMENT 1: Management Commitment				

Does the formal Statement include the name, position, and contact information, such as: e-mail address & telephone number of the person(s) to contact with questions concerning the legitimacy of a transaction or possible violations?

What management records will be maintained to verify compliance with procedures and processes (including the formal Statement)?

Who is responsible for keeping each of the management records?

How long must the records be retained?

Where will the records be maintained?

In what format will the records be retained?

Are adequate resources (time, money, people) dedicated to the implementation and maintenance of the EMCP?

Is management directly involved through regularly scheduled meetings with various units responsible for roles within the EMCP?

Is management involved in the auditing process?

Has management implemented a team of EMCP managers who meet frequently to review challenges, procedures and processes and who serve as the connection to the employees who perform the EMCP responsibilities?

Does the Statement describe where employees can locate the EMCP Manual (on the company intranet or specific person and location of hard copies)?

Are there written procedures to ensure consistent, operational implementation of this Element?

Is a person designated to update this Element, including the Management Commitment Statement, when management changes, or at least annually? (Note in comments the name of the person.)

Who are other employees who are held accountable for specific responsibilities under this Element? For example:
- Company Official charged with EMCP oversight and ongoing commitment to the program.
- Management Team Members who are responsible for connecting with all responsible employees in the EMCP.
- Persons charged with ensuring the EMCP is functioning as directed by management.

ELEMENT 1: Management Commitment	Y	N	U	Initials _____ Date _____ Comments

If the primary responsible person is unable to perform the responsibilities, is a secondary person designated to back up the primary designee? (If not, is a procedure in place to eliminate vulnerabilities of an untrained person proceeding with tasks that might lead to violations of the EAR?)

Do responsible persons understand the interconnection of their roles with other EMCP processes and where they fit in the overall export compliance system?

Is the message of management commitment conveyed in employee training through:
Orientation programs?
Refresher training?
Electronic training modules?
Employee procedures manuals?
Other?

Is management involved in EMCP training to emphasize management commitment to the program?

Determination:

ELEMENTS 2 and 5: Risk Assessment and Cradle- to-Grave Export Compliance Security and Screening	Y	N	U	Initials _____ Date _____ Comments

Are there written procedures for ensuring compliance with product and country export restrictions?

Do procedures include reexport guidelines or any special instructions?

Is there a written procedure that describes how items are classified under ECCNs on the CCL?

A. Does a technical expert within the company classify the items?

B. If your company does not manufacture the item, does the manufacturer of the item classify it?

C. Is there a written procedure that describes when a classification will be submitted to BIS and who will be responsible?

D. Is there a written procedure that describes the process for seeking commodity jurisdiction determinations?

ELEMENTS 2 and 5: Risk Assessment and Cradle-to-Grave Export Compliance Security and Screening	Y	N	U	Initials _____ Date _____ Comments
Is an individual designated to ensure that product/country license determination guidance is current and updated?				
Is there a distribution procedure to ensure all appropriate users receive the guidance and instructions for use?				
Is there a list that indicates the name of the persons responsible for using the guidance?				
Is a Matrix or Decision Table for product/country license determinations used?				
Are the instructions provided easily understood and applied?				
Do the instructions provided specify who, when, where, and how to check each shipment against the matrix?				
Does the matrix/table display ECCNs and product descriptions?				
Appropriate shipping authorizations, License Required, License Exception (specify which), or NLR?				
Does the matrix communicate License Exception parameters/restrictions?				
Are license conditions and restrictions included within the matrix/table?				
Does the matrix/table cross reference items to be exported with license exceptions normally available (based on item description and end destination)?				
Does the matrix/table clearly define which license exceptions are normally available for each item (also clearly state which license exceptions may not be used due to General Prohibitions)?				
Are embargoed destinations displayed?				
Is country information in the table up-to-date?				
Are item restrictions displayed? (i.e., technical parameter limitations, end-user limitations)				
Is the matrix automated?				
Is a person designated for updating the tool?				
Are reporting prompts built into the matrix/table?				
Are Wassenaar reports required? Does the matrix/table denote when they are required?				
Is the matrix manually implemented?				
If so, is a person designated to update the tool?				

ELEMENTS 2 and 5: Risk Assessment and Cradle-to-Grave Export Compliance Security and Screening	Y	N	U	Initials _____ Date _____ Comments
Is there a "hold" function to prevent shipments from being further processed, if needed?				
Is there a procedure to distribute and verify receipt of license conditions?				
Is there someone designated to distribute and follow-up with acknowledgment verification?				
Is there a response deadline defined when conditions are distributed?				
Are there written procedures to ensure that checks and safeguards are in place within the internal process flows, and are there assigned personnel responsible for all checks?				
Is the order process and all linking internal flows displayed visually in a series of flow charts?				
Is there a narrative that describes the total flow process?				
Are the following checks included in the internal process?				
• Pre-order entry screen checks performed (i.e., know your customer red flags)				
• Denied Persons				
• Entity List				
• Unverified List				
• Specially Designated Nationals List				
• Boycott language				
• Nuclear End-Uses				
• Certain Rocket Systems and Unmanned Air Vehicles End-Uses				
• Chemical and Biological Weapons End-Uses				
• Product/Country Licensing Determination				
• Diversion Risk Check				
Do the order process and other linking processes include a description of administrative control over the following documents: Shipper's Export Declarations (SED)/AES Records, Shipper's Letter of Instruction (SLI)? Airway bills (AWB) and/or Bills of Lading, Invoices?				
Does the procedure explain the order process and other linking processes from receipt of order to actual shipment?				

ELEMENTS 2 and 5: Risk Assessment and Cradle-to-Grave Export Compliance Security and Screening	Y	N	U	Initials _____ Date _____ Comments
Does the procedure include who is responsible for each screen/check throughout the flow?				
Does the procedure describe when, how often, and what screening is performed?				
Are hold/cancel functions implemented?				
Does the procedure clearly indicate who has the authority to make classification decisions?				
Are supervisory or EMCP Administrator sign-off procedures implemented at high risk points?				
Does the company have an on-going procedure for monitoring compliance of consignees, end-users, and other parties involved in export transactions?				
Determination:				

ELEMENTS 2 and 5: Risk Assessment and Cradle-to-Grave Export Compliance Security and Screening

Review orders/transactions against the Denied Persons List (DPL)	Y	N	U	Initials _____ Date _____ Comments
Is there a written procedure to ensure screening of orders/shipments to customers covering servicing, training, and sales of items against the DPL?				
Are personnel/positions identified who are responsible for DPL screening (consider domestic and international designee)?				
Is there a procedure to stop orders if a customer and/or other parties are found on the DPL?				
Is there a procedure to report all names of customers and/or other parties found on the DPL?				
Do the procedures include a process for what is used to perform the screening, and if distribution of hard copies is required, who is responsible for their update and distribution?				
Is the DPL checked against your customer-base?				
A. Are both the customer name and principal checked?				
B. Is there a method for keeping the customer-base current?				
C. Is there a method for screening new customers?				

**ELEMENTS 2 and 5: Risk Assessment and Cradle-
to-Grave Export Compliance Security and Screening**

Review orders/transactions against the Denied Persons List (DPL)	Y	N	U	Initials _____ Date _____ Comments

Is the DPL checked on a transaction-by-transaction
basis?
  A. Is the name of the ordering party's firm and
     principal checked?
  B. Is the end-user's identity available? If so, is a
     DPL check done on the end-user?
  C. Is the check performed at the time an order is
     accepted and/or received?
  D. Is the check performed at the time of shipment?
  E. Is the check performed against backlog orders
     when a new or updated DPL is published?

Does documentation of screen (whether hard copy
or electronic signature) include:
  A. Name of individuals performing the checks?
  B. Dates screen-checks performed?
  C. Date of current denied person's information
     used to perform the check?
  D. Is the date of the DPL used to check the
     transaction documented? Is it current?

Are other trade-related sanctions, embargoes, and
debarments imposed by agencies other than the
Department of Commerce checked?
  A. Department of Treasury (Office of Foreign
     Assets Control):
     1. Specially Designated Terrorists?
     2. Specially Designated Nationals and Foreign
        Terrorist Organizations?
  B. Department of State:
     1. Trade-related sanctions (Bureau of Politico-
        Military Affairs)?
     2. Suspensions & debarments (Center for
        Defense Trade, Office of Defense Trade
        Controls)?

Are domestic transactions screened against the
DPL?

Determination:

ELEMENTS 2 and 5: Risk Assessment and Cradle-to-Grave Export Compliance Security and Screening

Diversion Risk Profile (DRP) See EAR Part 732, Supplements 1 & 3	Y	N	U	Initials _____ Date _____ Comments
Are there procedures to screen orders for diversion risk red flag indicators?				
Is a checklist used based upon the red flag indicators?				
Does the written screening procedure identify the responsible individuals who perform the screen checks?				
Is the DRP considered at all phases of the order processing system?				
Is a transaction-based DRP performed?				
Is a customer-based DRP performed?				
Is a checklist documented and maintained on file for each and every order?				
Is a checklist documented and maintained on file in the customer profile?				
Is the customer base checked at least annually against the red flag indicators or when a customer's activities change?				
General Prohibition 6—Prohibits export/reexports of items to embargoed destinations without proper license authority. Are embargoed-destinations prohibitions communicated on the product/country matrix and part of the red flag indicators?				
General Prohibition 10—Prohibits an exporter from proceeding with transactions with knowledge that a violation has occurred or is about to occur. Is there anything that is suspect regarding the legitimacy of the transactions?				

Determination:

ELEMENTS 2 and 5: Risk Assessment and Cradle-to-Grave Export Compliance Security and Screening

Prohibited nuclear end-uses/users, EAR, Section 744.2	Y	N	U	Initials _____ Date _____ Comments
Are there written procedures for reviewing exports and reexports of all items subject to the EAR to determine, prior to exporting, whether they might be destined to be used directly or indirectly in any one or more of the prohibited nuclear activities?				
Are personnel/positions identified who are responsible for ensuring screening of customers and their activities against the prohibited end-uses?				
Does the procedure describe when the nuclear screen should be performed?				
A. Is your nuclear screen completed on a transaction-by-transaction basis?				
B. Is the screen conducted against an established customer base? If yes, is there a procedure for screening each new customer before the new customer is added to that customer base?				
C. Is the nuclear screen completed before a new customer is approved?				
Is there a list of all employees responsible for performing nuclear screening?				
Does the check include documentation with the signature/initials of the person performing the check, and the date performed, to verify consistent operational performance of the check?				
Is the customer base checked and the check documented at least annually in the Customer Profiles? (See EMCP Guidelines, Diversion Risk Screen.)				
Is it clear who is responsible for the annual check?				
Is there a procedure to verify that all responsible employees are performing the screening?				
Are nuclear checklists (and/or other tools) distributed to appropriate export-control personnel for easy, efficient performance of the review?				
Have export/sales personnel been instructed on how to recognize situations that may involve prohibited nuclear end-use activities?				

ELEMENTS 2 and 5: Risk Assessment and Cradle-to-Grave Export Compliance Security and Screening

Prohibited nuclear end-uses/users, EAR, Section 744.2				Initials _____ Date _____
	Y	**N**	**U**	**Comments**
Does the procedure include what to do if it is known that an item is destined to a nuclear end-use/user?				
Determination:				

ELEMENTS 2 and 5: Risk Assessment and Cradle-to-Grave Export Compliance Security and Screening

Rocket Systems & Unmanned Air Vehicles **Prohibited missile end-uses/users, EAR,** **Section 744.3**				Initials _____ Date _____
	Y	**N**	**U**	**Comments**
Are there written procedures for reviewing exports and reexports of all items subject to the EAR to determine, prior to exporting, whether the items are destined for a prohibited end-use?				
Are personnel/positions identified who are responsible for ensuring screening of customers and their activities against the prohibited end-users/users?				
Does the procedure describe when the missile systems and unmanned air vehicles screen should be performed?				
Does the procedure include a check against the Entity List?				
If yes, is there a procedure to maintain documented Entity List screen decisions on file to verify consistent operational review?				
A. Is your rocket/UAV screen completed on a transaction-by-transaction basis?				
B. Is the screen conducted against an established customer base? If yes, is there a procedure for screening each new customer before the new customer is added to that customer base?				
C. Is the rocket/UAV screen completed before the new customer is approved?				
Does the check include documentation with the signature/initials of the person performing the check, and the date performed, to verify consistent operational performance of the check?				

**ELEMENTS 2 and 5: Risk Assessment and Cradle-
to-Grave Export Compliance Security and Screening**

Rocket Systems & Unmanned Air Vehicles **Prohibited missile end-uses/users, EAR,** **Section 744.3**	Y	N	U	**Initials** _____ **Date** _____ **Comments**
Is the customer base checked and the check documented at least annually in the Customer Profiles?				
Is it clear who is responsible for the annual check?				
Is there a list of all employees responsible for the annual check?				
Is there a procedure to verify that all responsible employees are performing the screening?				
Are missile systems and unmanned air vehicles checklists (and/or other tools) distributed to appropriate export-control personnel for easy, efficient performance of the review?				
Have export/sales personnel been instructed on how to recognize prohibited missile systems and unmanned air vehicles end-use activities?				
Does the procedure include what to do if it is known that an item is destined to a prohibited end-use/user?				

Determination:

**ELEMENTS 2 and 5: Risk Assessment and Cradle-
to-Grave Export Compliance Security and Screening**

Prohibited chemical & biological weapons **(CBW) end-uses/users, EAR, Section 744.4**	Y	N	U	**Initials** _____ **Date** _____ **Comments**
Are there written procedures for reviewing exports and reexports of all items subject to the EAR for license requirements, prior to exporting, if the item can be used in the design, development, production, stockpiling, or use of chemical or biological weapons?				
Are personnel/positions identified who are responsible for ensuring screening of customers and their activities against the prohibited end-use/users?				
Does the procedure describe when the chemical & biological weapons screen should be performed?				

ELEMENTS 2 and 5: Risk Assessment and Cradle-to-Grave Export Compliance Security and Screening

Prohibited chemical & biological weapons (CBW) end-uses/users, EAR, Section 744.4	Y	N	U	Initials _____ Date _____ Comments
A. Is your chemical & biological weapons screen completed on a transaction-by-transaction basis?				
B. Is the screen conducted against an established customer base? If yes, is there a procedure for screening each new customer before the new customer is added to that customer base?				
C. Is your chemical & biological weapons screen completed before the new customer is approved?				
Does the check include documentation with the signature/initials of the person performing the check, and the date performed, to verify consistent operational performance of the check?				
Is the customer base checked and the check documented at least annually in the Customer Profiles?				
Is it clear who is responsible for the annual check?				
Is there a list of all employees responsible for performing chemical & biological weapons screening?				
Is there a procedure to verify that all responsible employees are performing the screening?				
Are chemical & biological weapons checklists (and/or other tools) distributed to appropriate export-control personnel for easy, efficient performance of the review?				
Have export/sales personnel been instructed on how to recognize prohibited chemical & biological weapons end-use activities?				
Does the procedure include what to do if it is known that an item is destined to a prohibited end-use/user?				
Determination:				

ELEMENTS 2 and 5: Risk Assessment and Cradle-to-Grave Export Compliance Security and Screening

Review orders/transactions against Antiboycott Compliance Red Flags	Y	N	U	Initials _____ Date _____ **Comments**
Is there a written procedure to screen transactions and orders/shipping documents for restrictive trade practice or boycott language included in Part 760 of the EAR?				
Are personnel/positions identified who are responsible for performing this screen?				
Is the antiboycott screening performed by using a profile check list?				
Does the checklist include the following: A. The firm's name? (as "Consignee") B. Name/initials of personnel performing the screen check? C. Date screen check is performed?				
Is there a procedure to "hold" orders if there is a red flag during the processing of orders?				
Is a person designated to resolve red flags or report them to the BIS Office of Antiboycott Compliance?				
Have all units that might possibly come into contact with the red flags been trained to identify the red flags?				
Are antiboycott red flags included in training materials?				
Determination:				

ELEMENTS 2 and 5: Risk Assessment and Cradle-to-Grave Export Compliance Security and Screening

Review customers & other parties against the Entity List	Y	N	U	Initials _____ Date _____ **Comments**
Is there a written procedure to screen transactions against the Entity List to determine whether there are any license requirements in addition to normal license requirements for exports or reexports of specified items to specified end-users, based on BIS' determination that there is an unacceptable risk of use in, or diversion to, prohibited proliferation activities?				

**ELEMENTS 2 and 5: Risk Assessment and Cradle-
to-Grave Export Compliance Security and Screening**

Review customers & other parties against the Entity List	Y	N	U	Initials _____ Date _____ Comments
Is the screening documented, including the following?				
A. The firm's name?				
B. Names/initials of individuals performing the check?				
C. Date checks are performed?				
D. Is screen check combined and performed with another check (e.g., Denied Persons List check)?				
Is the Federal Register monitored daily for the addition of new entities to the Entity List?				
If matches occur, is there a "hold" function implemented within the order processing system that stops the order until a decision is made as to license requirements?				
Determination:				

ELEMENT 3: A Formal Written EMCP	Y	N	U	Initials _____ Date _____ Comments
Are there written procedures that describe how information will flow among all the Elements to help ensure EMCP effectiveness and accountability?				
Is the written EMCP developed and maintained with input from all the corporate stakeholders in the export process?				
Do the written procedures clearly describe detailed step-by-step processes that employees are expected to follow, and are contingencies addressed?				
Are the written procedures reviewed for update at least annually and when major changes occur?				
Are the written and operational procedures consistent?				
Has an Administrator been designated for oversight of the EMCP?				

ELEMENT 3: A Formal Written EMCP	Y	N	U	Initials _____ Date _____ Comments
Is there a table that identifies individuals, their positions, addresses, telephone numbers, e-mail addresses, and their respective export transaction and compliance responsibilities?				
Does it include all domestic sites				
Does it include all international sites?				
Is a person designated as responsible for management and maintenance of this Element?				
Is a person assigned responsibility for distribution of information related to this Element?				
Is a person assigned to retain the records?				
Is the length of time the records are to be retained included?				
Is the location of where the records are to be retained included?				
Is the format of the records to be retained included?				
If the primary responsible persons are unable to perform the assigned responsibilities, are secondary persons designated to back-up the primary designees?				
Where there are no backup designees, are there procedures in place to prevent untrained/unauthorized personnel from taking action?				
Are all EMCP tasks clearly summarized in this Element and consistent with detailed information in other corresponding Elements?				
Does each employee designated with tasks understand the importance of his/her role related to the overall export compliance system?				
Do the responsible persons understand how the processes they are responsible for connect to the "next" process? ("...and then what happens next?")				
Do all the appropriate personnel have the ability to hold a questionable transaction?				
Are the necessary systems to allow employees to perform their tasks readily available to them?				
Is training for understanding and use of the EMCP provided on a regular basis to the necessary employees, and are records of the training kept?				

				Initials _____ Date _____
ELEMENT 3: A Formal Written EMCP	Y	N	U	**Comments**
Based on an organization chart and assignment of tasks, does it appear that there are conflicts of interest in the chain of command and the tasks to be performed?				
Determination:				

				Initials _____ Date _____
ELEMENT 4: Training	Y	N	U	**Comments**
Are there written procedures that describe an ongoing program of export transaction/ compliance training and education?				
Do the written procedures clearly describe detailed step-by-step processes that employees are expected to follow?				
Is a qualified individual designated to conduct training and to update the training materials? (Note in comments the name of the person.)				
If the primary responsible person is unable to perform the responsibilities, is a secondary person designated to back-up the primary designee? (If not, is a procedure in place to eliminate vulnerabilities of an untrained person proceeding with tasks that might lead to violations of the EAR?)				
Is there a schedule to conduct training (including date, time, and place)?				
Does the training component of the EMCP include what training materials are used (module, videos, and manuals)?				
Are training materials accurate, consistent, and current with operational company policy, procedures and processes? (If not, note in the comments section what corrective actions are needed.)				

	Initials _____

				Date _____
ELEMENT 4: Training	Y	N	U	**Comments**

Are attendance logs used for documentation which
   includes agenda, date, trainer, trainees, and
   subjects?

Is frequency of training defined?

Is a list of employees/positions defined who should
   receive export control/compliance training?

Are responsible persons trained to understand the
   interconnection of their roles with other EMCP
   processes and where they fit in the overall export
   transaction/compliance program?

Is the list of employees/positions to be trained
   consistent with other elements?

Is a person identified and responsible for keeping
   the training records?

Is the location of where these training records are to
   be maintained included?

Is the format of how these training records will be
   maintained noted?

Do training methods include:
  • Orientation for new employees?
  • Formal (structured setting, agenda, modules
    used)?
  • Informal (less structured basis, verbal, daily,
    on-the-job exchanges)?
  • Circulation of written memoranda and e-mails
    to a small number of personnel (usually group
    specific instruction)?
  • Refresher courses and update sessions
    scheduled?
  • Employee desk procedure manuals?
  • Back-up personnel training?

ELEMENT 4: Training	Y	N	U	Initials _____ Date _____ Comments

Does content of training materials include:
- Organizational structure of export-related departments and functions?
- Message of management commitment—Policy Statement?
- The role of the EMCP administrator and key contacts?
- U.S. export/reexport regulatory requirements?
- EMCP company operating procedures?
- The purpose and scope of export controls?
- Licenses and conditions/license exceptions and parameters?
- Regulatory changes and new requirements?
- Destination restrictions?
- Item restrictions?
- End-use and end-user prohibitions?
- How to perform and "document" screens and checklists?
- Various process flows for each element?
- New customer review procedures?
- Identification and description of non-compliance?

Determination:

ELEMENT 6: Recordkeeping (EAR, Part 762)	Y	N	U	Initials _____ Date _____ Comments

Are there written procedures to comply with recordkeeping requirements?

Do the written procedures clearly describe detailed step-by-step processes that employees are expected to follow?

Are all records in each process included in the records maintained?

Are the written procedures reviewed for update at least annually and when significant changes occur?

Are the written and operational procedures consistent?

ELEMENT 6: Recordkeeping (EAR, Part 762)	Y	N	U	Initials _____ Date _____ Comments
Is there a designated employee responsible for management and maintenance of this element? Is name and contact information provided?				
Identify all other employees who are held accountable for specific responsibilities under this recordkeeping element?				
Do the designated employees know who is responsible for the next action to be taken in the process?				
If the primary responsible person is unable to perform the responsibilities, is a secondary person designated to back up the primary designee?				
Where there are no backup designees, are there procedures in place to prevent untrained/ unauthorized personnel from taking action?				
Do employees understand the importance of their roles related to the overall recordkeeping requirement?				
Do employees have the appropriate budgetary, staff, and supporting resources to perform their responsibilities?				
Do employees have access to all the appropriate systems, tools, databases, and records to perform their responsibilities and ensure compliance with recordkeeping procedures?				
Is appropriate and specific training provided regarding this element?				
Is the training included on an annual schedule of employee training?				
Have appropriate parties been identified who will retain records? Are names and contact information provided?				
Has the length of time for record-retention been identified?				
Have secure physical and electronic storage locations for records been identified for the retention of records?				
Have determinations been made regarding the formats that all of the different types of records will be retained in?				
Is there a list of records that are to be maintained (see Guidelines and below for checklists)?				

	Initials _____
	Date _____
ELEMENT 6: Recordkeeping (EAR, Part 762) Y N U	Comments

Does the procedure include a list of records to
  maintain, including the following Administrative
  Records:

Commodity Classification records?

Commodity Jurisdiction letters?

Advisory Opinion letters?

Copy of the EMCP?

BIS 748P, Multipurpose Application Form?

BIS 748P-A, Item Appendix?

BIS 748P-B, End-User Appendix?

BIS 711, Statement by Ultimate Consignee and
  Purchaser? Electronic version BIS 748P, Simplified
  Network Application Process (SNAP) ACCN
  Number?

Accompanying attachments, rider or conditions?
  International Import Certificates?

End-user Certificates?

License Exception TSR Written Assurance? AES
  Electronic Filing Authorization?

High Performance Computer Records?

Transmittal and acknowledgment of license condition?

Log administering control over use of Export/
  Reexport license?

Is a log maintained to ensure return or commodities
  previously exported under License Exception
  TMP?

Is a log maintained to ensure License Exception LVS
  limits are not exceeded?

Humanitarian Donations GFT Records?

Are there instructions for the accurate completion
  and filing of the following Transaction Records:

  1. Commercial Invoices?

  2. AES electronic filing authorization?

    a. Description of items(s)

    b. ECCN(s)

    c. License Number

    d. License Exception Symbols or Exemptions

    e. Schedule B Number(s)

  3. Air Waybills and/or Bills of Lading Value of
    Shipments

Is there conformity regarding the above documents?

Determination:

ELEMENT 7: Audits/Assessments	Y	N	U	Initials _____ Date _____ Comments
Are written procedures established to verify ongoing compliance?				
Is there a qualified individual (or auditing group) designated to conduct internal audits?				
Is there a potential conflict of interest between the auditor and the division being audited?				
Is there a schedule for audits?				
Are internal reviews performed annually, every six months, quarterly, etc.?				
Is there a step-by-step description of the audit process?				
Is a standard audit module or self-assessment tool used?				
If yes, does the audit module or self-assessment tool evaluate: Corporate management commitment in all aspects of the audit not just the Written Policy Statement Element?				
If yes, does the audit module or self-assessment tool evaluate: Formalized, written EMCP procedures compared to operational procedures?				
If yes, does the audit module or self-assessment tool evaluate: Accuracy & conformity of export transaction documents by random sampling or 100% verification?				
If yes, does the audit module or self-assessment tool evaluate: Whether there is a current, accurate product/license determination matrix consistent with the current EAR and Federal Register notices?				
If yes, does the audit module or self-assessment tool evaluate: Whether correct export authorizations were used for each transaction?				
If yes, does the audit module or self-assessment tool evaluate: Maintenance of documents, as required in the written EMCP?				
If yes, does the audit module or self-assessment tool evaluate: Whether internal control screens were performed and documented as required in the EMCP?				
If yes, does the audit module or self-assessment tool evaluate: Whether there are flow charts of the various processes for each element?				

ELEMENT 7: Audits/Assessments	Y	N	U	Initials _____ Date _____ Comments
If yes, does the audit module or self-assessment tool evaluate: What is used to provide verification that the audits were conducted?				
If yes, does the audit module or self-assessment tool evaluate: Whether there is a procedure to stop/ hold transactions if problems arise?				
If yes, does the audit module or self-assessment tool evaluate: Whether all key export-related personnel are interviewed?				
If yes, does the audit module or self-assessment tool evaluate: Whether there are clear, open communications between all export-related divisions?				
If yes, does the audit module or self-assessment tool evaluate: Whether there is daily oversight over the performance of export control checks?				
If yes, does the audit module or self-assessment tool evaluate: Sampling of the completed screens performed during the order processing and/or new (or annual) customer screening?				
If yes, does the audit module or self-assessment tool evaluate: Whether export control procedures and the EMCP manual are consistent with EAR changes that have been published?				
If yes, does the audit module or self-assessment tool evaluate: Whether the company's training module and procedures are current with EAR and Federal Register notices?				
Is there a written report of each internal audit?				
Are there written results of the review?				
Is the appropriate manager notified, if action is needed?				
Are spot checks/informal self-assessments performed? Are they documented?				
Is there evidence of a conflict of interest between the reviewer and the division being reviewed?				
Are records of past audits maintained to monitor repeated deficiencies?				

ELEMENT 7: Audits/Assessments	Y	N	U	Initials _____ Date _____ Comments
Is there a "best practice" that should be shared with other divisions in the company to improve effectiveness and efficiency of export controls and promote consistency of procedures?				
Are other departments aware of their export-control-related responsibilities, e.g., legal dept., human resources, information management, etc.?				
Determination:				

ELEMENTS 8 and 9: Reporting, Escalation, and Corrective Action	Y	N	U	Initials _____ Date _____ Comments
Are there internal procedures in place to notify management within the company if a party is determined to be in non-compliance? Is contact information provided for each official in the chain?				
Does the company policy/guidelines address accountability and consequences for noncompliant activity? Are the appropriate incentives, rewards, requirements, and penalties in place and is an appropriate business culture of compliance being fostered to facilitate notification of any possible noncompliance?				
Are there internal procedures in place to notify the appropriate U.S. Government officials (e.g., Export Administration's Office of Exporter Services (OEXS), Export Enforcement, etc.) when non-compliance is determined?				
Has a central corporate point-of-contact been defined for all communications with the U.S.G.?				
Is the management chain clearly defined for Voluntary Self-Disclosures (VSDs) and are there clear guidelines for VSDs?				
Do all employees receive export control awareness training (including for potential deemed exports and hand-carry scenarios)? Does this training detail reporting, escalation, and corrective action requirements?				

				Initials _____ Date _____
ELEMENTS 8 and 9: Reporting, Escalation, and **Corrective Action**	Y	N	U	**Comments**
Is there a 24-hour mechanism for notifying compliance management of possible export violations or problems?				
Does the company have an anonymous reporting mechanism for employees?				
Do compliance guidelines provide defined criteria for when a formal internal investigation is required? If yes, are the procedures to be followed defined? Are the reporting and documentation requirements defined?				
Do compliance guidelines include policy and procedures for follow-up reporting to management and the reporting employee? Is there a process for evaluating lessons learned?				
Determination:				

Appendix D: The Post-9/11 Global Framework for Cargo Security*

United States International Trade Commission
Journal of International Commerce and Economics

This paper reviews changes in global cargo security policies following September 11, 2001. The events of 9/11 led to the establishment of new protocols for tracking and screening cargo both in the United States and in foreign countries. These protocols have been incorporated into international frameworks such as those under the World Customs Organization (WCO), and in country-specific programs such as the Container Security Initiative (CSI) and the Customs-Trade Partnership Against Terrorism (C-TPAT) administered by the United States. In addition, a host of foreign countries, including Australia, Canada, Sweden, and New Zealand have introduced new cargo security programs following 9/11 or have strengthened previously existing programs. Many of these countries aim to harmonize their cargo security standards with those of the United States. Although substantial progress has been made in the development of post-9/11 cargo security programs, some have expressed concern regarding the programs' efficacy, their costs to business, and their effects on cross-border trade. At present, post-9/11 cargo security programs continue to be refined, which may ultimately lead to changes in the direction and implementation of these programs.

* From Joann Peterson and Alan Treat (Web version: March 2014). Joann Peterson (joann.peterson @usitc.gov) and Alan Treat (alan.treat@usitc.gov) are International Trade Analysts in the Office of Industries. The views presented in this article are solely those of the authors, and do not necessarily represent the opinions of the US International Trade Commission or of any of its Commissioners.

INTRODUCTION

This article surveys changes in cargo security policies following the terrorist attacks of September 11, 2001. The events of 9/11 led the United States and its trade partners to re-assess and strengthen the global cargo security regime, resulting in new protocols for tracking, screening, and inspecting containerized imports and exports (Schmitz 2007).* These protocols have entered international frameworks such as those under the World Customs Organization (WCO), and have led to two new prominent U.S. programs; the Container Security Initiative (CSI) and the Customs-Trade Partnership Against Terrorism (C-TPAT). Several U.S. trade partners have either established programs similar to those of the United States or participated in the mutual recognition of these programs.

Despite progress in the development and implementation of post-9/11 cargo security programs, however, concerns remain regarding their efficacy, their costs to business, and their effects on cross-border trade. For example, while the primary goal of post-9/11 programs is to prevent the cross-border movement of terrorist-related weapons, some have found that nonuniform security procedures among C-TPAT members and inadequate screening equipment at certain CSI ports may compromise this objective (GAO 2005). Separately, it is unclear whether the benefits of participation in post-9/11 cargo security programs outweigh their costs to participants. In particular, a 2007 study conducted by the University of Virginia found that whereas the annual costs to U.S. importers of participation in C-TPAT were more than $30,000, the benefits of such participation, including increased supply chain security and fewer customs inspections, had not yet been fully realized (CBP 2007b). Finally, a recent Canadian study found that while post-9/11 cargo security programs have had no measurable impact on the volume of cross-border trade between the United States and Canada, such programs have resulted in increased border delays and therefore higher costs for firms engaged in U.S.-Canada trade (CBP 2007b).

Following a discussion of international agreements that address cargo security, this article will review U.S.- and foreign-country-based cargo

---

* In general, the objective of cargo security measures is to prevent the cross-border shipment of dangerous or illicit goods such as weapons of mass destruction (WMD), drugs, chemicals intended for destructive use, counterfeit or undeclared merchandise, firearms, currency, and hazardous materials.

security programs developed after 9/11. The article will then outline the primary challenges and concerns of current programs, as plans to expand the global framework for cargo security move forward.

INTERNATIONAL AGREEMENTS ON CARGO SECURITY

The events of 9/11 precipitated a change in cargo security measures at national borders. Prior to 9/11, customs authorities were responsible primarily for clearing imported goods after such goods arrived at the border. They did so through the review of entry documentation accompanying such goods at the time of importation and, if necessary, their physical inspection. In contrast, the cargo security programs developed after 9/11 emphasize preshipment examination of exports. In particular, these programs require that exporters provide customs documentation in advance of their shipment of goods to the importing country. Such advanced documentation assists customs authorities employing sophisticated and multilayered risk assessment techniques to determine whether to admit goods at the border or to hold them for further inspection.*

Although advance information requirements and mandatory screening procedures can disrupt the flow of cross-border trade, recent international conventions aim, for example, to harmonize customs practices across countries and to require that individual customs administrations employ efficient, technologically advanced, and unburdensome procedures for inspecting and clearing cargo (De Wulf and Sokol 2005, xv).

After the events of September 11, 2001, the WCO ratified the revised Kyoto Convention on the Simplification and Harmonization of Customs Procedures and introduced a new set of protocols for cargo security called the Framework of Standards to Secure and Facilitate Trade (SAFE) (WCO 2006).† The objective of these documents was to address the specific security needs of the post-9/11 customs environment while

---

* In August 2007, President Bush signed the 9/11 Commission Recommendations Act, which requires that, by 2012, all U.S.-bound containerized cargo must be scanned by X-ray machine before entering the United States. For more information, see subsequent section on U.S.-based cargo security policies Natter 2007.

† The revised Kyoto Convention, which was drafted in June 1999 and entered into force in February 2006, is an updated version of the International Convention on the Simplification and Harmonization of Customs Procedures (Kyoto Convention) of 1974. As of January 2007, 52 countries were parties to the agreement. WCO Instruments and Programmes.

strengthening procedures to facilitate the movement of goods across borders (Widdowson 2007). Building upon core principles found in the 1974 Kyoto Convention, the revised convention established guidelines to facilitate cross-border trade in response to the rapid growth in the volume and pace of international commerce. Among other things, the revised convention recommended that customs administrations (1) use electronically based systems to process and clear goods; (2) employ risk management techniques in selecting goods for inspection; (3) cooperate with customs authorities from other countries; and (4) ensure that customs-related laws and regulations are transparent and made readily available to the public (WCO 2000, 2005). The revised Kyoto Convention encouraged customs authorities to advance beyond the role of gatekeeper to that of the trade facilitator (Widdowson 2007).

In June 2005, the members of the WCO adopted the SAFE Framework,* which further expanded trade facilitation principles in the Kyoto Convention and introduced new provisions on cargo security in response to 9/11 (Schmitz 2007). Like the Kyoto Convention, the WCO Framework viewed customs administrations as playing a key role in facilitating trade. The framework has two customs-centered supports: the customs-to-customs network and the customs-to-business partnership. Both support the international supply chain.†

The customs-to-customs network uses automated techniques to screen high-risk cargo; and the customs-to-business partnership sets up procedures to precertify shippers through an authorized economic operator (an AEO program).‡ The network and the partnerships help traders to realize the four primary concepts of the framework: (1) the harmonization of advance cargo information requirements across parties to the agreement; (2) the use of risk management techniques; (3) the inspection of outbound cargo upon the request of an importing country; and (4) the establishment

---

* The SAFE framework was developed jointly by customs administrations and the private sector. As of February 2007, 144 of the 171 members of the WCO were signatories to the agreement (Schmitz 2007).

† A supply chain is defined as a network of interrelated activities including the production, transport, and storage of goods.

‡ Authorized economic operator (AEO), or trusted shipper, programs are an important component of trade facilitation measures in that they permit importers, exporters, manufacturers, and transportation firms who have met precertification requirements to clear their cargo quickly through customs. AEO programs also aim at mutual recognition, where a certified shipper from one country may benefit from expedited customs processing in another country. Kulisch 2006, 32; and Edmondson 2007, 17.

BOX A4.1   RISK MANAGEMENT*

Risk management focuses on identifying and implementing measures to limit exposure to risk, or the likelihood of an event occurring with a negative or unwanted outcome. In trade, the focus of risk management is to systematically identify imports and exports that represent the greatest risk of noncompliance of customs laws and regulations, as well as the greatest risk to national security and safety.

By using multiple risk management strategies, U.S. and foreign customs agencies can identify and target those areas that pose the greatest risk, and allocate resources accordingly. U.S. and foreign cargo security programs generally implement similar risk management strategies based on the following: collecting data elements and detailed shipment information from a variety of sources; analyzing and assessing risk using rules-based computer programs and customs targeting teams; prescribing action, such as undertaking non-intrusive or physical inspection or seizure; and tracking and monitoring the risk management process and its outcomes (Laduba 2005).

In the United States, trade data and detailed shipment information are gathered from various government data sources in the Automated Targeting System (ATS), a vast database that uses targeting rules and criteria based on intelligence to filter through cargo data and flag high-risk shipments. Electronic manifests submitted 24 hours prior to foreign lading allow U.S. Customs and Border Protection to assess cargo risk earlier prior to U.S. arrival (CBU, n.d.). In addition, U.S. cargo security partnerships such as C-TPAT and CSI aim to mitigate risk by strengthening supply chain security in the case of the former, and by prescreening U.S.-bound cargo at foreign ports prior to departure for the latter.

Risk management techniques allow customs to identify shipments that represent little to no risk, and thus focus limited resources on shipments that pose the greatest risk of noncompliance. In contrast

---

* Risk management procedures had been used by customs administrations prior to 9/11, but their use has expanded with the introduction of post-9/11 programs such as CSI and C-TPAT.

to inspection based on a shipment's risk profile, the aim of full inspection is either to physically inspect or scan 100 percent of imported containers. The 9/11 Commission Recommendations Act of 2007, signed into law August 3, 2007, mandates the scanning of 100 percent of all maritime cargo containers entering U.S. ports by 2012. Some industry observers believe that cargo inspection based on risk management is a more practical method to balance cargo security with the flow of legitimate (i.e., low or no risk) trade than 100 percent inspection of imported containers (Anderson 2007). Others question the cost of implementing 100 percent inspection, and who should pay for it (e.g., importers or exporters) (Lane 2007).

of new programs to expedite customs processing for commercial shippers (CRS 2006).

The cargo security principles included in the WCO SAFE Framework are designed to encourage rather than to impede cross-border trade (WCO 2005). The customs-to-customs network of the agreement outlines 11 substandards, or guidelines, for customs authorities to follow in implementing cargo security measures (WCO 2005). These guidelines recommend, for example, that (1) customs authorities use noninvasive equipment for the inspection of cargo; (2) establish automated systems for risk assessment; (3) develop consistent methods to distinguish high-risk from low-risk cargo; (4) require advance electronic information on cargo and container shipments; and (5) establish performance measures to track the efficacy of cargo security programs. The guidelines on risk management and cargo inspection, in particular, address trade facilitation concerns in that they recommend, to the extent possible, that customs authorities implement security procedures that do not interfere with cross-border trade flow (WCO 2005).

Similarly, the customs-to-business partnership fulfills the dual objectives of trade facilitation and cargo security. The partnership helps private-sector entities such as importers, exporters, freight forwarders, and transportation companies to complete self-assessments of their internal security regime. Those companies whose procedures meet specific criteria for protecting supply chains from the movement of dangerous goods are eligible for expedited customs processing under an AEO, or trusted shipper, program. By requiring that shippers inspect goods that are purchased from foreign manufacturers as they are prepared for outgoing shipment, the customs-to-business partnership enables customs authorities to engage the private sector in securing the international supply chain (WCO 2005).

Appendix E: Trade Facilitation Principles under the World Trade Organization*

Although the World Trade Organization (WTO) General Agreement on Tariffs and Trade (GATT) does not address cargo security directly, the provisions of the agreement on trade facilitation under articles V, VIII, and X are complementary to cargo security measures under the WCO (WCO, Information Note 2007). Article V addresses freedom of transit and states that a country should permit cargo that originates from or is destined for another country to pass through the territory of the former without being delayed by local customs authorities. Article VIII recommends that countries simplify import and export procedures, including customs documentation requirements. Article X requests transparency in the publication of a country's customs-related rules and regulations (GATT 1986, 12). These provisions correspond closely with WCO recommendations on trade facilitation, including the cooperation between national customs authorities, the simplification of customs procedures, and the assurance of predictability in customs operations (WCO Information n.d.a.). Under the SAFE Framework, the WCO introduced implementation guidelines for GATT Article VIII, in particular, that form the basis of post-9/11 cargo security measures, such as those pertaining to the electronic processing of customs documentation, the use of risk management, and the pre-authorization of commercial shippers.

In August 2004, the WTO initiated trade facilitation negotiations to strengthen members' commitments under articles V, VIII, and X. Several members submitted proposals on specific aspects of these articles: for example, Canada on the importance of coordination between national customs agencies; Korea on the reduction of administrative burdens in customs processing; and Japan on the pre-arrival

---

* From World Trade Organization. As of July 2007, 151 countries were members of the WTO.

examination of cargoes and the use of risk management (WTO 2005 a,b,c,d).

Trade facilitation negotiations under the WTO remain ongoing, with members working toward the development of a draft text on key principles under articles V, VIII, and X to be finalized by the conclusion of the Doha Round (WTO 2005a).

Appendix F: Cargo Security Provisions under the International Maritime Organization*

Acknowledging the importance of the maritime sector to international trade, the International Maritime Organization (IMO) established new security measures following the events of 9/11 to ensure the safety of maritime ports and cargo.[†] These measures are outlined in the International Ship and Port Facility (ISPS) Code, which entered into force on July 1, 2004.[‡] The objective of the ISPS Code is to establish a set of uniform measures to be implemented jointly by governments, port facility operators, and shipping firms for the assessment of and response to security threats to international ports.[§] The code is divided into two parts: the first part contains mandatory guidelines on security plans to be established by ships, shipping firms, and ports. National governments are responsible for overseeing the implementation. The second part of the framework provides recommendations on how to execute port security plans (Australian Government 2007). Plans developed and implemented by contracting parties to the ISPS Code are intended to pre-empt security threats to maritime trade (IMO FAQ 2007). As such, participants in the code are requested to develop plans based on three predefined threat levels to port security (for example, "normal," "heightened," or "exceptional"),

---

* From *International Maritime Organization*. The International Maritime Organization (IMO) was established by the Safety of Life at Sea Convention (SOLAS), adopted in 1948. A specialized agency of the United Nations (UN), the IMO maintains regulations regarding maritime safety, security, and technical cooperation, as well as environmental protection (IMO 2007).

[†] According to one estimate, more than 80 percent of world trade is transported by sea. The global maritime industry consists of 46,000 vessels and over 4,000 ports (OECD 2007).

[‡] The International Ship and Port Facility (ISPS) Code was adopted as an amendment to the 1974 IMO Safety of Life at Sea (SOLAS) Convention and based on provisions of U.S. legislation entitled the Maritime Transportation Security Act (MTSA) of 2002. Contracting parties to SOLAS, which number 148 countries, must comply with ISPS regulations. However, compliance by parties non-contracting to SOLAS is voluntary (CRS 2006).

[§] Ibid.

and to use risk assessment to determine which threats represent the highest vulnerability to ships and ports and, therefore, which merit a response (IMO FAQ 2007).

Compliance with the ISPS Code is estimated to lead to significant costs for participant countries. One study assesses such costs as reaching nearly $300 million in the first year of participation, and $700 million in each subsequent year. However, these costs are reportedly outweighed by the potential benefits of compliance with ISPS regulations, which include not only the avoidance of a shutdown in port operations due to a security threat, but in faster vessel turnaround times and expedited customs processing (OECD 2003).

AIR CARGO SECURITY MEASURES

Post-9/11 security measures on air cargo have been discussed both at the national and international level, but unlike measures for maritime cargo, such measures have not been codified under a single agreement. Prior to 9/11, the International Civil Aviation Organization (ICAO) established standards for shippers, freight forwarders, and transportation firms to maintain the security of cargo while in transit. The standards also included recommendations to facilitate the cross-border movement of goods.* Among the recommendations established by ICAO and outlined in the Chicago Convention are, where possible, the use of risk management techniques over the physical inspection of cargo, the acceptance of customs documentation in electronic formats, and the use of "authorized importers" to expedite customs processing. In addition, the Chicago Convention mandates that both airports and airlines establish security programs and that contracting states to ICAO cooperate in matters of air cargo security (Buzdugan 2006).

More recently, the International Air Transport Association (IATA), whose membership includes 250 global airlines, developed a list of best practices with regard to the protection of air cargo and created an internal working group to establish a strategic plan on air cargo security and trade

---

* The International Civil Aviation Organization (ICAO) was established under the Convention on International Civil Aviation (also known as the Chicago Convention), signed in December 1944. ICAO is under UN auspices, and its purpose is to maintain standards on aviation safety and security.

facilitation (IATA 2006, 2007). IATA initiatives emphasize all-cargo versus passenger air transport* and aim to ensure that cargo security measures, such as screening and clearance procedures, are harmonized across countries both to ensure their maximum efficacy and their minimal interference with air transport operations (Peck 2006; Task Force 2007).

---

* Although up until recently, emphasis had been placed on the screening of air passenger baggage, recent U.S. legislation entitled the 9/11 Commission Recommendations Act, signed into law by President Bush on August 3, 2007, requires that all cargo transported in the storage cabins of passenger planes be screened (e.g., by X-ray, explosive detection systems [EDS], physical search, or canine inspection) by 2010. Earlier legislation proposed by the U.S. Senate recommended the screening of cargo transported by both passenger aircraft and air freighters. See Air Cargo Security Act 2003; Natter 2007; and Putzger 2007, 40–42.

Appendix G: United States– Based Cargo Security Policies*

CUSTOMS-TRADE PARTNERSHIP AGAINST TERRORISM (C-TPAT) AND THE CONTAINER SECURITY INITIATIVE (CSI)

Shortly after 9/11, the U.S. Government introduced two programs to secure the movement of imports into the United States: the Customs-Trade Partnership Against Terrorism (C-TPAT) and the Container Security Initiative. C-TPAT, launched in April 2002, is a voluntary program with participation by all members of the supply chain—including manufacturers, transportation firms, customs brokers, and warehouse and port terminal operators—who are required to complete security self-assessments and security enhancements to meet the criteria of the program.[†] The idea behind C-TPAT is that by engaging private-sector participants to help screen low-risk cargo, the U.S. Customs and Border Protection (CBP) agency[‡] can focus its resources on detaining high-risk shipments that represent the greatest security threat (Feldman 2007). Participants in C-TPAT include U.S. companies as well as U.S.-based affiliates of foreign companies, all of whom must be involved in the movement of goods between U.S. and non-U.S. ports. As of June 2007, there were 7200 companies that were members of the C-TPAT program (Lodbell 2007).

---

[*] From U.S. Customs and references cited herein.

[†] A company that applies for voluntary membership in C-TPAT is required to sign a 16-page memorandum of understanding stating that it will follow security guidelines established by the program and will submit a security profile regarding procedures it uses to protect its supply chain, including information from its suppliers. CBP 2007; Tuttle 2007.

[‡] The CBP agency was established under the Department of Homeland Security in 2003 to help deter the movement of terrorist and terrorist weapons across U.S. borders. Prior to 2003, the U.S. Customs Service resided under the Department of the Treasury. CBP 2007.

In general, companies that participate in C-TPAT benefit from fewer container searches and faster customs processing of goods that are imported into the United States. In addition, companies under C-TPAT are eligible to participate in the Free and Secure Trade (FAST) program, created to expedite the movement of goods between the U.S.-Canadian and the U.S.-Mexican borders, and a maritime "greenlane" to reduce customs wait times for cargo arriving at U.S. seaports.* Once more, companies that have achieved a higher level or higher tier status within C-TPAT, receive additional customs benefits, such as a guarantee of expedited customs processing during times of elevated security threat levels, and a further reduction in the number of cargo inspections.† According to a 2007 study conducted by the University of Virginia at the request of CBP, the annual cost to a U.S. importer of compliance with C-TPAT is more than $30,000. Approximately 33 percent of the companies surveyed for the study stated that the benefits of the program outweigh the costs, compared with 16 percent who stated that the costs exceed the benefits. Twenty-four percent of the companies surveyed believed that the costs and benefits of participation in C-TPAT are roughly equal (CRS 2007). At the same time, many small- and medium-sized businesses have noted that the costs of compliance with C-TPAT are high enough to deter them from participating in the program (Lodbell 2007).

Under the Container Security Initiative (CSI), begun in January 2002, CBP representatives are placed at foreign seaports where they work with local customs officials to prescreen U.S.-bound containerized cargo (CBP 2007d). Containers are prescreened, in particular, to determine if they are used to transport terrorists or terrorist weapons to the United States. The prescreening process includes a review of customs documentation, along with other intelligence information, to determine which containerized cargo poses a security threat and, if warranted, requires the use of x-ray machines or radiation detection devices to examine the contents of such cargo (CBP 2007d). Potentially dangerous cargo may be further subject to

---

* For a discussion of the FAST program and the greenlane for maritime cargo, see subsequent sections on Mutual Assistance Programs and Post-9/11 Cargo Security Legislation, respectively.

† The C-TPAT program consists of three tiers of participation. Tier 1 participants are those companies that have passed a preliminary review of their supply chain security based on a written profile submitted to the CBP agency and are certified to participate in C-TPAT. Tier 2 participants undergo an on-site inspection by CBP to ensure that their security procedures are sufficient to protect against a terrorist weapon being transported through their supply chain and are then validated as C-TPAT members. Tier 3 participants are certified and validated members of C-TPAT that have security procedures in place which exceed criteria established by CBP under the C-TPAT program. They are rewarded with the most extensive customs benefits. CRS 2006; Feldman 2007.

physical inspection and/or withheld from shipment. At present, 58 foreign ports participate in CSI, with the majority of ports being in Asia and Europe (CBP 2006, 2007g).* The program also allows for reciprocity: customs officials from Canada and Japan are currently stationed at U.S. ports to screen U.S.-outbound containerized cargo destined for these countries. Like C-TPAT, participation in CSI has a trade facilitative effect in that it reduces customs processing at U.S. ports of destination and expedites the clearance of those containers that have been pre-screened at foreign ports (CBP 2007d). The estimated costs to an individual port of participation in CSI were \$230,000 in 2005, which is reported to be significantly less than the amount of annual revenue that would be lost by a port closure due to a terrorist attack (CBP 2006).

POST-9/11 CARGO SECURITY LEGISLATION

Finally, following 9/11, several U.S. policies were set up to address cargo security. The first of these policies is the Maritime Transportation Security Act (MTSA) of 2002, which requires that participants in the U.S. maritime sector, including operators of passenger vessels, cargo vessels, and ports complete security assessments of their facilities and establish procedures to counter the threat of terrorist attacks (DHS 2003). The act recommends that participants deploy specific safety measures to ensure the security of their facilities, such as the screening of both passengers and baggage, the establishment of identification procedures for onsite personnel, and the use of surveillance equipment. In addition, regulations under MTSA provide for the implementation of the Automatic Identification System (AIS), which monitors vessel movement through the electronic exchange of ship-to-ship and ship-to-shore information (DHS 2003).

Also in 2002, the CPB introduced the Operation Safe Commerce (OSC) program and the 24-Hour Advance Manifest Rule. Operation Safe Commerce provides government funding for private-sector initiatives to better secure containerized cargo moving into and out of U.S. ports. Such initiatives may include the development of information systems to

---

* For a listing of ports in the CSI program, see CBP 2007a. Ports that participate in CSI are selected on the basis of the volume of goods that they export to the United States, and whether or not their geographic location makes them likely to be the source of terrorist activity. See CBP 2006, 2007.

track and monitor cargo or the use of electronic seals on cargo containers. Participants in the program represent all levels of the supply chain, including customers, shippers, and transportation firms (DOT 2002). Separately, the 24-hour rule requires ships and nonvessel operating common carriers (NVOCCs)* to provide CBP with a declaration of the items within a U.S.-bound cargo container 24 hours before the container is loaded onto a vessel. The rule permits U.S. Customs to determine if a specific container represents a security threat and, consequently, whether it should be denied further shipment (CBP 2003; Maersk n.d.).

In 2005, the U.S. Senate introduced the GreenLane Maritime Cargo Security Act and, in 2006, the Secure Freight Initiative. The GreenLane Maritime Cargo Security Act provides additional customs benefits to C-TPAT participants if the participants meet certain criteria regarding the screening and inspection of cargo (U.S. Congress 2006; Heritage 2007). These benefits include priority customs processing, reduced cargo or container searches, and the expedited release of goods through customs. The Secure Freight Initiative calls for the increased scanning of U.S.-inbound containers for nuclear or radiological weapons. Under this initiative, nuclear detection equipment is deployed in overseas ports to scan containers before they are transported to the United States. Currently seven foreign ports—including Hong Kong, and those in Honduras, Korea, Oman, Pakistan, Singapore, and the United Kingdom—participate in the program (DHS 2006; CBP 2007c). Finally, also in 2006, Congress passed the Security and Accountability for Every (SAFE) Port Act, which built upon previous U.S. legislation to secure maritime ports and cargo. Among other things, the Act codified into law C-TPAT required the placement of radiation detection equipment in 22 U.S. ports, established a new identification card system for employees at 40 U.S. ports, and set aside $400 million in government funding for port security grants (Edmundson 2006; White House 2007).

FOREIGN-COUNTRY-BASED PROGRAMS

Countries outside of the United States have either updated or introduced new cargo security programs following 9/11. Some of these programs

---

* Nonvessel operating common carriers (NVOCCs) purchase cargo space from shipping lines at wholesale rates and resell such space at retail rates to shipping customers.

contain measures that are compatible with provisions under the U.S.-based program C-TPAT. The following section discusses cargo security programs in the EU, Sweden, Australia, New Zealand, and Canada.

The European Union

In 2005, the European Union introduced a series of measures aimed at protecting the internal EU market, securing international supply chains, and facilitating legitimate cross-border trade through improved customs procedures. These measures, which are embodied within the EU Customs Security Program, introduce three changes to the Community Customs Code* by (1) requiring traders† to provide customs authorities with advance electronic information prior to the import of goods to or the export of goods from the EU (pre-arrival and pre-departure declarations); (2) creating a uniform risk management approach based on common risk-selection criteria for EU-Member States; and (3) creating an AEO program to provide reliable and customs-compliant traders with simplified customs procedures to facilitate legitimate cross-border trade (EC 2006a). Each measure will enter into force at a different time. For example, a new framework to establish EU-wide risk-based procedures entered into force in early 2007, with computerized risk management systems scheduled to be put into place by 2009. At the same time, provisions regarding the AEO program entered into force on January 1, 2008, while requirements for traders to submit to customs authorities advance information on all goods entering or leaving the EU will become mandatory on January 7, 2009 (EC 2006a).

Under the AEO program, reliable and customs-compliant traders will benefit from the streamlining of EU-Member State customs procedures and/or from facilitation with customs controls related to supply chain security or from both (EC 2006a,b). Benefits for operators granted AEO status—dependent on the type of AEO certificate granted—include, among others, the simplification of customs procedures, fewer physical

---

* The Community Customs Code contains the basic customs legislation of the EU customs territory.

† A trader refers to a supply chain participant involved in the cross-border movement of goods. Such entities include, for example, manufacturers, importers, exporters, freight forwarders, warehousing firms, customs agents, and transportation firms.

inspections and documentation requirements, and priority treatment for shipments (EC 2006b, 7, 14; 2006c, L360/67–68).*

Under the program, EU-Member States will be able to grant AEO status to an economic operator involved in the international supply chain that is able to demonstrate a history of compliance with customs requirements, appropriate record-keeping standards, proven financial solvency, and adequate security and safety standards (EC 2005). Economic operators eligible for AEO status include manufacturers, exporters, freight forwarders, warehousing firms, customs agents, transportation firms, and importers. The program is voluntary; economic operators may apply for AEO status through an application process to determine program eligibility based on the criteria outlined above. The application process involves a security self-assessment followed by a formal assessment by the customs authority of an economic operators' risk. The risk assessment is based on the Compliance Partnership Customs and Trade (COMPACT) framework, a methodology that incorporates risk mapping along with security guidelines established under the AEO program.†

Sweden

In addition to the security measures adopted by the European Union at the supranational level, Sweden, an EU-member country, has developed the Stairsec program aimed at improving customs compliance and supply chain security. The Stairsec program is an integrated supply chain security program developed within Sweden's existing Stairway customs accreditation program, which focuses on increasing the quality of customs compliance (Tullvereket 2002). The objective of the Stairsec program is to increase supply chain security through an accreditation process for all private-sector stakeholders in the international supply chain, including importers and exporters, brokers, forwarders independent of transport mode (e.g., air, sea, and land), and terminals. Stairsec became operational

---

* Types of AEO certificates include customs simplification certificates, security and safety certificates, and joint certificates. Holders of either the AEO security and safety certificate or a joint certificate may benefit from reduced data information requirements and prior notification for physical inspection of shipments (effective July 9, 2009).

† The COMPACT framework acts as a pre-audit to determine an economic operator's eligibility for AEO status. If AEO status is granted, customs authorities issue an AEO certificate to the operator. However, if customs authorities conclude that the security profile of an AEO applicant is high risk and requires additional improvements, then the applicant is asked to address such improvements and re-apply for assessment under COMPACT. See EC 2006b.

with the certification of pilot operators on January 15, 2004, following the CSI-certification of the Port of Gothenburg in May 2003. Currently, more than 40 Swedish companies are certified in Stairsec or are in the processing of becoming so (Tukkverket n.d.a.). According to former U.S. CBP Commissioner Robert Bonner, Stairsec mirrors closely the objectives of C-TPAT (Bonner 2004). The two programs are compatible, and discussions between Sweden and the United States on ways C-TPAT and Stairsec can be further harmonized are ongoing (Tullverket n.d.b.).

Australia

Australia's Frontline program, established in 1990, is a cooperative effort between the Australian Customs Service and Australian private-sector firms to deter illegal activities such as drug trafficking, wildlife and flora smuggling, money laundering, and the illegal importation and exportation of prohibited items (Australian Customs 2003). After 9/11, the program shifted its primary focus from the prevention of the movement of narcotics to counterterrorism although the former remains an important program objective (Embassy of Australia 2007a). The Frontline program currently has 705 members that are involved in international trade and transport, including shippers, freight forwarders, airlines, customs brokers, warehousing firms, air couriers, and postal and port authorities (Parliament 2003; Embassy of Australia 2007a). The program is voluntary in nature although membership is essentially by invitation from the Australian customs administration (Parliament 2003). Companies sign a memorandum of understanding (MOU) with customs to formalize the agreement. However, the MOU is not a legally binding or enforceable contract (Australian Customs 2007a). Program participants receive awareness training on illegal drugs and activities and correspond regularly with Australian customs to report any suspicious activities.

Within the context of the WCO SAFE Framework, Australia is conducting an AEO pilot program involving Australian customs, industry, and foreign customs administrations in the Asia-Pacific Economic Cooperation (APEC) region. The aim of the pilot program is to test the AEO application and assessment processes for the security accreditation of supply chain operators (e.g., importers, exporters, freight forwarders, and customs brokers), with the ultimate objective of achieving mutual recognition between Australian Customs and other customs administrations participating in the AEO pilot program (Australian Customs 2007b).

New Zealand

In 2004, the New Zealand Customs Service initiated the Secure Exports Scheme (SES), an export-oriented voluntary partnership between customs and exporters to strengthen security measures that protect goods against tampering when containers are packed and uploaded for shipment (Australian Customs 2007b). To participate in the program, potential SES participants are required to submit advance export information and maintain security measures approved by New Zealand's customs administration in return for greenlane status, or expedited customs processing.* SES partners' security measures comply with standards outlined in the WCO SAFE Framework.

On July 1, 2007 the United States and New Zealand signed a Mutual Recognition Agreement (MRA) under which C-TPAT and SES-certified trading partners receive reciprocal benefits from each other's program. SES-certified trading partners will be eligible for direct benefits such as faster customs clearance times for exports arriving in the United States and reduced customs inspections (New Zealand Embassy 2007).

Canada's Partners in Protection (PIP) Program

Administered by Canada's Border Services Agency (CBSA), the Partners in Protection (PIP) program is a voluntary initiative between CBSA and private-sector firms engaged in international trade to enhance border security, increase awareness of customs compliance issues, help detect and prevent smuggling of contraband goods, and combat organized crime and terrorism (CBSA 2007c). In a cooperative effort based on a voluntary MOU, CBSA and PIP partners develop joint action plans, conduct assessments of security measures, and participate in security awareness sessions (CBSA 2007c). PIP participants benefit from reduced shipment processing times and improved security levels. PIP participants also become eligible to participate in the FAST program developed jointly between Canada and the United States (CBSA 2007a). The Canadian Government plans to harmonize measures established under the PIP program with those of C-TPAT with the eventual goal of mutual recognition between the two programs (CBSA 2007a; Anderson 2007).

---

* The program requires that participants meet formal security guidelines established by New Zealand's customs administration, but also recognizes and incorporates participants' existing security practices (New Zealand Customs 2006; Secker 2007).

Mutual Assistance Programs

Mutual assistance programs are established to harmonize cargo security practices between two or more countries thereby increasing the effectiveness of such practices, while at the same time facilitating the cross-border flow of goods. The United States currently participates in two separate mutual assistance programs: the U.S.-EU Mutual Assistance Agreement and the Free and Secure (FAST) Program between the United States–Canada and the United States–Mexico.

U.S.-EU Mutual Assistance Agreement

In April 2004, the United States and European Union reached an agreement to improve cargo security on a reciprocal basis while ensuring equal levels and standards of control for U.S. and EU ports and operators (Europa 2004). The objective of the agreement is to achieve mutual recognition of C-TPAT and the EU-AEO program. The agreement expanded the existing U.S.-EU Customs Cooperation and Mutual Assistance in Customs Matters Agreement (CMAA), signed in 1997, to include supply chain security (Europa 2004). The new agreement established a U.S.-EU Joint Customs Cooperation Committee (JCCC) and two working groups to identify and examine activities to achieve the objectives outlined in the agreement, including minimum standards for CSI ports, common risk criteria, and trade partnership programs (EC 2007b). In 2007, the 8th U.S.-EU JCCC formalized a work plan to move toward mutual recognition, including an in-depth comparison of C-TPAT and the AEO program, a pilot program to identify and assess any differences between the two programs, and a draft plan outlining additional steps to take toward mutual recognition prior to the formal implementation of the AEO program in 2008 (EC 2007b; EU-U.S. 2007).

Free and Secure (FAST) Program between the United States–Canada and the United States–Mexico

As noted earlier, the FAST program comprises two bilateral initiatives between the United States and Canada and the United States and Mexico that allow pre-approved eligible or low-risk shipments to cross the U.S.–Canadian and U.S.–Mexican borders with greater speed through dedicated highway lanes and with reduced customs inspections (CBSA 2007b; CBP 2007f). Participants eligible for expedited goods clearance under the FAST program include importers, transportation firms, and drivers that are enrolled in C-TPAT and/or the PIP program for U.S.-Canadian highway carriers, or that are enrolled in C-TPAT for U.S.-Mexican highway carriers. By allowing expedited transborder shipments from carriers certified in C-TPAT and/or the PIP program, the FAST program aims to promote increased supply chain security while facilitating legitimate cross-border trade, permitting U.S. Customs to focus resources on high-risk shipments.

Assessment of Post-9/11 Cargo Security Programs

Although cargo security programs had been in place prior to the events of September 11, 2001, post-9/11 cargo security initiatives differ from earlier programs in three important ways. First, although like previous programs, post-9/11 efforts generally target the movement of illegal or dangerous cargo, their primary emphasis is on preventing the cross-border transport of terrorist weapons of mass destruction (WMD). Second, while earlier cargo security programs focused on the role of national customs administrations in policing the transborder movement of goods, post-9/11 programs have engaged private-sector supply chain participants—from manufacturers to importers to transportation providers—in achieving this objective. As such, post-9/11 programs offer a more holistic approach to cargo security by recognizing both the need for cooperation between private-sector entities and customs administrations and by acknowledging the importance of "behind-the-border measures" in securing the international supply chain. Finally, whereas post-9/11 programs have introduced new and additional procedures for screening and clearing cargo through customs, many of these programs also contain trade facilitation components. As noted, such components may be based on the pre-authorization of shippers, the use of risk management techniques, or the simplification of customs documentation requirements. Post-9/11 programs therefore attempt to strike a balance between security and facilitation, recognizing that rather than being mutually exclusive, the two objectives may be mutually reinforcing.

Despite progress in the development of cargo security programs six years after the events of 9/11, some key concerns remain. In particular, participants in post-9/11 cargo security programs have asked whether these programs are effective in securing the international supply chain; what their impact is on cross-border trade; and whether the benefits of compliance with post-9/11 programs outweigh their costs to participants.

Recent studies evaluating post-9/11 cargo security programs offer at least partial answers to these questions. For instance, on the question of efficacy, a May 2005 report completed by the United States Government Accountability Office (GAO) reviewed both the C-TPAT and CSI programs and found that certain factors may compromise their effectiveness in preventing the movement of terrorist weapons. For example, the report stated, among other things, that uniform standards for assessing the supply chain security of C-TPAT members are not in place; that screening equipment used at some CSI ports may not be capable of detecting weapons of mass destruction (WMD); and that ship manifest data, used by CSI officials to prescreen containerized cargo, may often be inaccurate and thereby ineffective in identifying dangerous goods. However, improvements to both these programs continue to be made, some of which may address the above issues (GAO 2005).

Separately, regarding the effect of cargo security measures on cross-border trade, a study conducted by the Conference Board of Canada found that while tighter security along the U.S.-Canadian border has had no measurable impact on the volume of Canadian exports to the United States, it has in many cases increased the overall costs to firms of engaging in U.S.-Canada trade. Some of these costs result directly from companies' compliance with new security measures; others are indirect costs, such as those arising from increased border delays (Conference 2007). Finally, on the issue of whether the benefits of participation in cargo security programs outweigh the costs to individual participants, a study cited earlier in this article by the University of Virginia on C-TPAT found that while the costs of C-TPAT membership are high, compliance with the program may result in several potential benefits to participants such as increased supply chain security, fewer customs inspections, enhanced reputation with customers, and improved inventory control. However, although these so-called "secondary" benefits are important to C-TPAT participants, the majority of the companies surveyed for the study indicated that such benefits have not yet been fully realized (CBP 2007e).

CONCLUSION

Following the events of 9/11, many programs have been developed both at the international and national level to ensure the secure movement of

TABLE AG.1

Selected Post-9/11 Programs on Cargo Security and Trade Facilitation

Program	Year Implemented	Country of Origin	Main Objectives	Participants
The Revised Kyoto Convention	2006	Global	–Customs/trade facilitation –Simplification and harmonization of customs procedures across countries	–52 member countries as of January 2007
WCO SAFE Framework	2005	Global	–Customs/trade facilitation –Supply chain security	–144 member countries as of February 2007
IMO International Ship and Port Facility Security (ISPS) Code	2004	Global	–Maritime port security –Cargo/supply chain security	–National governments –Maritime port facility operators –Shipping firms
International Civil Aviation Organization (ICAO)	(a)	Global	–Air cargo security –Customs/trade facilitation	–Airlines and airports of contracting parties to ICAO
Customs-Trade Partnership Against Terrorism (C-TPAT)	2002	United States	–Security of cargo transported by land, air, and sea into the United States –Supply chain security	–Importers, manufacturers, transportation and logistics firms, customs brokers, warehouse and port terminal operators[b]
Container Security Initiative (CSI)	2002	United States	–Cargo security for U.S.-inbound maritime containers	–Maritime port facility operators of U.S. trade partners[c]

(Continued)

TABLE AG.1 (CONTINUED)

Selected Post-9/11 Programs on Cargo Security and Trade Facilitation

Program	Year Implemented	Country of Origin	Main Objectives	Participants
European Union's Authorized Economic Operator (AEO) Program	2008[d]	European Union	–Customs/trade facilitation –Supply chain security	–Importers, exporters, manufacturers, customs brokers, transportation firms of EU member-states
Stairsec	2004	Sweden	–Customs/trade facilitation –Supply chain security	–Importers, exporters, customs brokers, freight forwarders, and terminal operators
Frontline Program	1990[e]	Australia	–Cargo security, with a new focus on counter-terrorism following 9/11	–Shipping firms, freight forwarders, airlines, customs brokers, warehousing firms, postal and port authorities
Secure Exports Scheme (SES)	2004	New Zealand	–Strengthen and ensure security of New Zealand's containerized exports to its trading partners	–New Zealand's Customs Service and firms involved in exporting goods from New Zealand
U.S.-EU Mutual Assistance Agreement	2004	United States, European Union	–Mutual recognition and harmonization of customs procedures	–Customs administrations and port terminal operators in the United States and the European Union

(Continued)

TABLE AG.1 (CONTINUED)

Selected Post-9/11 Programs on Cargo Security and Trade Facilitation

Program	Year Implemented	Country of Origin	Main Objectives	Participants
Free and Secure (FAST) Program	2002/2003[f]	United States, Canada, and Mexico	–Expedited customs clearance for firms operating between the U.S.-Canadian and U.S.-Mexican borders	–Trucking firms operating along highways between the U.S.-Canadian and U.S.-Mexican borders
Partners in Protection (PIP) Program	1995[g]	Canada	–Enhance security with respect to cargo crossing the Canadian border –Increase customs compliance	–Canadian customs authority and firms involved in U.S.-Canadian cross-border trade

Source: Compiled by USITC staff from various sources.

[a] The agreement establishing ICAO, known as the Chicago Convention, was introduced in 1944. Annexes to the Chicago Convention, including those on air cargo security, have been subsequently amended as recently as 2006.

[b] Although C-TPAT is a U.S.-based program, Canadian and Mexican manufacturers are eligible to enroll in the program, as are highway transportation carriers operating between the United States and Canada and the United States and Mexico.

[c] As of October 2007, 58 foreign maritime ports were participating in the CSI program.

[d] Year the program enters into force.

[e] Although originally introduced in 1990, Australia's Frontline program was revised in response to 9/11.

[f] FAST-Canada was introduced in December 2002, and FAST-Mexico was introduced in September 2003.

[g] According to officials from the Canada Border Services Agency, membership in the PIP program increased notably in the aftermath of 9/11. In 2008, security criteria under PIP will be revised so that the program meets standards under the WCO SAFE Framework and is also more closely aligned with the U.S.-based C-TPAT program.

goods across borders. The United States appears to be at the forefront of these efforts, and has established the most comprehensive cargo security programs to date. Although post-9/11 programs have as their primary focus preventing the cross-border movement of dangerous cargo and, in particular, terrorist-related weapons via the international supply chain, they also contain trade facilitation measures designed to expedite customs processing and enhance trade. Nonetheless, current cargo security programs face certain implementation challenges that some claim may compromise their effectiveness and minimize their potential benefits to participants. Overall, however, as many cargo security programs continue to be refined, conclusions regarding their efficacy, their costs to business, and their effects on trade will likely change, in turn influencing the future direction of these programs.

REFERENCES

American Shipper and Shippers Newswire. 2007. Many Companies Claim C-TPAT Security Program Generates ROI. 2007. April 18. http://www.americanshipper.com (accessed September 6, 2007).

Anderson, Mary. 2007. Canada/U.S. trade special report: Bold leadership for cross-border business. *Canada Sailings.* July 2. http://www.canadiansailings.com/full_story.cfm?articleid=0004&issue=0722&origin=arc_art&cfid=15681344&cftoken=729788 (accessed September 14, 2007).

Asia Pacific Customs News. 2006. New Zealand's secure exports scheme: A success.

Australian Customs Service. 2007a. Frontline fact sheet. Presentation, 86th Annual Conference and Expo, American Association of Exporters and Importers (AAEI). http://www.customs.gov.au/webdata/resources/files/FS_frontline_help_protect_aus_borders1.pdf (accessed August 21, 2007).

———. 2007b. Supply chain security pilot. http://www.customs.gov.au/site/page.cfm?u=5689 (accessed September 7, 2007).

Australian Government, Department of Transport and Regional Services. 2002. International ship and port facility code. December 13. http://www.dotars.gov.au (accessed August 21, 2007).

Bonner, Robert. 2004. Homeland security: The U.S. and the EU are working to protect global trade from terrorism. *European Affairs.* Spring. http://www.ciaonet.org/olj/ea/2004_spring/2004_spring_15.html (accessed September 12, 2007).

Buzdugan, Maria. 2006. Existing and emerging air cargo security and facilitation issues and concerns. http://www.tiaca.org (accessed June 20, 2007).

Canada Border Services Agency (CBSA) website. 2007a. Partners in protection fact sheet. January. http://www.cbsa.gc.ca/media/facts-faits/048-eng.html.

———. 2007b. Staff email official correspondence. October 19.

———. 2007c. Partners in protection. http://www.cbsa.gc.ca/general/enforcement/partners/menu-e.html (accessed September 12, 2007).

Conference Board of Canada. 2007. Reaching a Tipping Point? Effects of Post-9/11 Border Security on Canada's Trade and Investment June. http://www.conferenceboard.ca (accessed September 10, 2007).

Congressional Research Service (CRS). 2006. Port and supply-chain security initiatives in the United States and abroad. Policy Research Report prepared by Leigh B. Boske, Lyndon B. Johnson School of Public Affairs, University of Texas at Austin. http://www.nitl.org/LBJSecurityReport.pdf (accessed June 20, 2007).

Edmondson, R.G. 2006. Congress gets it done. *Journal of Commerce*. October 9.

———. 2007a. Piece by piece on WCO framework. *Journal of Commerce*. February 12.

———. 2007b. A 100 percent mess. *Journal of Commerce*. July 30. http://www.joc.com (accessed July 30).

Embassy of Australia. 2007a. Washington, DC, embassy official staff telephone interview. September 17.

———. 2007b. Washington, DC, embassy official staff email correspondence. September 18.

Embassy of New Zealand. 2007. New Zealand and United States' customs sign trade security arrangement. Washington, DC. July 2. http://www.nzembassy.com/news.cfm?i=3618&c=31&l=86&CFID=7532784&CFTOKEN=66692305 (accessed September 7, 2007).

Europa. 2004. Press release. Customs: Commission Welcomes Signature of Agreement with United States on Expanding Co-operation to Trade Security. Press release IP/04/525 (April 22, 2004). http://europa.eu/rapid/pressReleasesAction.do?reference=IP/04/525&format=HTML&aged=0&language=en&guiLanguage=en (retrieved September 12, 2007).

EC, DG. n.d. Taxation and Customs website, Customs and Security. http://ec.europa.eu/taxation_customs/customs/policy_issues/customs_security/index_en.htm#csp (accessed September 12, 2007).

European Commission (EC). 2005. Commission Regulation No. 648/2005 of the European Parliament and of the Council of 13 April 2005 amending Council Regulation (EEC) No. 2913/92 establishing the Community Customs Code. April 13, 2005. http://eur-lex.europa.eu/LexUriServ/LexUriServ.do?uri=CELEX:32005R0648:en:HTML (accessed August 20, 2007).

———. 2006. Directorate-General. (DG). Taxation and Customs Union, Authorised economic operators: The AEO COMPACT model. Working Document TAXUD/2006/1452 (June 13). http://ec.europa.eu/taxation_customs/resources/documents/customs/policy_issues/customs_security/AEO_compact_model_en.pdf (accessed September 10, 2007).

———. 2007. DG. Taxation and Customs website, Customs and Security. http://ec.europa.eu/taxation_customs/customs/policy_issues/customs_security/index_en.htm#csp (accessed September 12, 2007).

———. 2006a. Supply Chain Security: EU Customs' Role in the Fight Against Terrorism. http://ec.europa.eu/taxation_customs/resources/documents/common/publications/info_docs/customs/customs_security_en.pdf (accessed September 10, 2007).

———. 2006b. Commission Regulation No. 1875/2006, article 14(a), L 360/67B68. December 19.

———. 2007a. Directorate-General (DG) Taxation and Customs, Authorised Economic Operators Guidelines, June 29.

———. 2007b. Customs and Security. http://ec.europa.eu/taxation_customs/customs/policy_issues/customs_security/index_en.htm#csp (accessed September 10, 2007).

European Union-U.S. Joint Customs Cooperation Committee (JCCC). 2007. Working Group on Mutual Recognition. Terms of reference. January 22. http://ec.europa.eu /taxation_customs/resources/documents/customs/policy_issues/customs_security /TOR_MR_en.pdf (accessed September 12, 2007).

Feldman, Lenny. 2007. C-TPAT and border security: The very latest from CBP. *World Trade Interactive.* June 15.

General Agreement on Tariffs and Trade (GATT). 1986. Geneva. July.

GreenLane Maritime Cargo Security Act 2005. 109th Congress, 1st Session, S. 2008, November 15. http://www.theorator.com/bills109/s2008.html (accessed August 30, 2007).

Heritage Foundation. 2006. GreenLane maritime cargo security act: A good first attempt. January 26. http://www.heritage.org (accessed August 30, 2007).

International Air Transport Association (IATA). 2007. Cargo services conference resolutions manual. http://www.iata.org (accessed August 29, 2007).

———. 2006. Simplifying Air Cargo: Cargo Security Strategy. 2006/07BYear 1. http:// www.iata.org (accessed August 21, 2007).

International Maritime Organization (IMO). 2007a. FAQ on ISPS code and maritime security. http://www.imo.org/Safety/mainframe.asp?topic_id=897 (accessed April 26, 2007).

———. 2007b. IMO adopts comprehensive maritime security measures. http://www.imo .org/Safety/mainframe.asp?topic_id=583 (accessed August 21, 2007).

Journal of Commerce Online. 2007. Task force to develop airfreight security strategy. April 9. http://www.joc.com (accessed August 29, 2007).

Kulisch, Eric. 2006. WCO to spell out security rules. *American Shipper.* May.

Labuda, Janet. 2000. Risk management and you. *U.S. Customs Today*, December. http:// www.cbp.gov/custoday/dec2000/risk.htm (accessed August 7, 2007).

Lane, Michael. 2007. Who pays? How much? *Journal of Commerce.* March 19. http://www .joc.com (accessed July 30, 2007).

Lobdell, Karen. 2007. Race for global trade security: Taking security to the next level, presentation. 86th Annual Conference and Expo, American Association of Exporters and Importers (AAEI), DrinkerBiddleGardner&Carton, June 18. New York.

Maersk Logistics. n.d. AU.S. 24-hour rule. http://www.maersklogistics.com (accessed August 30, 2007).

Natter, Ari. 2007. Security at a cost. *Traffic World.* August 13.

New Zealand Customs Service. 2007. Secure exports scheme. http://www.customs.govt .nz (accessed September 7, 2007).

Official Journal of the European Union. 2005. Article 5(a) of Regulation (EC) No. 648/2005 of the European Parliament and of the Council of 13 April 2005 amending Council Regulation (EEC) No. 2913/92 establishing the Community Customs Code, Official Journal of the European Union L 117 (May 4, 2005), 0013B0019. http:// eur-lex.europa.eu/LexUriServ/LexUriServ.do?uri=CELEX:32005R0648:en:HTML (accessed September 10, 2007).

Organization for Economic Co-operation and Development (OECD). 2003a. Price of Increased Maritime Security Is Much Lower than Potential Cost of Major Terrorist Attack. Directorate for Science, Technology and Industry. July 21. http://www.oecd .org (accessed August 23, 2007).

———. 2003b. *Security in Maritime Transport: Risk Factors and Economic Impact*, Maritime Transport Committee, July. http://www.oecd.org (accessed August 23, 2007).

Parliament of Australia. 2003. Senate Legal and Constitutional Legislation Committee, hearing on Australian Customs Service, response to Senator Ludwig (Question No. 98). February 10. http://www.aph.gov.au (accessed August 22, 2007).

Peck, William G. 2006. Don't forget air cargo security. *JOC Online*. October 9. http://www.joc.com (accessed August 29, 2007).

Putzger, Ian. 2007. Questions on Airfreight Security. *Journal of Commerce*. September 17.

Schmitz, Michael. 2007. WCO Director of Compliance and Facilitation, speech on the WCO Framework of Standard and the Implementation of United Nations Security Council Resolution 1540, New York, February 23.

Secker, John. 2007. Supply chain security: Perspective of New Zealand Customs. PowerPoint presentation given at the Secure Trade in the APEC Region (Star V) Conference, Sydney, Australia, June 27–28. http://www.apec2007star.org/pdf/presentations/John_Secker.pdf (accessed September 7, 2007).

Tullverket (Swedish Customs). 2002. The Stairway: The customs system for improved service, higher quality, optimal logistics and more efficient controls. October. http://www.tullverket.se/NR/rdonlyres/624AABD4-3D38-44BA-AC7A-35288A6F3E44/0/stairway_utv_folder2002.pdf (accessed September 9, 2007).

———. n.d.a. Stairsec background. http://www.tullverket.se/en/Business/the_stairsec/Background.htm (accessed August 22, 2007).

———. n.d.b. The Stairsec: CSI-coordinator. http://www.tullverket.se/en/Business/the_stairsec/CSI_coordinator.htm (accessed September 12, 2007).

Tuttle, George R. n.d. Customs-trade partnership against terrorism (C-TPAT). Law Offices of George R. Tuttle. http://www.tuttlelaw.com (accessed September 7, 2007).

U.S. Customs and Border Protection (CBP). 2003. Enforcement of 24-hour rule begins February 2. News release. January 30. http://www.cbp.gov (accessed August 30, 2007).

———. 2006. Container security initiative: 2006–2011 Strategic Plan. August. http://www.cbp.gov (accessed September 7, 2007).

———. 2007a. C-TPAT frequently asked questions. http://www.cbp.gov (accessed September 4, 2007).

———. 2007b. Snapshot: A summary of CBP facts and figures. April. http://www.cbp.gov (accessed September 7, 2007).

———. 2007c. Hong Kong to scan U.S.-bound goods for radiation as part of secure freight initiative. news release. July 27. http://www.cbp.gov (accessed September 4, 2007).

———. 2007d. Fact sheet, August 29. http://www.cbp.gov (accessed September 7, 2007).

———. 2007e. Customs-trade partnership against terrorism: Cost/Benefit Survey. Prepared by the Center for Survey Research, University of Virginia, August. http://www.cbp.gov/xp/cgov/import/commercial_enforcement/ctpat/ (accessed September 10, 2007).

———. 2007f. FAST fact sheet. September. http://www.cbp.gov/xp/cgov/import/commercial_enforcement/ctpat/fast (accessed September 12, 2007).

———. 2007g. Ports in CSI. September 25. http://www.cbp.gov/xp/cgov/border_security/international_activities/csi/ports_in_csi.xml (accessed October 3, 2007).

———. n.d. The 2% myth. http://www.cbp.giv/xp/cgov/border_security/antiterror_iniatives/2myth.xml (accessed August 7, 2007).

U.S. Government Accounting Office (GAO). 2005. Key Cargo Security Programs Can Be Improved. Statement of Richard M. Stana, Director, Homeland Security and Justice Issues. Testimony Before the Permanent Subcommittee on Investigations, Committee on Homeland Security and Governmental Affairs, U.S. Senate. Homeland Security: May 26. http://www.gao.gov (accessed September 14, 2005).

U.S. Department of Homeland Security (DHS). 2003. Protecting America's Ports: Maritime Transportation Security Act of 2002. http://www.uscg.mil/news/Headquarters /MTSAPressKit.pdf (accessed August 30, 2007).

———. 2006. DHS and DOE launch secure freight initiative. News release. December 7. http://www.dhs.gov (accessed August 30, 2007).

U.S. Department of Transportation (DOT) and U.S. Customs Service. 2002. DOT and Customs launch "Operation SAFE commerce" program. News release. November 20. http://www.dot.gov/affairs/dot10302.htm (accessed August 30, 2007).

U.S. Senate. 2003. Air Cargo Security Act (Introduced in Senate). 108th Congress. 1st Session, S. 165, January 15.

The White House. Office of the Press Secretary. 2007. President Bush signs SAFE port act. News release. October 13. http://www.whitehouse.gov/news/releases/2006 (accessed June 7, 2007).

Widdowson, David. 2007. Changing role of Customs: Evolution or revolution? *World Customs Journal.* March. http://www.worldcustomsjournal.org (accessed June 20, 2007).

World Bank. 2000. *Kyoto Convention*, Chapter 7: Application of Information Technology. http://www.wcoomd.org. Date of entry into force—February 3, 2007.

———. 2005. *Customs Modernization Handbook.* Edited by Luc De Wulf and Jose B. Sokol.

World Customs Organization (WCO). 2005. *Framework to secure and facilitate trade.* June. http://www.wcoomd.org (accessed February 15, 2007).

———. n.d.a. Information note: WCO instruments and GATT articles V, VIII and X. http://www.wcoomd.org (accessed August 10, 2007).

———. n.d.b. WCO instruments and programmes: Customs procedures and trade facilitation. http://www.wcoomd.org (accessed August 7, 2007).

World Shipping Council. 2002. Comments of the World Shipping Council regarding Operation Safe Commerce, Submitted to the Department of Transportation, Transportation Security Administration, December 5. http://www.wsc.org (accessed August 31, 2007).

World Trade Interactive. 2007. CBP announces operations at two Panamanian ports. 2007. October 1.

World Trade Organization. (WTO). 2005a. Negotiating Group on Trade Facilitation, Clarification and Improvement of Article VIII of the GATT: Reducing Administrative Burdens. TN/TF/W/18, March 16.

———. 2005b. Possible Commitments on Border Agency Coordination, Communication from Canada, TN/TF/W/20. March 18.

———. 2005c. Explanatory Note on Risk Management: Japan's Experience, TN/TF/W/42. June 3.

———. 2005d. Explanatory Note on Pre-Arrival Examination: Japan's Experience, TN/ TF/W/53. July 15.

———. 2007. Summary Minutes of the Meeting. TN/TF/M/17, May 11.

Appendix H: North American Free Trade Agreement*

Free-trade agreements represent a leverage method to gain competitive advantage in global trade, opening the door for growth and expansion. The following overview of the North American Free Trade Agreement (NAFTA) between the United States, Canada, and Mexico presents the details necessary to comprehend this important trade-facilitation law that encourages international partnerships.

On January 1, 1994, the NAFTA entered into force. All remaining duties and quantitative restrictions were eliminated, as scheduled, on January 1, 2008. NAFTA created the world's largest free trade area, which now links 450 million people producing $17 trillion worth of goods and services.

Trade between the United States and its NAFTA partners has soared since the agreement entered into force. U.S. goods and services trade with NAFTA totaled $1.2 trillion in 2012 (latest data available). Exports totaled $597 billion; imports totaled $646 billion. The U.S. goods and services trade deficit with NAFTA was $49 billion in 2012.

The United States has $1.1 trillion in total (two ways) goods trade with NAFTA countries (Canada and Mexico) during 2013. Goods exports

---

* From the author's personal notes.

totaled $527 billion; goods imports totaled $613 billion. The U.S. goods trade deficit with NAFTA was $86 billion in 2013.

Trade in services with NAFTA (exports and imports) totaled $134 billion in 2012 (latest data available). Services exports were $89 billion; services imports were $45 billion. The U.S. services trade surplus with NAFTA was $44 billion in 2012.

EXPORTS

- The NAFTA countries (Canada and Mexico), were the top two purchasers of U.S. exports in 2013 (Canada, $300.3 billion, and Mexico, $226.2 billion).
- U.S. goods exports to NAFTA in 2013 were $526.5 billion, up 3.5% ($18 billion) from 2012 and up 97% from 2003. It was up 271% from 1993 (pre-NAFTA). U.S. exports to NAFTA accounted for 33.3% of overall U.S. exports in 2013.
- The top export categories (two-digit harmonized system [HS]) in 2013 were machinery ($83.8 billion), vehicles (parts) ($73.3 billion), electrical machinery ($63.4 billion), mineral fuel and oil ($47.7 billion), and plastic ($28.3 billion).
- U.S. exports of agricultural products to NAFTA countries totaled $39.4 billion in 2013. Leading categories include processed food ($2.6 billion), fresh fruits ($2.5 billion), beef and beef products ($2.1 billion), pork and pork products ($2.1 billion), dairy products ($2.0 billion), and fresh vegetables ($2.0 billion).
- U.S. exports of private commercial services* (i.e., excluding military and government) to NAFTA were $88.6 billion in 2012 (latest data available), up 5.4% ($4.5 billion) from 2011, and up 109% since 2002. It was up 223% from 1993 (pre-NAFTA).

IMPORTS

- The NAFTA countries were the second and third largest suppliers of goods imports to the United States in 2013 (Canada, $332.1 billion, and Mexico, $280.5 billion).

- U.S. goods imports from NAFTA totaled $612.5 billion in 2013, up 1.8% ($11 billion) from 2012 and up 70% from 2003. It was up 305% from 1993 (pre-NAFTA). U.S. imports from NAFTA accounted for 27.0% of overall U.S. imports in 2013.
- The five largest categories in 2013 were mineral fuel and oil (crude oil) ($144.2 billion), vehicles ($115.3 billion), electrical machinery ($65.3 billion), machinery ($62.4 billion), and special other (returns) ($15.8 billion).
- U.S. imports of agricultural products from NAFTA countries totaled $39.4 billion in 2013. Leading categories included fresh vegetables ($5.8 billion), snack foods (including chocolate) ($4.7 billion), fresh fruit (excluding bananas) ($3.3 billion), processed fruit and vegetables ($2.6 billion), and red meats (fresh/chilled/frozen) ($2.4 billion).
- U.S. imports of private commercial services* (i.e., excluding military and government) were $44.9 billion in 2012 (latest data available), up 6.1% ($2.6 billion) from 2011 and up 52% since 2002. It was up 171% from 1993 (pre-NAFTA).

TRADE BALANCES

- The U.S. goods trade deficit with NAFTA was $86.0 billion in 2013, a 7.5% decrease ($7 billion) over 2012. The U.S. goods trade deficit with NAFTA accounted for 12.5% of the overall U.S. goods trade deficit in 2013.
- The United States had a services trade surplus of $43.7 billion with NAFTA countries in 2012 (latest data available), up 4.6% from 2011.

INVESTMENT

- U.S. foreign direct investment (FDI) in NAFTA countries (stock) was $452.5 billion in 2012 (latest data available), up 7.1% from 2011.
- U.S. direct investment in NAFTA countries is led by the nonbank holding companies, manufacturing, and finance/insurance sectors.

- NAFTA countries FDI in the United States (stock) was $240.2 billion in 2012 (latest data available), up 7.3% from 2011.
- NAFTA countries direct investment in the United States is in the finance/insurance, banking, and manufacturing sectors.
- Sales of services in NAFTA by majority U.S.-owned affiliates were $163.3 billion in 2011 (latest data available), while sales of services in the United States by majority EU-owned firms were $79.5 billion.

Appendix I: Terms of Trade*

Following are basic terms of trade to help guide you through any international trade deal!

ad valorem tariff: A tariff calculated "according to value," or as a percentage of the value of goods cleared through customs; for example, 15% ad valorem means 15% of the value of the entered merchandise.

ATA Carnet: A.k.a. "merchandise passport"; a document that facilitates the temporary importation of products into foreign countries by eliminating tariffs and value-added taxes (VATs) or the posting of a security deposit normally required at the time of importation.

commodity: Any article exchanged in trade but most commonly used to refer to raw materials, including such minerals as tin, copper, and manganese and bulk-produced agricultural products such as coffee, tea, and rubber.

consumers: Individuals or groups that use economic goods and services, thus deriving utility from them.

consumer goods: Goods that directly satisfy human desires (as opposed to capital goods). An automobile used for pleasure is considered a consumer good. An automobile used by a business person to deliver wares is considered a capital good.

consumption: The purchase and utilization of goods or services for the gratification of human desires or in the production of other goods or services. The consumer may be an individual, a business firm, a public body, or other entity.

countervailable subsidy: Foreign governments subsidize industries when they provide financial assistance to benefit the production, manufacture, or exportation of goods. Subsidies can take many forms, such as direct cash payments, credits against taxes, and loans at terms that do not reflect market conditions. The statute and regulations establish standards for determining when an unfair subsidy has been conferred. The amount of subsidies the foreign producer receives from the government is the basis for the subsidy rate by which the subsidy is offset, or "countervailed," through higher import duties.

---

* From Department of Commerce and the author's prior work.

countervailing duties (CVDs): Specific duties imposed on imports to offset the benefits of subsidies to producers or exporters in the exporting country.

demand: The quantity of an economic good that will be bought at a given price at a particular time in a specific market. Demand in a market economy is strongly influenced by consumer preference or the individual choices of many independent buyers, based upon their perceptions of value for price.

dumping: A situation where a foreign producer sells a product in the United States at a price that is below that producer's sales price in the country of origin (home market), or at a price that is lower than the cost of production. The difference between the price (or cost) in the foreign market and the price in the U.S. market is called the dumping margin. Unless the conduct falls within the legal definition of dumping as specified in U.S. law, a foreign producer selling imports at prices below those of American products is not necessarily dumping.

exports: Goods and services produced in one country and sold in other countries in exchange for goods and services, gold, foreign exchange, or settlement of debt. Countries devote their domestic resources to exports because they can obtain more goods and services with the international exchange they earn from the exports than they would from devoting the same resources to the domestic production of goods and services.

free trade: A theoretical concept that assumes international trade unhampered by government measures such as tariffs or nontariff barriers. The objective of trade liberalization is to achieve "freer trade" rather than "free trade," it being generally recognized among trade-policy officials that some restrictions on trade are likely to remain in effect for the foreseeable future.

goods: Inherently useful and relatively scarce articles or commodities produced by the manufacturing, mining, construction, and agricultural sectors of the economy. Goods are important economically because they may be exchanged for money or other goods and services.

harmonization: The process of making procedures or measures applied by different countries—especially those affecting international trade—more compatible, as by effecting simultaneous tariff cuts applied by different countries so as to make their tariff structures more uniform.

import: The inflow of goods and services into a country's market for consumption. A country enhances its welfare by importing a broader range of higher-quality goods and services at lower cost than it could produce domestically. The expansion of world trade since the end of World War II has therefore been a principal factor underlying a general rise in living standards in most countries.

Incoterms: A set of rules that define the responsibilities of sellers and buyers for the delivery of goods under sales contracts for domestic and international trade. They are published by the International Chamber of Commerce (ICC) and are widely used in international commercial transactions. The most recent version of Incoterms, Incoterms 2010, was launched in September 2010 and became effective on January 1, 2011.

The two main categories of Incoterms 2010 are now organized by modes of transport. Used in international as well as in domestic contracts for the first time, the new groups aim to simplify the drafting of contracts and help avoid misunderstandings by clearly stipulating the obligations of buyers and sellers.

Group 1: Incoterms That Apply to Any Mode of Transport

EXW: ex works

FCA: free carrier

CPT: carriage paid to

CIP: carriage and insurance paid to

DAT: delivered at terminal

DAP: delivered at place

DDP: delivered duty paid

Group 2: Incoterms That Apply to Sea and Inland Waterway Transport Only

FAS: free alongside ship

FOB: free on board

CFR: cost and freight

CIF: cost, insurance, and freight

market access: The ability of domestic providers of goods and services to penetrate a related market in a foreign country. The extent to which the foreign market is accessible generally depends on the existence and extent of trade barriers.

market economy: The national economy of a country that relies on market forces to determine levels of production, consumption, investment, and savings without government intervention.

market forces: Shifts in demand and supply that are reflected in changing relative prices, thus serving as indicators and guides for enterprises that make investment, purchase, and sales decisions.

services: Economic activities—such as transportation, banking, insurance, tourism, telecommunications, advertising, entertainment, data processing, and consulting—that normally are consumed as they are produced, as contrasted with economic goods that are more tangible. Service industries, which are usually labor intensive, have become increasingly important in domestic and international trade since at least the 1920s. Services account for about two-thirds of the economic activity of the United States and for a rapidly increasing percentage of U.S. exports.

subsidy: An economic benefit granted by a government to domestic producers of goods or services, often to strengthen their competitive position.

supply: The quantity of an economic good that sellers will make available at a given price at a certain time in a specific market. A supply schedule indicates the quantity of an economic good that might enter the market at all possible prices at a particular time. Supply in a market economy is principally determined by the response of many individual entrepreneurs and firms to their perceptions of opportunities for earning profits.

surplus: The amount of a commodity that cannot be absorbed in a given market at the existing price.

tariff: A duty (or tax) levied upon goods transported from one customs area to another either for protective or revenue purposes. Tariffs raise the prices of imported goods, thus making them generally less competitive within the market of the importing country unless that country does not produce the items so tariffed.

trade barriers: Government laws, regulations, policies, or practices that either protect domestic products from foreign competition or artificially stimulate exports of particular domestic products.

Appendix J: Finding Qualified Buyers and Expanding into Overseas Markets*

By now, your company has identified its most promising markets and devised a strategy to enter those markets. As discussed earlier, your company may sell directly to a customer or may use the assistance of an in-country representative (agents or distributors) to reach the end user. This section describes some of the sources that can help you find buyers, evaluate trade shows and missions, and generate sales.

U.S. DEPARTMENT OF COMMERCE WORLDWIDE BUYER-FINDING PROGRAMS

The U.S. Department of Commerce can help exporters identify and qualify leads for potential buyers, distributors, joint-venture partners, and licensees from both private and public sources. Along with its experts in various products, countries, and programs, the U.S. Department of Commerce has an extensive network of commercial officers posted in countries that represent 95% of the market for U.S. products.

Programs available through the U.S. Department of Commerce, including those of the U.S. Commercial Service, are listed in this section. Exporters should contact the nearest Export Assistance Center for more information or call the Trade Information Center at (800) USA-TRADE (800-872-8723). Information on these programs is also available at the Commercial Service website.

BuyUSA.gov Matchmaking

BuyUSA.gov matchmaking is a convenient online program of the U.S. Commercial Service that matches U.S. exporters with buyers and importers in overseas markets. On the basis of the profiles that companies send

---

* From Department of Commerce.

to BuyUSA.gov, U.S. exporters receive the information that they need to contact potential importers in the overseas markets they select. There is no need to search a database or return to check for new importers; when an importer registers with a profile that matches your export objectives, BuyUSA.gov matchmaking will automatically notify you. Whether you contact the potential importers is up to you, so you will not receive unwanted contacts by registering for the program.

Commercial News USA

Commercial News USA (CNUSA) is the official U.S. Department of Commerce showcase for American-made products and services. It provides worldwide exposure for U.S. products and services through an illustrated catalog-magazine and through electronic bulletin boards. CNUSA is designed to help U.S. companies promote products and services to buyers in more than 145 countries. Each issue of the free bimonthly catalog-magazine reaches an estimated 400,000 readers worldwide. CNUSA is mailed directly to qualified recipients and is also distributed by Commercial Service personnel at U.S. embassies and consulates throughout the world.

CNUSA can help your company make sales. Its features include the following:

- **Direct response.** New customers around the world will read about your product or service and will receive information that enables them to contact you directly. Address-coded trade leads make it easy to track results.
- **Built-in credibility.** Distributed by U.S. Commercial Service officials at embassies and consulates, CNUSA enjoys exceptional credibility.
- **Follow-up support.** The U.S. Department of Commerce offers free individual export counseling at any of the Export Assistance Centers across the country. For the center nearest you call (800) USA-TRADE (800-872-8723), or visit www.export.gov/eac/.

For more information, visit the CNUSA home page.

Featured U.S. Exporters

Featured U.S. Exporters (FUSE) is a directory of U.S. products presented on the websites of many U.S. Commercial Service offices around the world. It gives your company an opportunity to target markets in specific countries in the local language of business. This service is offered free of charge to qualified U.S. exporters seeking trade leads or representation in certain markets. To find out if your company qualifies and to request a free listing, visit www.buyusa.gov/home/fuse.html.

Customized Market Research

Customized market research reports use the Commercial Service's world-wide network to help U.S. exporters evaluate their sales potential in a market, choose the best new markets for their products and services, establish effective marketing and distribution strategies in their target markets, identify the competition, determine which factors are most important to overseas buyers, pinpoint impediments to exporting, and understand many other pieces of critical market intelligence. These customized reports will be built to your specifications. To order a customized market research report, contact your local Export Assistance Center (see www.export.gov/eac/).

Gold Key Matching Service

The Gold Key Matching Service is a customized buyer-finding solution offered by the Commercial Service in key export markets around the world. The service includes orientation briefings; market research; appointments with potential partners; interpreter services for meetings; and assistance in closing the deal, shipping the goods, and getting paid. To request a Gold Key Matching Service, contact your local Export Assistance Center (see www.export.gov/eac/).

International Company Profiles

An International Company Profile (ICP) is a background report on a specific foreign firm that is prepared by commercial officers of the United States Commercial Service at American embassies and consulates. These reports include the following:

- Information on the firm
- Year established
- Relative size
- Number of employees

- General reputation
- Territory covered
- Language capabilities
- Product lines handled
- Principal owners
- Financial references
- Trade references

Each ICP also contains a general narrative report by the U.S. Commercial Service officer who conducted the investigation concerning the reliability of the foreign firm.

The ICP service is offered in countries that lack adequate private-sector providers of credit and background information on local companies. Credit reports on foreign companies are available from many private-sector sources, including (in the United States) Dun and Bradstreet and Graydon International. For help in identifying private-sector sources of credit reports, contact your nearest Export Assistance Center.

International Partner Search

With the U.S. Commercial Service's International Partner Search, teams of experts in more than 80 countries work to find you the most suitable strategic partners. You provide your marketing materials and a background on your company. The Commercial Service uses its strong network of international contacts to interview potential partners and to provide you with a list of up to five prescreened companies. By working only with pre-screened firms that are interested in buying or selling your products and services, you save valuable time and money.

The International Partner Search allows you to obtain high-quality market information in 15 days. The search yields information on each potential partner's size, sales, years in business, and number of employees, as well as a statement from each potential partner on the marketability of your product or service. You will also receive complete contact information on key individuals among the potential partners who are interested in your company. To obtain more information or to order an International Partner Search, contact your local Export Assistance Center.

DEPARTMENT OF COMMERCE TRADE-EVENT PROGRAMS

Some products, because of their nature, are difficult to sell unless the potential buyer has an opportunity to examine them in person. Sales letters and brochures can be helpful, but an actual presentation of products in the export market may prove more beneficial. One way for your company to actually present its products to an overseas market is by participating in trade events such as trade shows, fairs, trade missions, matchmaker delegations, and catalog exhibitions.

Trade fairs are "shop windows" where thousands of firms from many countries display their goods and services. They serve as a marketplace where buyers and sellers can meet with mutual convenience. Some fairs, especially in Europe, have a history that goes back centuries. Also, it is often easier for buyers from certain regions of the world to gather in Europe than the United States.

Attending trade fairs involves a great deal of planning. The potential exhibitor must take into account the following logistic considerations:

- Choosing the proper fair out of the hundreds that are held every year
- Obtaining space at the fair, along with designing and constructing the exhibit
- Shipping products to the show, along with unpacking and setting up
- Providing proper hospitality, such as refreshments, along with maintaining the exhibit
- Being able to separate serious business prospects from browsers
- Breaking down, packing, and shipping the exhibit home at the conclusion of the fair

A trade magazine or association can often provide information on major shows. Whether privately run or government sponsored, many trade shows have a U.S. pavilion that is dedicated to participating U.S. businesses. For additional guidance, contact your local Export Assistance Center or visit www.export.gov/tradeevents. You can find a complete list of trade events online, and you can search by country, state, industry, or date.

Examples of trade shows are Medtrade, which takes place annually and is geared toward the healthcare services sector, and the Automotive Aftermarket Industry Week, which is also held annually and is attended by companies in various parts of the automotive industry.

International Buyer Program

The International Buyer Program (IBP) supports major domestic trade shows featuring products and services of U.S. industries with high export potential. Commercial Service officers recruit prospective foreign buyers to attend selected trade shows. The shows are extensively publicized in targeted markets through embassy and regional commercial newsletters, catalog-magazines, foreign trade associations, chambers of commerce, travel agents, government agencies, corporations, import agents, and equipment distributors.

As a U.S. exhibitor at an IBP event, you will receive many valuable free benefits, including the following:

- Opportunities to meet with prospective foreign buyers, representatives, and distributors from all over the world who have been recruited by U.S. Commercial Service specialists in more than 150 cities overseas
- Worldwide promotion of your products and services through the Export Interest Directory, which is published by the show organizers and distributed to all international visitors attending the show
- Access to hundreds of current international trade leads in your industry
- Hands-on export counseling, marketing analysis, and matchmaking services by country and industry experts from the U.S. Commercial Service
- Use of an on-site international business center, where your company can meet privately with prospective international buyers, sales representatives, and business partners and can obtain assistance from experienced U.S. Commercial Service staff members

Each year, the Commercial Service selects and promotes more than 30 trade shows representing leading industrial sectors, including information technology, environmental products and services, medical equipment and supplies, food processing and services, packaging, building and construction products, sporting goods, and consumer products.

For more information, visit www.export.gov/ibp.

Trade Fair Certification Program

The U.S. Department of Commerce's Trade Fair Certification program is a partnership arrangement between private-sector show organizers and the International Trade Administration to assist and encourage U.S. firms to promote their products at appropriate trade fairs abroad. Certification of a U.S. organizer signals to exhibitors, visitors, and the government of the host country that the event is an excellent marketing opportunity and that participants will receive the support of the U.S. government. Certified organizers are authorized to recruit and manage a U.S. pavilion at the show. They are especially focused on attracting small and medium-sized U.S. firms that are new to the market. Certified organizers can help with all aspects of freight forwarding, customs clearance, exhibit design, and on-site services.

Certified organizers receive government assistance, such as the following:

- Designation as the official U.S. pavilion
- Authorized use of an official Commercial Service certification logo
- On-site support and counseling for U.S. exhibitors from the U.S. embassy commercial staff
- Local market information and contact lists
- Press releases and other promotion actions
- Advertising and marketing assistance from Commerce Department's Export Assistance Centers
- Support letters from the secretary of commerce and the president of the United States when appropriate
- Exhibitor briefings
- Opening ceremonies, ribbon-cuttings, and dignitary liaison

For more information, visit www.export.gov/tradeevents.

Trade Missions

The U.S. Department of Commerce organizes or supports numerous trade missions each year. The missions involve travel to foreign countries by U.S. companies and Commerce Department employees. Participants meet face to face with prescreened international businesspeople in the market they travel to. Trade missions save U.S. companies time and money by allowing them to maximize contact with qualified distributors, sales representatives, or partners. U.S. Commercial Service missions are industry specific and target two to four countries per trip. Commercial Service specialists abroad will prescreen contacts, arrange business appointments, and coordinate logistics in advance. This preparatory effort is followed up by a one-week trip by the U.S. company to personally meet with the new prospects.

To learn more about trade missions, and for a list of upcoming trade missions, visit www.export.gov/tradeevents.

International Catalog Exhibition Program

The U.S. Commercial Service's International Catalog Exhibition program offers U.S. companies a convenient, affordable way to stimulate interest in their products and services while never leaving the office. Commercial Service trade specialists located in international markets will translate the company profile into the local language, display the company's marketing materials, collect sales leads from interested local buyers, and then assist the U.S. company as it follows up with the local contacts. There are three types of catalog events:

- Multistate catalog exhibitions target four or more promising international markets, promote U.S. exports in 20 or more high-demand product and service sectors, and leverage the partnership between the Department of Commerce and state economic development agencies.
- American Product Literature Centers target a single promising international market, focus on a single industry sector, and typically take place at a leading industry trade show.
- U.S. embassy and consulate–sponsored catalog exhibits target a single promising international market and are managed by a U.S. embassy or consulate.

For all three types of catalog events, the U.S. Commercial Service will coordinate support from local chambers of commerce, industry associations, and other trade groups; provide trade leads generated by each exhibition; and help capitalize on leads by providing any needed export assistance. For a complete list of catalog events, visit www.export.gov /tradeevents.

U.S. DEPARTMENT OF AGRICULTURE, FOREIGN AGRICULTURAL SERVICE

Through a network of counselors, attachés, trade officers, commodity analysts, and marketing specialists, the Department of Agriculture's

Foreign Agricultural Service (FAS) can help arrange contacts overseas and provide marketing assistance for companies that export agricultural commodities. Extensive information on the FAS is also available on the Internet. Visit the Department of Agriculture's FAS web site at www.fas .usda.gov.

U.S. AGENCY FOR INTERNATIONAL DEVELOPMENT

The U.S. Agency for International Development (USAID) administers programs that offer export opportunities for U.S. suppliers of professional technical assistance services and commodities. Opportunities to export commodities are available through the commodity import programs that USAID operates in select USAID-recipient countries and through USAID's direct procurement of commodities. In addition, USAID funds may be available in certain recipient countries to finance developmentally sound projects involving U.S. capital goods and services. For exporters traveling to developing countries where a USAID program is in place, information is available on funds, projects under consideration, and contacts. Talk to someone at the nearest Export Assistance Center or call (800) USAID-4U (800-872-4348). The USAID website may be accessed at www.usaid.gov.

U.S. TRADE AND DEVELOPMENT AGENCY

The U.S. Trade and Development Agency (TDA) assists in the creation of jobs for Americans by helping U.S. companies pursue overseas business opportunities. Through the funding of feasibility studies, orientation visits, specialized training grants, business workshops, and various forms of technical assistance, TDA helps American businesses compete for infrastructure and industrial projects in emerging markets.

TDA's mission is to help companies get in on the ground floor of export opportunities and to make them competitive with heavily subsidized foreign companies. Because of its focused mission, TDA considers only infrastructure and industrial projects that have the potential to mature into significant export opportunities for American companies and to create jobs in the United States. Projects are typically in the areas of agriculture, energy and power, health care, manufacturing, mining and minerals development, telecommunications, transportation, and environmental services.

To be considered for TDA funding, projects

- Must face strong competition from foreign companies that receive subsidies and other support from their governments
- Must be a development priority of the country where the project is located and have the endorsement of the U.S. embassy in that nation
- Must represent an opportunity for sales of U.S. goods and services that is many times greater than the cost of TDA assistance
- Must be likely to receive implementation financing and have a procurement process open to U.S. firms

Contact TDA at (703) 875-4357, or visit its website at http://www.ustda .gov/ for more information.

STATE AND LOCAL GOVERNMENT ASSISTANCE

Most states can provide an array of services to exporters. Many states maintain international offices in major markets; the most common locations are in Western Europe and Japan. Working closely with the commercial sections of U.S. embassies in those countries, state foreign offices can assist exporters in making contacts in foreign markets, providing such services as the following:

- Specific trade leads with foreign buyers
- Assistance for trade missions, such as itinerary planning, appointment scheduling, travel, and accommodations
- Promotional activities for goods or services, including representing the state at trade shows
- Help in qualifying potential buyers, agents, or distributors

In addition, some international offices of state development organizations help set up and promote foreign buyer missions to the United States, which can be effective avenues of exporting with little effort. Attracting foreign investment and developing tourism are also very important activities of state foreign offices. More and more cities and counties are providing these same services.

PROMOTION IN PUBLICATIONS AND OTHER MEDIA

A large and varied assortment of magazines covering international markets is available to you through U.S. publishers. They range from specialized international magazines relating to individual industries, such as construction, beverages, and textiles, to worldwide industrial magazines covering many industries. Many consumer publications produced by U.S.-based publishers are also available. Several are produced in national-language editions (e.g., Spanish for Latin America), and some offer "regional buys" for specific export markets of the world. In addition, several business directories published in the United States list foreign representatives geographically or by industry specialization.

Publishers frequently supply potential exporters with helpful market information, make specific recommendations for selling in the markets they cover, help advertisers locate sales representation, and render other services to aid international advertisers.

Many of these magazines and directories are available at libraries, Export Assistance Centers, or the U.S. Department of Commerce's reference room in Washington, D.C. State departments of commerce, trade associations, business libraries, and major universities may also provide such publications.

FACT: Most U.S. exporters simply take orders from abroad rather than vigorously marketing their products or services.

INSIGHT: U.S. government agencies, particularly the U.S. Commercial Service, can help you strategically increase your international sales by identifying and qualifying leads for potential buyers, distributors, and other partners.

FACT: According to the World Health Organization, diarrhea causes 1.6 million deaths every year—the vast majority among children under five years. Those deaths are related to unsafe water, sanitation, and hygiene. More than a billion people lack access to a clean water source.

INSIGHT: By building infrastructure in the developing world, U.S. companies are improving the quality of life of millions of people and are saving lives.

Appendix K: Example of Landed-Cost Modeling Standard Operating Procedure*

Effective January 1, 2016, all divisions of XYZ Corp. will utilize a landed-cost calculator for import shipments in determining the "true and real" cost to XYZ Corp. when comparing vendor options in the decision-making process. It is critical that we comprehensively understand what our total costs are in making the decisions on where, what, and how much we buy from overseas or domestic suppliers. We also need to document this process in our product files.

Following is an outline of what landed costs are as an overview in general, followed by some additional thoughts on specifically sourcing from China, where the majority of our imports derive from. This SOP concludes with a draft calculator that should be utilized as a guide for actually determining landed costs for our products.

WHAT IS LANDED COST?

Establishing landed costs for the products a company has in their profile can be difficult and convoluted. All businesses that import or export need to understand what the total cost of goods is for what they are buying or selling. In order to accurately calculate the landed cost, all factors beyond the obvious primary price must be considered. Calculating landed cost is critical in understanding what a product actually costs and therefore what it can be sold for. Landed cost also impacts margin considerations, which are one of the most important aspects of managing a business in a public market.

---

* From U.S.T.R.

LANDED COST DEFINITION

Landed cost is the total cost of a product once it has arrived at the purchaser's door. This list of components that are needed to determine landed costs include the original cost of the item, all brokerage and logistics fees, complete shipping costs, customs duties, tariffs, taxes, insurance, currency conversion, crating costs, and handling fees. Not all of these components are present in every shipment, but all that exist must be considered part of the landed cost.

Clearly it is advantageous to reduce the cost of each or any component of landed cost. Each one will allow the purchaser to lower their final selling price or increase the margin associated with their sale.

When considering the landed cost or true cost of any item that is shipped internationally, there are components that need to be included. For instance, determining harmonized tariff (HTS) codes is essential for over 98% of global trade. Once the HTS code is obtained, the applicable duties and tariffs can be established. Accuracy of these harmonized codes is of significant importance as misclassification will result in incorrect tariff codes, incorrect duties, and possible customs delays and fines. When customs delays and fines are levied, they themselves need to be calculated into the landed cost model as demurrage, penalties, etc.

Global trade management, supply-chain management, and international logistics all have many moving parts. In this economic climate, trade agreements may also be entered into to obtain preferential tariff treatment. These trade agreements are ultimately based on the HTS code. Trade agreements and HTS codes vary from place to place, cost of fuel can drastically affect shipping costs, currency valuations ebb and flow constantly, and the list of variables goes on and on. Limiting the variables to a manageable few will streamline operations and keep overall cost structures as stable as possible.

Additional variables such as, but not limited to, quantity purchased, choice of Incoterm, insurance, inland freight charges, storage, and warehousing all impact landed costs but are often not considered by purchasing and sourcing personnel at the time of product acquisition.

Controlling costs, ensuring timely deliveries and customs compliance are serious issues that every international business is concerned with. Landed cost is a significant component of all of these concerns. Establishing a landed cost model is not just important; it is essential.

ADDITIONAL CONSIDERATIONS

How to Calculate Landed Cost When Importing from China

From an importer's viewpoint, made in China is a good choice for many products that can sell locally or online with a good profit. While XYZ Corp. purchases goods from all over the world and this diversity will continue to grow, China presents itself as one of the largest sources of imported goods.

Making sure we are earning the correct margins on merchandise sales from China is a key responsibility of all purchasing and sourcing managers. Additionally, supply chain and logistics considerations must be contemplated. Therefore those XYZ Corp. managers with these specific responsibilities must include these additional factors as part of their landed cost model.

Congruently, XYZ Corp.'s trade-compliance consultants must be in the information loop, as total costs will be impacted by various areas in import and export trade compliance issues, such as, but not limited to, vendor choices, selection of Incoterm, and the HTS codes utilized.

Both seasoned and new-to-China buyers focus only on product purchase price and then get an unexpected and ugly surprise when they have an accumulation of additional costs when the goods arrive at destination. These costs were not planned for in the budget nor when margins were considered.

Locating and selecting a supplier is just the first step. Buyers need to calculate a landed cost of the product they are purchasing before actually importing it. This is the only way to avoid going through the *trouble of importing and then finding out you spent more to buy the product than you can sell it for.*

This outline will help us to better understand the true cost of the product you are buying from China. We go back to landed cost being the total cost of a product once it has arrived at the purchaser's door. This list of components that are needed to determine landed cost includes *the original cost of the item, all brokerage and logistics fees, complete shipping costs, customs duties, tariffs, taxes, insurance, currency conversion, crating costs,* and *handling fees.* Not all of these components are present in every shipment, but all that are must be considered part of the total cost.

The responsibilities for specific costs is determined by the Incoterm as outlined in the chart below.

Incoterms 2010

	A	B	C	D	E	F	G	H	I	J	K	L	M
1	Incoterm	Loading on truck	Export-customs declaration	Carriage to port of export	Unloading of truck in port of export	Loading charges in port of export	Carriage to port of import	Unloading charges in port of import	Loading on truck in port of import	Carriage to place of destination	Insurance	Import-customs clearance	Import taxes
2	EXW	Buyer	Buyer	Buyer	Buyer	Buyer	Buyer	Buyer	Buyer	Buyer	N/A	Buyer	Buyer
3	FCA	Seller	Seller	Seller	Buyer	Buyer	Buyer	Buyer	Buyer	Buyer	N/A	Buyer	Buyer
4	FAS	Seller	Seller	Seller	Seller	Buyer	Buyer	Buyer	Buyer	Buyer	N/A	Buyer	Buyer
5	FOB	Seller	Seller	Seller	Seller	Seller	Buyer	Buyer	Buyer	Buyer	N/A	Buyer	Buyer
6	CFR	Seller	Seller	Seller	Seller	Seller	Seller	Buyer	Buyer	Buyer	N/A	Buyer	Buyer
7	CIF	Seller	Seller	Seller	Seller	Seller	Seller	Buyer	Buyer	Buyer	Seller	Buyer	Buyer
8	DAT	Seller	Seller	Seller	Seller	Seller	Seller	Seller	Buyer	Buyer	N/A	Buyer	Buyer
9	DAP	Seller	Seller	Seller	Seller	Seller	Seller	Seller	Seller	Seller	N/A	Buyer	Buyer
10	CPT	Seller	Seller	Seller	Seller	Seller	Seller	Seller	Seller	Seller	N/A	Buyer	Buyer
11	CIP	Seller	Seller	Seller	Seller	Seller	Seller	Seller	Seller	Seller	Seller	Buyer	Buyer
12	DDP	Seller	Seller	Seller	Seller	Seller	Seller	Seller	Seller	Seller	N/A	Seller	Seller

The Incoterms rules are intended primarily to clearly communicate the tasks, costs, and risks associated with the transportation and delivery of goods. The table indicates who has the responsibilities for fees at different points in an international transaction.

If the delivered duty paid (DDP) purchaser's receiving site is chosen as the Incoterm, there will be no need to do any additional landed-cost calculation as all costs will be included in the purchasing. However, there is a considerable amount of money that is added into the costing model that may be going into the seller's pocket as additional profit as you may not be receiving the best pricing on variables such as freight and trucking.

This is the reason most importers will choose free-on-board (FOB) outbound gateway as an Incoterm. In an FOB purchase the supplier will deliver the cargo to the outbound gateway, border crossing, port, or airport and the importer will take over from that point. Imports from China are typically purchased on a FOB or free-carrier (FCA) outbound gateway basis.

Utilizing an FOB/FCA Incoterm allows the importer to choose the international carrier, customs broker, freight forwarder and trucker. For example:

- Cost of goods—variable depending on unit price and quantity
- Import assistance company—variable depending on level of service
- Freight—variable depending on volume, port its coming from/going to, time of year, freight company used, etc.; allow $2000–$5000
- Duty—variable percentage of the value customs puts on your goods
- Tax (goods and services tax or value-added tax) – $ variable percentage of (the customs value of cost of goods + freight + insurance + customs duty)
- Insurance
- Inland freight
- Customs-clearance fees
- Other charges including document fees, wharfage, etc.—estimate an additional 3%–6% on top of everything else

Import Customs Duties and Taxes

A common mistake made by purchasers is to ask the supplier in China to confirm the taxes and duties in the destination country. Suppliers may not be knowledgeable about how your government would classify the given product and what additional regulations may apply to that commodity that would add additional costs, such as antidumping fees, applicability of harbor maintenance, and merchandise-processing fees. In the United States, Customs and Border Protection (CBP) holds XYZ Corp. totally responsible for making the correct harmonized tariff declaration at the time of import.

In order to determine the applicable rate of duty for a particular product, you need to identify the harmonized tariff schedule number for that product.

1. *Determining the Harmonized Tariff Code for your Product*

The HTS is part of an international classification system that provides a common, but not exact, numbering system for customs. The HTS and country of origin of the item will determine the applicable rate of duty.

It should be noted that the HTS numbers are also referred to as *tariff codes, customs codes, harmonized codes, export codes, import codes,* and *harmonized commodity descriptions.* When there is a code representing the product, that code is the HTS number.

HTS numbers can vary from country to country. The code that your supplier provides is a starting point. Generally that starting point will be accurate to the first four or six numbers, known as the chapter, heading, and subheading.

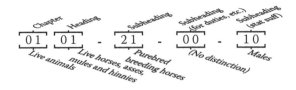

It is a U.S. entry requirement that the HTSUS be included on the invoice presented to CBP. The applicable duty amount will be determined by the HTS, country of origin, and the declared value. Knowing the right HTS number for products is of central importance to the importing process. The incorrect HTS number may not only delay customs clearance but could also incur unexpected costs.

2. *Declared Value*

Most duties and taxes are percentages calculated based ad valorem, according to value. The customs value is based on the invoice value. For U.S. Customs, the FOB/FCA value is the value to be declared at the time of import. How that value is arrived at will depend on the circumstances of the purchase. The most common valuation method is transaction value, the price paid or payable.

Duty/Tax-Free Amount (De Minimis Value)

The de minimis value of the destination country is the declared value of your shipment below to which duties and taxes will not apply. If you are importing a shipment with a total declared value less than this de minimis amount, duties and taxes will not apply. A customs clearance is still required but duties and taxes do not apply. Certain products may be subject to other types of fees or taxes, i.e., alcohol and tobacco.

Each country has its own threshold for determining if a shipment will move without the payment of duties and taxes.

- Australia: AUD 1000
- Canada: CAD 20
- Europe: EUR 22
- Japan: USD 130
- United Kingdom: GBP 15
- United States: USD 200

It is the importer's responsibility to be certain that the correct declared value is stated on the invoice presented to customs. This responsibility cannot be shifted to the Chinese supplier.

3. *Import Customs Duties*

Import duty is a customs tax levied on the imported items. Imports from most countries are dutiable at the most favored nation rate under Column 1 General. Tariff rates for goods originating from countries that qualify for preferential tariff treatment are found under Column 1 Special. Goods originating from countries that do not fall under normal trade relations or preferential tariff treatment are found under Column 2.

Harmonized tariff schedule of the United States (2012)

Annotated for statistical reporting purposes

VI

28-3

Heading/ subheading	Stat. suffix	Article description	Unit of quantity	Rates of duty		2
				1		
				General	Special	
		I. CHEMICAL ELEMENTS				
2801		Fluorine, chlorine, bromine and iodine:				
2801.10.00	00	Chlorine...	kg............	Free		25%
2801.20.00	00	Iodine..	kg............	Free		Free
2801.30		Fluorine: bromine:				
2801.30.10	00	Fluorine..	kg............	3.7%	Free (A, AU, BH, CA, CL, E, IL, J, JO, MA, MX, OM, P, PE)	25%

Goods originating in China fall under the Column 1 duty rates.

Duty Calculation

While the HTSUS reflects the applicable duty rates for items, there may be additional factors that override the duty rate in the HTS. These are called antidumping duties. Antidumping duties are a surcharge on the applicable duty rate. Antidumping duties are a form of protection of a particular commodity being manufactured.

For example, for global imports of stainless steel sinks, the normal rate of duty is 3.4% ad valorem. However, stainless steel sinks originating from China are subject to antidumping duties of 39.98% in addition to the ad valorem rate of 3.4%. This means a shipment of sinks valued at $50,000 from China would incur duties payable to CBP in the amount of $21,690.00 as opposed to $1700.00 if those same stainless steel sinks originated from another country.

Division	Description	HTS Code	Country of Origin	Duty Rate	Antidumping Rate
Tiger	TV mounts	8302.50.0000	China	Free	n/a
Tiger	Monitors	8473.30.5100	China	Free	n/a
Tiger	Keyboards	8471.60.2000	China	Free	n/a
Global	Plastic bins	3926.90.9980	China	53%	n/a
Global	Stainless steel sinks	7324.10.0010	China	3.40%	39.87%
Global	Hand trucks	8716.80.5010	China	3.20%	n/a

4. *Import Taxes*

While the United States does not have VAT or goods and services tax (GST) for import shipments, the United States does have fees that are applicable at the time of import.

All goods moving into the United States will be assessed a merchandise-processing fee (MPF) in addition to any duties owed. The MPF is assessed at 0.3464% of the value of the shipment. MPF maxes out at $485 and there is a minimum of $25 for all import shipments. For import shipments that are American Goods Being Returned or fall under NAFTA the merchandise processing fee is waived.

Imports moving into the United States by vessel are subject to a harbor-maintenance fee (HMF). This fee is calculated at 0.3464% of the value of the shipment and does not have a maximum payable amount as with the MPF.

5. *Insurance*

All goods to be imported from China and worldwide are insured by our master cargo insurance policy. This protects our merchandise on an all-Risk warehouse-to-warehouse basis. Specific insuring terms and conditions can be found from our corporate risk management department in Port Washington.

For landed-cost calculation purposes, we would utilize $10 per $100 of insured value. If a purchase is valued at US$50,000, then the insurance cost is calculated at US$50,000 divided by $100 × $10 = US$50.

6. *Inland Freight*

Our merchandise will typically arrive at an ocean port, an airport, or the border. It will then move from that point to our final destination distribution location in Las Vegas, Robbinsville, Buford, Jefferson, or Naperville.

That inland freight cost must be obtained from our international transportation provider and included in the landed cost model.

CONCLUSION

Protecting our profits and growing our business are key responsibilities of everyone involved in sourcing, purchasing, merchandising, logistics, or supply chain. Making sure we are aware of all our costs and then applying sound practice to lower costs and risks are all primary responsibilities. Understanding landed-cost modeling is necessary to control margins and accomplish our XYZ Corp.'s corporate goals.

Landed-Cost Calculator

Category	Cost
FOB/FCA cost of goods purchased	
Pickup at supplier	
Inland transportation to a port or airport	
Origin terminal and port fees	
Export licensing, documentation, and duties	
Ocean, air, or truck international freight	
Import clearance, documentation, and handling	
Duties	
Merchandise-processing fee	
Harbor-maintenance fee	
Antidumping duties (if applicable)	
Terminal and port fees at destination	
Examination fees (if applicable)	
Import security filing (if applicable)	
Cargo insurance	
Inland transportation to importer's location	
Storage/warehousing/distribution	

Appendix L: Example of International Marketing Plan Workbook

The purpose of the international marketing plan workbook is to prepare your business to enter the international marketplace. Ask yourself: Should I expand my company through exporting? Do I have any products or services I can export? This workbook will lead you step by step through the process of exporting your product to an international market.

The workbook is divided into sections. Each section should be completed before you start the next. After you have completed the entire workbook, you will be ready to develop an international marketing plan to export your product. The remaining sections of this guide will assist you in determining where and how to find the resources to begin exporting successfully.

PLANNING

Why complete this workbook and write a plan?

Five reasons why it will be worth your time and effort:

1. Careful completion of this workbook will help evaluate your level of commitment to exporting.
2. The completed workbook can help you assess your products' potential for the global market.
3. The workbook gives you a tool to help you better manage your international business operations successfully.
4. The completed workbook will help you communicate your business ideas to persons outside your company. It is an excellent starting point for developing an international financing proposal.

5. With a plan the business is able to stay focused on primary objectives and has a measuring tool for results as each step is achieved.

Can I hire someone to do this for me?

No! Nobody will do your thinking or make decisions for you. This is *your* business. If the marketing plan is to be useful, it must reflect *your* ideas and efforts.

Why is planning so important?

The planning process forces you to look at your future business operations and anticipate what will happen. This process better prepares you for the future and makes you more knowledgeable about your business. Planning is vital for marketing your product in an international marketplace and at home.

Any firm considering entering into international business transactions must understand that doing business internationally is not a simple task. It is stimulating and potentially profitable in the long term but requires much preparation and research prior to the first transaction.

What qualities should a business have in considering products or services for the international market?

A business needs to be

1. Successful in its present domestic operation;
2. Willing to commit its resources of time, people, and capital to the export program (entry into international markets may take as long as two years of cash outflow to generate profit); and
3. Sensitive and aware of the cultural differences in doing business in other countries.

Approach your export operations in the same way you would your domestic operations—using sound business fundamentals. Developing an international marketing plan helps you assess your present market situation, business goals, and commitment. This will increase your opportunities for success.

A marketing plan is a process, not a product. It must be revised on a continual basis as your knowledge increases about international markets. You will be surprised how much easier it is to update a marketing plan after the first one is written. Planning is a continuous process. Plus, after a revision or two, you will know more about your international business market opportunities to export products.

GOAL SETTING

Identifying business goals can be an exciting and often challenging process. It is, however, an important step in planning your entry into the international marketplace. The following exercise is an additional step to help clarify your short- and long-term goals.

Step 1: Define long-term goals.

A. What are your long-term goals for this business in the next five years? Example: Increase export sales by __% annually or __% market share or __% profitability or return on assets

_____
_____
_____
_____
_____
_____
_____
_____
_____
_____

B. How will the international trade market help you reach your long-term goals?

_____
_____
_____
_____

Step 2: Define short-term goals.

A. Select one or two target markets; research product standards and certification requirements; and make modifications, if needed, to get product export ready.

_____
_____
_____
_____
_____
_____

B. What are your two-year goals for your international business products/services?

Examples: Modify product for metric definition; expand international opportunities from initial penetration of a market to other similar markets.

_____
_____
_____
_____
_____

Step 3: Develop an action plan with timelines to reach your short-term goals.

_____
_____
_____
_____
_____

IDENTIFYING PRODUCTS WITH EXPORT POTENTIAL

List below the products your company sells that you believe have export potential. Write down why you believe each product will be successful in the international marketplace. The reasons should be based on your current knowledge, rather than any research.

Products/Services	Reasons for Export Success
1. _____	1. _____
2. _____	2. _____
3. _____	3. _____

Based on reasons for export success, select one or more products you believe might have the best prospects for exporting.

Decision Point: These products have export potential.
If YES, go on to next steps.

Yes   No

Step 1: Select the most exportable products to be offered internationally.

To identify products with export potential, you need to consider products that are sold successfully in the domestic market. The product should fill a targeted need for the purchaser in export markets according to price, value to customer/country, and market demand.

    A. What are the major products my business sells?
       1.
       2.
       3.
    B. What product(s) do you feel have the best potential for international trade?
       1.
       2.
       3.

Step 2: Evaluate the product(s) to be offered internationally.

    A. What makes your product(s) attractive for an overseas market?
       1.
       2.
       3.
    B. Why do you believe international buyers will purchase your company's products?
       1.
       2.
       3.

DETERMINING YOUR COMPANY'S EXPORT READINESS

Pros and Cons of Market Expansion

Brainstorm a list of pros and cons for expanding your market internationally. Based on your current assumptions about your company, your company's products, and any market knowledge, determine your probability of success in the international market.

Pros   **Cons**

1. _____   1. _____
2. _____   2. _____
3. _____   3. _____
4. _____   4. _____
5. _____   5. _____

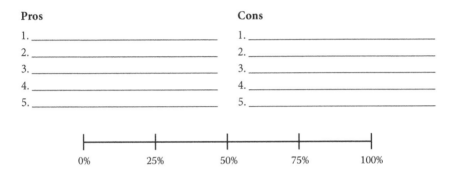

    0%   25%   50%   75%   100%

YOUR BUSINESS/COMPANY ANALYSIS

Step 1: Why is your business successful in the domestic market? Give specific reasons. What is your company's annual growth rate?

    1.

    2.

    3.

Step 2: What are the competitive advantages of your products or business over the domestic and international businesses? List them.

    1.

    2.

    3.

Step 3: What is your level of commitment and that of your company's top management to expanding into international markets? How much

preparation time, planning, and resources are you willing to commit to implementing an export program?

  1.
  2.
  3.

INDUSTRY ANALYSIS

Step 1: Find export data available on your industry.

Go online to the U.S. Department of Commerce's website (http://www .export.gov) or search for trade statistics on Industry Canada's website (http://strategis.ic.gc.ca/sc_mrkti/ibin/compare.html).

  1.
  2.
  3.

Step 2: Research how competitive your industry is in the global markets.

Locate industry sector reports available at http://www.export.gov, evaluate import-export statistics from the Bureau of Census (http://www .census.gov) or contact your trade association, or the nearest U.S. Export Assistance Center.

  1.
  2.
  3.

Step 3: Find your industry's growth potential internationally.

Talk to companies in your industry or trade association, read industry-specific magazines, attend a national trade fair, and look for industry reports at the website http://www.export.gov.

  1.
  2.
  3.

Step 4: Research federal or state government market studies that have been conducted on your industry's potential international markets.

Obtain information available through the U.S. Department of Commerce at http://www.export.gov; or contact your local U.S. Export Assistance Centers (EACs), Small Business Administration (SBA), or Small Business Development Center (SBDC) office, or your trade association.

1.
2.
3.

DEVELOPING YOUR EXPORT MARKETING PLAN

Read the sections "Goal Setting" and "Identifying Products with Export Potential" of this guide before completing this section.

Step 1: Select the best countries to market your product.

Since the number of world markets to be considered by a company is very large, it is neither possible nor advisable to research them all. Thus, your firm's time and money are spent most effectively by using a sequential screening process.

Your first step in this process is to select the more commercially attractive countries for your product. Preliminary screening involves defining the physical, political, economic, and cultural environment. You can find country research at http://www.export.gov; the website has Country Commercial Guides for each country where there is a Foreign Commercial Service presence. In addition, the Department of State has background reports on each country at http://www.state.gov, as does the Central Intelligence Agency's *World Factbook*, which can be accessed at http://www.cia.gov.

1. Select three countries you think have the best market potential for your product.
2. Review the market factors for each country.
3. Research data/information for each country.

4. Rate each factor on a scale of 1–5 with 5 being the best.
5. Select a target market country (C) based on your ratings (R).

Market Factor Assessment	Country	Rating	Country	Rating
Demographic/Physical Environment				
• Population size, growth, density				
• Urban and rural distribution				
• Climate and weather variations				
• Shipping distance				
• Product-significant demographics				
• Physical distribution and communication network				
• Natural resources				
Political Environment				
• System of government				
• Political stability and continuity				
• Ideological orientation				
• Government involvement in business				
• Attitudes toward foreign business (trade restrictions, tariffs)				
Competitive Environment				
• Uniqueness of your product/service				
• Pricing of competitive products (nontariff barriers, bilateral trade agreements)				
• National economic and development priorities				
• Regulatory or quality standards for imports				
Economic Environment				
• Overall level of development				
• Economic growth; GNP, industrial sector				
• Role of foreign trade in the economy				
• Currency: inflation rate, availability, controls, stability of exchange rate				
• Balance of payments				
• Per capita income and distribution				
• Disposable income and expenditure patterns				

(Continued)

Market Factor Assessment	Country	Rating	Country	Rating
Social/Cultural Environment				
• Literary rate, educational level				
• Existence of middle class				
• Similarities and differences in relation to home market				
• Language and other cultural considerations				
Market Access				
• Limitations on trade: high levels, quotas				
• Documentation and import regulations				
• Local standards, practices, and other nontariff barriers				
• Patents and trademark protection				
• Preferential treaties				
• Legal considerations for investment, taxation, repatriation, employment, code of laws				
Product Potential				
• Customer needs and desires				
• Local production, imports, consumption				
• Exposure to and acceptance of product				
• Availability of linking products				
• Industry-specific key indicators of demand				
• Attitudes toward products of foreign demand				
• Competitive offerings				
Local Distribution and Production				
• Availability of intermediaries				
• Regional and local transportation facilities				
• Availability of manpower				
• Conditions for local manufacture				

Indicators of population, income levels, and consumption patterns should be considered. In addition, statistics on local production trends, along with imports and exports of the product category, are helpful for assessing industry market potential. Often, an industry will have a few key indicators or measures that will help determine the industry strength and demand within an international market. A manufacturer of medical equipment, for example, may use the number of hospital beds, the number of surgeries, and public expenditures for health care as indicators to assess the potential for this product.

Why do you believe international buyers will purchase your company's products?

_____

_____

Step 2: Research how competitive your industry is in the global markets.

Much of this information can be obtained from an industry trade association for your particular industry.

A. What is your present U.S. market percentage?

_____

_____

_____

B. What are the projected sales for similar products in your chosen international markets for the coming year?

_____

_____

C. What sales volume will you project for your products in these international markets for the coming year?

_____

_____

D. What is the projected growth in these international markets over the next five years?

_____

_____

_____

Step 3: Identify customers within your chosen markets.

    A. What companies, agents, or distributors have purchased similar products?

    _____

    _____

    B. What companies, agents, or distributors have made recent requests for information on similar products?

    _____

    _____

    C. What companies, agents, or distributors would most likely be prospective customers for your export products?

    _____

    _____

Step 4: Determine the method of exporting.

    A. How do other U.S. firms sell in the markets you have chosen?

    _____

    _____

    B. Will you sell directly to the customer?

    _____

    _____

    C. Who will represent your firm?

    _____

    _____

    D. Who will service the customers' needs?

    _____

    _____

Step 5: Building a distributor or agent relationship.

Plan to travel to the country in question as many times as is necessary to build a successful relationship.

    A. Will you appoint a rep or distributor to handle your export market? Consider legal advice from the Export Legal Assistance Network (ELAN). A free initial consultation is available by request through a U.S. Export Assistance Center.

    _____

    _____

B. What facilities does the agent or distributor need to service the market?

_____

_____

C. What type of client should your agent or distributor be familiar with in order to sell your product?

_____

_____

D. What territory should the agent or distributor cover?

_____

_____

E. What financial strength should the agent or distributor have?

_____

_____

F. What other competitive or noncompetitive lines are acceptable or not acceptable for the agent or distributor to carry?

_____

_____

G. How many sales representatives does the agent or distributor need and how often will they cover the territory?

_____

_____

H. Will you use an export management company (EMC) to do your marketing and distribution for you?

Yes   No

EMCs do not have to represent your company exclusively on a worldwide basis. Rather, they sometimes can represent you in specific regional markets. For example, you might contract with an EMC to sell your products in Latin American markets, while you continue to handle direct export sales to Europe and Asia.

If yes, have you developed an acceptable sales and marketing plan with realistic goals you agree to?

Yes   No

Comments:

_____

_____

MARKETING YOUR PRODUCT/SERVICE

Given the market potential for your products in international markets, how is your product or service distinguished from others—attractive or competitive?

A. What are your product's advantages?

_____

_____

B. What are your product's disadvantages?

_____

_____

C. What are your competitors' products' advantages?

_____

_____

D. What are your competitors' products' disadvantages?

_____

_____

E. What needs does your product fill in a foreign market?

_____

_____

F. What competitive products are sold abroad and to whom?

_____

_____

G. How complex is your product? What skills or special training are required to
   1. Install your product?

   _____

   _____

   2. Use your product?

   _____

   _____

   3. Maintain your product?

   _____

   _____

   4. Service your product?

   _____

   _____

H. What options and accessories are available?

_____

_____

I. Has an aftermarket been developed for your product?

_____

_____

J. What other equipment does the buyer need to use your product?

_____

_____

K. What complementary goods does your product require?

_____

_____

L. If your product is an industrial good,
   1. What firms are likely to use it?

   _____

   _____

   2. What is the useful life of your product?

   _____

   _____

   3. Is use or life of product affected by climate? If so, how?

   _____

   _____

   4. Will geography affect product purchase; for example, transportation problems?

   _____

   _____

   5. Will the product be restricted abroad; for example, tariffs, quotas, or nontariff barriers?

   _____

   _____

M. If your product is a consumer good,
   1. Who will consume it? How frequently will the product be bought?

   _____

   _____

   2. Is consumption affected by climate?

   _____

   _____

3. Is consumption affected by geography; for example, transportation problems?

_____

_____

4. Will there be product-related requirements, i.e., product certification, testing, special government approval, quotas, etc.?

_____

_____

5. Does your product conflict with traditions, habits, or beliefs of customers abroad?

_____

_____

SUPPORT FUNCTIONS

To achieve efficient sales offerings to buyers in the targeted markets, you should address several concerns regarding

Step 1: Identify product concerns.

A. Can the potential buyer see a functioning model or sample of your products that is substantially the same as would be received from production?

Yes   No

Comments:

_____

_____

_____

_____

B. What product labeling requirements (metric measurements, AC or DC electrical, voltage, etc.) must be met?

Keep in mind that the European Union countries now require three languages on all new packaging and Mexico requires labels in Spanish, while Canada requires labels in French and English under the North American Free Trade Agreement.

_____

_____

C. When and how can product conversion requirements be obtained?

_____

_____

D. Can the product be delivered on time as ordered?

Yes   No

This is especially important if letters of credit are used as a payment method.

Comments:

_____

_____

Step 2: Identify literature concerns.

A. If required, can you produce product literature in a language other than English?

Yes   No

B. Do you need a product literature translator to handle the technical language?

Yes   No

C. What special concerns should be addressed in sales literature to ensure quality and informative representation of your product?

Keep in mind that translations should reflect the linguistic nuances of the country where the literature will be used.

_____

_____

Step 3: Identify customer relations concerns.

A. What are delivery times and method of shipment?

_____

_____

B. What are payment terms? Will financing be necessary to support either the preshipment (production) or postshipment (accounts receivable) working capital needed for these orders? If so, are you aware of export financing programs offered by the SBA and the Export-Import Bank?

_____

_____

C. What are the warranty terms? Will inspection/acceptance be required?

_____

_____

D. Who will service the product when needed?

_____

_____

E. How will you communicate with your customer: through a local agent or fax? via the Internet?

_____

_____

F. Are you prepared to give the same order and delivery preferences to your international customers that you give to your domestic customers?

Yes   No

MARKETING STRATEGY

In international sales, the chosen terms of sale are most important. Where should you make the product available: at your plant; at the port of exit; landed at the port of importation; or delivered free and clear to the customer's door? The answer to this question involves determining what the market requires and how much risk you are willing to take.

Terms of sale have internationally accepted definitions; learn to be familiar with the most commonly used types and be prepared to include them in quotations. For definitions of Incoterms, see http://www.iccwbo.org/incoterms/faq.asp.

Pricing strategy depends on terms of sale and also considers value-added services of bringing the product to the international market.

Step 1: Define the international pricing strategy.

A. How do you calculate the landed (in country) price for each product?

_____

_____

B. What factors have you considered in setting prices?

_____

_____

C. Which products' sales are very sensitive to price changes?

_____

_____

D. How important is pricing in your overall marketing strategy?

_____

_____

E. What are your discount policies?

_____

_____

F. What terms of sale are best for your export product?

_____

_____

Step 2: Define the promotional strategy.

A. What advertising materials will you use?

_____

_____

B. What trade shows or trade missions will you participate in, if any?

_____

_____

C. What time of year and how often will foreign travel be made to customer markets?

_____

_____

Step 3: Define customer services.

A. What special customer services do you offer?

_____

_____

B. What types of payment options do you offer?

_____

_____

C. How do you handle merchandise that customers return?

_____

_____

SALES FORECAST

Forecasting sales of your product is the starting point for your financial projections. Use realistic estimates to produce a useful sales forecast. Remember that sales forecasts show volume only. Actual cash flow will be determined by the cash cycle which includes supplier terms, delivery dates, and payment terms and methods.

   Step 1: Fill up the "Units sold" row for markets 1, 2, and 3 for each year on the following worksheet.

   Step 2: Fill in the sales price per unit for products sold in markets 1, 2, and 3.

   Step 3: Calculate the total sales for each of the different markets (units sold × sales price per unit).

   Step 4: Calculate the sales (all markets) for each year—add down the columns.

   Step 5: Calculate the five year total sales for each market—add across the rows.

Sales Forecasts—First Five Years

	1	2	3	4	5
Market 1					
Units sold					
Sale price/unit					
Total sales					
Market 2					
Units sold					
Sale price/unit					
Total sales					
Market 3					
Units sold					
Sale price/unit					
Total sales					
Total Sales					
All markets					

COST OF GOODS SOLD

The cost of goods sold internationally will differ from the cost of goods sold domestically if significant product alterations will be required. These changes will affect costs in terms of material and direct and indirect labor costs.

Pass-Through Costs

To ascertain the costs associated with the different terms of sale, it will be necessary to consult an international freight forwarder. For example, a typical term of sale offered by a U.S. exporter is cost, insurance, and freight (CIF) port of destination. Your price can include all the costs to move the product to the port of destination and other costs necessary to complete the export transaction. However, many of these costs are incurred by the exporter to provide a service to the importer. For example, you can price your product ex works and let your customer worry about getting the product to their destination from your factory or warehouse. However, most exporters arrange many of the details (transportation, insurance, etc.) for their customers. These costs should be identified separately on the invoice and passed through with little or no markup.

A typical cost worksheet will include some of the following factors. These costs are in addition to the material and labor used in the manufacture of your product.

Export packing	Forwarding
Container loading	Export documentation
Inland freight	Consular legalization
Truck/Rail unloading	Bank documentation
Wharfage	Dispatch
Handling	Bank collection
Terminal charges	Cargo insurance
Ocean freight	Other miscellany
Bunker surcharge	Telex
Courier mail	Demurrage
Tariffs	Import duties

To complete this worksheet, you will need to use data from the sales forecast. Certain costs related to your terms of sale may also have to be considered. For example, include cost of capital if you are extending payment terms.

> Step 1: Fill up the "Units sold" row for markets 1, 2, and 3 for each year.
>
> Step 2: Fill in the cost per unit for products sold in markets 1, 2, and 3.
>
> Step 3: Calculate the total costs for each of the different markets (units sold × cost price per unit).
>
> Step 4: Calculate the cost of goods sold—all products for each year—add down the columns.
>
> Step 5: Calculate the five-year cost of goods for each market—add across the rows.

Cost of Goods Sold—First Five Years

	1	2	3	4	5
Market 1					
Units sold					
Cost per unit					
Total cost					
Market 2					
Units sold					
Cost per unit					
Total cost					
Market 3					
Units sold					
Cost per unit					
Total cost					
Cost of Goods Sold					
All markets					

INTERNATIONAL MARKETING EXPENSES

To determine marketing costs for your export products, you should include costs that apply only to international marketing efforts. For example, cost of domestic advertising of services that do not pertain to the international market should not be included. Examples of most typical expense categories for an export business are listed below. Some of the expenses will be first-year, start-up expenses; others will occur every year.

Step 1: Review the expenses listed below. These are expenses that will be incurred because of your international business. There may be other expense categories not listed—list them under "Other expenses."

Step 2: Estimate your cost for each expense category.

Step 3: Estimate any domestic marketing expense included that is not applicable to international sales. Subtract these from the international expenses.

Step 4: Calculate the total for your international overhead expenses.

	Cost			
Expense	**Market 1**	**Market 2**	**Market 3**	**Total Year 1**
Legal fees				
Accounting fees				
Promotional material				
Travel				
Communication				
Equipment/Fax/Internet				
Advertising allowances				
Promotional expenses				
Other expenses				
Total expenses				
Less domestic expenses included above, if any				
Total international marketing expenses				

PROJECTED INCOME STATEMENT—YEARS 1 TO 5, ALL MARKETS

You are now ready to assemble the data for your projected income statement. This statement will calculate your net profit or net loss (before income taxes) for each year.

Step 1: Fill in the sales for each year. You already have estimated these figures; just recopy them on the work sheet.

Step 2: Fill in the cost of goods sold for each year. You already have estimated these figures; just recopy them on the work sheet.

Step 3: Calculate the gross margin for each year (sales minus cost of goods old).

Step 4: Calculate the operating expenses specifically associated with the international marketing program for each year.

Step 5: Allocate the international division's portion of the firm's overall domestic operating expenses (international's portion of lighting, office floor space, secretarial pool, etc.).

	1	2	3	4	5
International sales					
Cost of goods sold					
Gross margin					
International operating expenses					
Legal					
Accounting					
Advertising					
Travel					
Trade shows					
Promotional material					
Supplies					
Communication equipment					
Interest					
Insurance					
Other					
International division's domestic expense allocation					
Total international operating expense					
Net profit before income taxes					

BREAK-EVEN ANALYSIS

The breakeven is the level of sales at which your total sales exactly cover your total costs, which includes nonrecurrent fixed costs and variable costs. This level of sales is called the break-even point (BEP) sales level. In other words, above the BEP sales level, you will make at net profit. If you sell less than the BEP sales level, you will have a net loss.

To calculate the break-even point, costs must be identified as being either fixed or variable. *Fixed expenses* are those that the business will incur regardless of its sales volume—they are incurred even when a business has no sales—and include such expenses as rent, office salaries, and depreciation. *Variable expenses* change directly and proportionately with a company's sales and include such expenses as cost of goods sold and sales commissions. Some expenses are semivariable in that they vary somewhat with sales activity but are not directly proportionate to sales. Semivariable expenses include utilities, advertising, and administrative salaries. Semivariable expenses ideally should be broken down into their fixed and variable components for an accurate break-even analysis. Once a company's expenses have been identified as either fixed or variable, the following formula is used to determine its break-even point.

$$\text{Break-Even Point} = \frac{\text{Total Fixed Expenses}}{1 - \dfrac{\text{Total Variable Expenses}}{\text{Sales Volume}}}$$

Note: In addition to a break-even analysis, it is highly recommended that a profit and loss analysis be generated for the first few actual international transactions. Since there are a great number of variables relating to costs of goods, real transactions are required to establish actual profitability and minimize the risk of losses.

TIMETABLE

This is a worksheet that you will need to work on periodically as you progress in the workbook. The purpose is to ensure that key tasks and objectives are identified and completed to ensure accomplishment of your stated goals.

Step 1: Identify key activities.

By reviewing other portions of your marketing plan, compile a list of tasks that are vital to the successful operation of your business. Be sure to include travel to your chosen market as applicable.

Step 2: Assign responsibility for each activity.

For each identified activity, assign one person primary responsibility for the completion of that activity.

Step 3: Determine scheduled start date.

For each activity determine the date when work will begin. You should consider how the activity fits into your overall plan as well as the availability of the person responsible.

Step 4: Determine scheduled finish date.

For each activity determine when the activity must be completed.

ACTION PLAN

Project/Task	Person	Start Date	Finish Date

SUMMARY

Step 1: Verify completion of previous pages.

You should have finished all the other sections in the workbook before continuing any further. You are now ready to summarize the workbook into an exporting plan for your company.

Step 2: Identify your international marketing plan audience.

What type of person are you intending to satisfy with this plan? a banker? the company's chief executive officer? The summary should briefly address all the major issues that are important to this person. You may want to have several different summaries, depending on who will read the marketing plan.

Step 3: Write a one-page summary.

You will now need to write no more than a page summarizing all the previous work sheets you have completed.

Determine which sections are going to be most interesting to your reader. Write one to three sentences that summarize each of the important sections. Keep in mind that this page will probably be the first read by this person. A brief summary of the most important information should make the reader want to read the rest of your plan.

Summarize the sections in the order that they appear in the workbook.

INTERNATIONAL MARKETING PLAN SUMMARY

_____

_____

_____

_____

_____

_____

_____

_____

_____

_____

_____

_____

_____

_____

_____

_____

_____

_____

_____

_____

_____

_____

_____

PREPARING AN EXPORT PRICE QUOTATION

Setting proper export prices is crucial to a successful international program; prices must be high enough to generate a reasonable profit, yet low enough to be competitive in overseas markets. Basic pricing criteria—costs, market demand, and competition—are the same for domestic and foreign sales. However, a thorough analysis of all cost factors going into producing goods for export, plus operating expenses, results in prices that are different from domestic ones (remember freight cost, insurance, etc., are *pass-through costs* identified separately and include little or no markup).

Marginal cost pricing is an aggressive marketing strategy often used in international marketing. The theory behind marginal cost concludes that if the domestic operation is making a profit, the nonrecurrent annual fixed costs are being met. Therefore, only variable costs and profit margin should be used to establish the selling price for goods that will be sold in the international market (this strategy is used for domestic pricing as well). This results in a lower price for international goods yet maintains the profit margin. The risk of this strategy becomes apparent when the domestic operation becomes unprofitable and cannot cover the fixed costs, as each incremental sale could result in a larger loss for the company. This is a complex issue that can yield substantial benefits to a company with manageable risks. Some effort should be made by management to understand this pricing strategy.

Cost Factors

In calculating an export price, be sure to take into account all the cost factors for which you, the exporter, are liable.

1. Calculate direct materials and labor costs involved in producing the goods for export.

2. Calculate your factory overhead costs, prorating the amount of over-head chargeable to your proposed export order.
3. Deduct any charges not attributable to the export operation, espe-cially if export sales represent only a small part of total sales.
4. Be sure operating expenses are covered by your gross margin. Some of these expenses directly tied to your export shipments may include the following:

Travel expenses	Catalogs, slide shows, video presentations
Promotional material	Export advertising
Commissions	Transportation expenses (usually pass-through costs)
Packing materials	Legal expenses[a]
Office supplies[a]	Patent and trademark fees[a]
Communications[a]	Taxes[a]
Rent[a]	Insurance[a]
Interest[a]	Provision for bad debts
Market research	Credit checks
Translation costs	Product modification
Consultant fees	Freight forwarder fees (usually pass-through costs)

[a] These items will typically represent the expenses of the total operation, so be sure to pro-rate these to reflect only the operating expenses associated with your export operation.

5. Allow yourself a realistic price margin for unforeseen production costs, operating expenses, unavoidable risks, and simple mistakes that are common in any new undertaking.
6. Also allow yourself a realistic profit or markup.

Other Factors to Consider

Market Demand

As in the domestic market, product demand is the key to setting prices in a foreign market. What will the market bear for a specific product or ser-vice? What will the estimated consumer price for your product be in each foreign market? If your prices seem out of line, try some simple product modifications to reduce the selling price, such as simplification of technol-ogy or alteration of product size to conform to local market norms. Also keep in mind that currency valuations alter the affordability of goods. A good pricing strategy should accommodate fluctuations in currency, although your company should quote prices in dollars to avoid the risks of currency devaluations.

Competition

As in the domestic market, few exporters are free to set prices without carefully evaluating their competitors' pricing policies. The situation is further complicated by the need to evaluate the competition's prices in each foreign market an exporter intends to enter. In a foreign market that is serviced by many competitors, an exporter may have little choice but to match the going price or even go below it to establish a market share. If, however, the exporter's product or service is new to a particular foreign market, it may be possible to set a higher price than normally charged domestically.

WORKSHEETS

Export Programs and Services

This worksheet helps you identify organizational resources that can provide programs and services to assist you in developing your international business plan and increase your export sales.

	Organizations					
Services	USDOC Office	SBDC	USEAC	Trade Associations	Colleges	World Trade Centers
Readiness-to-export assessment						
Market research studies						
Counseling						
Training seminars						
Education programs						
Publications						
Export guides						
Databases						
Trade shows						
Financing						
Partner search						

EXPORT COSTING WORKSHEET

Quote Preparation

Pricing is a reflection of all costs incurred and influenced by the competitiveness of the marketplace. The quotation must first determine the domestic ex works* costs and then identify the additional costs incurred to sell overseas.

Export Costing Worksheet

Reference Information

1. Our reference_____ 2. Customer reference_____

Customer Information

3. Name_____ 5. Cable address_____

4. Address_____ 6. Telex no._____

_____ 7. Fax no._____

_____ 8. E-mail address_____

Product Information　　　　　　　　　　*NAICS Code*_____

9. Product_____ 13. Dimensions_____×_____×_____

10. No. of units_____ 14. Cubic measure_____(sq.in.)

11. Net weight_____(unit) 15. Total measure_____

12. Gross weight_____ 16. H.S. no._____

Ex Works Costs

17. Direct materials_____

18. Direct labor_____

19. Factory burden_____

20. Cost of goods_____

21. Selling expenses_____(should be less than domestic sales)

22. General expenses_____(includes cost of money borrowed)

23. Administrative expenses_____

24. Export marketing costs (product changes, labeling)_____

25. Profit margin

26. Ex works price_____

(Continued)

---

* *Ex works* means that the seller fulfills his delivery obligation to the buyer when he has made the goods available at his factory, warehouse, or other place of business.

Export Costing Worksheet (Continued)

Additional Exporting Costs

27. Foreign sales commission (if applicable)

28. Special export packing costs (typically 1 to 1.5% above ex works price)

29. Special labeling and marking (to protect from moisture, theft, rough handling)

30. Inland freight to pier (normal domestic common carrier; should also carry insurance)

31. Unloading charges (include demurrage, if any)

32. Terminal charges (include wharfage, if any)

33. Consular documents (includes shippers export declaration [SED], export license, or certificate of origin)

34. Freight (port to port)—determined by freight forwarder

35. Freight forwarder fees (*must* be included)

36. Export Insurance (insurance for transit risk; also for credit risk, if credit worthiness of buyer is unknown)

37. Cost of credit (include credit reports, letter of credit costs, and amendments, if any)

Total additional export costs_____   Quote = Ex works price + Total of additional exporting cost

At the end of the day, the only thing you take with you is your reputation, which is mostly based upon how well and favorably you impact the well-being of those around you. Make every day a day you help someone along.

This may mean that you may cause some uncomfort, may be somewhat difficult or arduous, but usually it has to be done.

No matter what it is or what you do or how large or trivial, teach, coach, mentor, hold accountable, and lead others to be better citizens, parents, siblings, business colleagues and friends.

That joy and impact will be your salvation and legacy.

Thomas A. Cook

Index

For Product Safety Concerns and Information please contact our EU
representative GPSR@taylorandfrancis.com Taylor & Francis Verlag GmbH,
Kaufingerstraße 24, 80331 München, Germany

Printed and bound by CPI Group (UK) Ltd, Croydon, CR0 4YY

08/05/2025

01864404-0002